Ripperologist I

A new look at Whitechapel serial killer Jack the Ripper using modern day evidence, photographs and maps.

Stephen Bloom

CONTENTS

PREFACE	2
PHOTOGRAPHS OF THE PEOPLE INVOLVED	3
LIST OF ILLUSTRATIONS	4
1. WHERE IT ALL HAPPENED	5
2. THE FIRST VICTIM	14
3. THE SECOND VICTIM	26
4. THIRD (NON-CONICAL) VICTIM	37
5. THE THIRD VICTIM	48
6. THE FOURTH VICTIM	67
REFERENCES	82
INDEX	83

PREFACE

No! We still don't know who Jack the Ripper was, although there are some pretty convincing theories out there. I think I first became interested in the case after watching that Barlow & Watts TV series on the case in 1973 (still available on YouTube). I remember riding my motorcycle up to London from my parent's house in West Sussex sometime in 1976/77 and using an old Polaroid camera to photograph the murder sites – the pictures I no longer have. A year later I joined the RAF and on my journey to my training base my car gave up near Wolverhampton and I abandoned it at a garage, along with many of my belongings that I could not carry – including some ripper notes and books. A few years later the police asked me to drop by to explain the books – it was then the height of the Yorkshire Ripper investigation: Peter Sutcliffe.

But I was too young when the first Yorkshire Ripper murder took place to be involved, and the police discharged me with a smile; it was a pity they never returned to me the items taken from my broken down car by the garage attendants in Wolverhampton. Amongst them were my hand written notes from the Metropolitan police files that I had read at the public records office. So, I have always held a deep interest in the original Jack the Ripper case; me, and dozens of other ripperologists and theorists. Anyone who is keen can become one. What you need to do though is something slightly different from everyone else, and hopefully I have done so with this book 'Ripperologist.'

Okay, the photographs are few and far between and nobody has yet done a house clearance and come across a load of new pictures, diaries or police notes dated 1888. But modern technology, for example, enables us to accurately measure distances from one murder site to the next, and calculate whether the murderer could have killed twice in one night in the time scale reported by police. So, 'Ripperologist' will examine closely the killings, the time sequencing as well as the men involved, both civilians, police and in the last instance, brief theories as to who may have been responsible for the murders, and the failure to apprehend the person or persons guilty. Where possible, I have added maps of the various locations plus modern day aerial shots; also photographs or newspaper drawings where available of those who dealt with the crimes – for after all, it's nice to put a face to a name, isn't it?

Stephen Bloom, England 2017

PHOTOGRAPHS OF PEOPLE INVOLVED

All photos freely available on the world wide net, unless otherwise specified.

Sir Charles Warren @ 1886 courtesy Elliott & Fry

Wolf Vanderlinden / Donald Rumbelow tentatively identify this photograph as that of Frederick Abberline

Rear yard of 29 Hanbury Street (bottom photo): in all my time researching the Whitechapel killings I have never seen this photo with the door closed until now! Unable to find whose photo it is; likely a police photographer.

LIST OF ILLUSTRATIONS

The warren that was the east end of London: Durward Street was Bucks Row back then and Duval Street was Dorset Street

Bucks Row (now Durward Street) on the Mile End boundary

Location of Nichols body in Bucks Row

Bucks Row: the Board School – the person in black stands just three feet from the spot where Polly Nichols was found

A white sign painted on the wall commemorates Polly Nichols

Typical police ambulance

Brown's Stable Yard

No.29 Hanbury Street

Front of no.29; there are two doors, the one on the right enters the shop and the one on the left enters the rest of the building and the rear yard

Rear yard of no.29; the victim was found with her head at the foot of the bottom step, close to the wooden fence

Berner Street, today called Henriques Street

International Workingmen's Educational Club

Mitre Square; black dot is where body was found, X are street lamps, note the urinal in St James's Place

Ripper corner

108-119 Wentworth Model Dwellings Goulston Street: the entrance, the stairs and the buildings in the distance

Millers Court

Room 13 (enhanced computer picture)

The arched Millers Court entrance from Dorset Street (left) and room 13 (right), door (at side) and victim's windows through which her body was first seen

Millers Court layout

Dorset Street, showing Millers Court, room 13 and the local pubs 'The Britannia' and the 'Queen's Head.'

Still here today; The Queen's Head – but no longer a pub. The original facia can still be seen just behind the lamp post, above the boarding

1. WHERE IT ALL HAPPENED?

London, England, 1888 (dark dot) (courtesy Google earth).

Spitalfields & Whitechapel murder sites (courtesy Google earth).

Most of us know that the ghastly killings that took place in the autumn of 1888, during the reign of our gracious sovereign Queen Victoria, were called the 'Whitechapel' murders. Whitechapel was (and still is) a district in the east end of London; today, part of the borough of Tower Hamlets and home to a predominantly Bangladeshi community. Back in 1888, there was a predominantly Jewish and Irish community present. To the north of Whitechapel stands the parish of Spitalfields; here two prostitutes were murdered (Mary Kelly and Annie Chapman). Plus, there stood here the infamous flats in Goulston Street, where part of Catherine Eddowes' bloodstained clothing was discovered during the night of the so called 'double killing'. Eddowes was found butchered in Mitre Square, which came under the jurisdiction of the City of London police and not the Metropolitan police.

The Met's central station in Whitechapel was in Leman Street – a mere 365-yard dash (as the crow flies) from Berner Street (now Henriques Street) where Elizabeth Stride was found murdered and her killer disturbed before he ran away to Mitre Square in time to kill Eddowes – supposedly. Why might the murderer (known to all as Jack the Ripper – a made up journalistic name) choose Whitechapel and Spitalfields for his area of operation? If you look at the map below, you will see why – a warren, a labyrinth even, of narrow, mostly unlit streets and allies made movement easy in and out of the place.

But above all, despite certain small pockets in the east end where property was well maintained by the owners, the area housed the poor of London and in particular, about 1200 low cast prostitutes. These 'unfortunates' walked the streets day and night looking for customers willing to pay a few pennies for sex; most lived in common lodging houses that charged a similar amount for a bed for the night. A few, like murder victim Mary Kelly, paid 4s (shillings) a week for a room consisting of a bed, a bedside table, a chair, table and fire place. The higher class prostitutes frequented the west end of London.

Many of the newspapers of the time depicted the east end as being one vast slum inhabited by an immoral and criminal population; whereas the entire district was tarnished with the reputation of being a bed of vice, villainy, drunkenness and debauchery. We should remember too that many law abiding, hard-working people also lived in the area, and probably made up the majority of the population. It was in this sadly neglected area of east London that Jack the Ripper and his legend was spawned on 31st August 1888. This therefore is the area we are about to enter.

The police command set up

All but one of the ripper murders took place in Metropolitan police areas, this being mostly H Division, but the murder of Catherine Eddowes took place in the City of London police area, a different police force altogether, and so we must include the City police in our examination.

Senior Metropolitan police officers

Sir Charles Warren, GCMG, KCB, FRS, (below) an army officer of the Royal Engineers from 1857, was the Metropolitan police commissioner from 1886 until the day of Mary Kelly's murder in November 1888. Sir Charles was not an unintelligent man, being an engineer in various army capacities throughout his career. In 1884 he was promoted major general and saw brief service in Bechuanaland (Botswana), a British protectorate bordering South Africa before being recalled to England the following year.

Sir Charles Warren

Warren stood for election to parliament as an independent liberal, but lost. He was sent to Suakin, a port in north east Sudan on the west coast of the Red Sea, as commander, but had no sooner arrived when he was recalled to London again to become Metropolitan police commissioner in January 1886, following the resignation of Sir Edmund Henderson KCB. We shall examine Sir Charles later in more detail but needless to say, he turned out to be quite utterly unsuitable to his position as police commissioner.

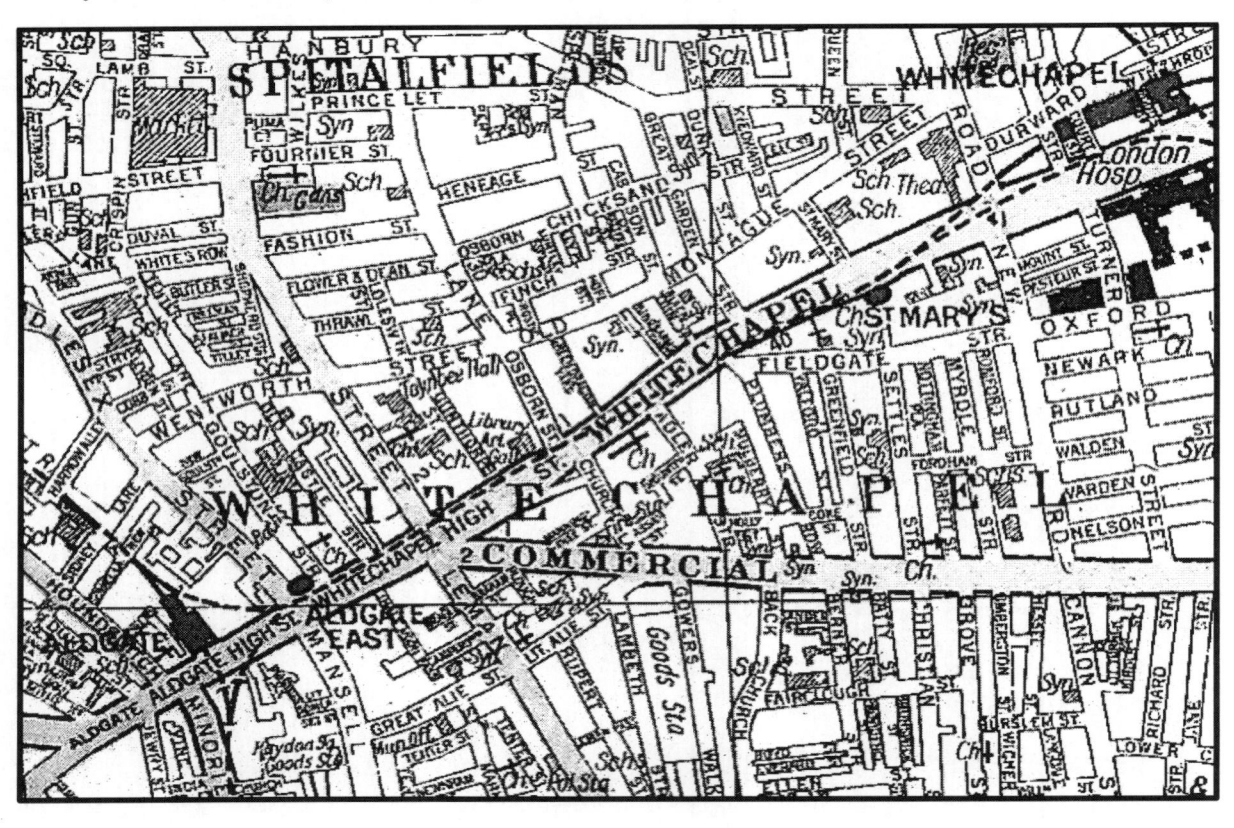

The warren that was the east end of London: Durward Street was Bucks Row back then and Duval Street was Dorset Street (unknown general map).

Sir Robert Anderson

Sir Robert Anderson was Assistant Commissioner (Crime) of the Metropolitan Police and was in charge of the detective department. Originally a barrister by training, he had served as a Home Office adviser on political crime. He was not particularly successful against the fenians (Irish separatists) who had been bombing and killing on the English mainland, but because of his knowledge he was assigned to assist James Monro in this task of combatting fenians; Monro at the time being Assistant Commissioner (Crime) of the Metropolitan Police. James Monro never got along with Sir Charles Warren, who vetoed Monro's choice of chief constable for CID Crime, Melville MacNaghten – of whom we shall come across later.

Monro thus resigned and Sir Robert took his place as Assistant Commissioner (Crime). Monro resigned on 31st August 1888, which was also the date of the first known ripper killing. On taking his new post, Sir Robert immediately went on an extended vacation to Switzerland (later Paris, to be nearer home), leaving others in charge. He was called back after just a month because of increased bad publicity over the east-end killings and his absence from duty. We shall examine Sir Robert and his efforts to capture the murderer later in more detail. Needless to say, as the murders increased during his absence (three additional women were killed during his sojourn abroad) Sir Charles Warren assigned Chief Inspector Donald Swanson to command the CID investigations from Scotland Yard.

James Monro

James Monro played no small part in the ripper killings. From 1884 until the murder of the first ripper victim, Polly Nichols on 31st August 1888, he was the first ever Assistant Commissioner (Crime) for the Met. He was thus in charge of the criminal detective department at Scotland Yard and was answerable, as had been his predecessor Sir Charles Edward Howard Vincent KCMG CB DL, directly to the Home Secretary and not Sir Charles Warren! This caused friction between the head of the Met and the head of CID Scotland Yard. As we have seen already, it was Monro's decision to appoint Sir Melville Leslie MacNaghten CB KPM to the post of Chief Constable (CID) that was vetoed by Sir Charles Warren. This caused friction between the two men and also new Home Secretary Henry Matthews, 1st Viscount Llandaff PC, QC.

The result was that Monro resigned and Sir Robert Anderson was appointed in his place, as mentioned earlier. However, Henry Matthews kept Monro on as head of the Special Branch, and when Sir Charles Warren resigned in November 1888, James Monro was appointed in his place as Met Commissioner. You can see now that the men at the very top of the Met were quarrelsome, jealous individuals who were highly educated (for that time) as soldiers and barristers, but none had any real police experience at all. Not so the men below them who did the donkey work of the investigation, and these we shall examine next before looking at the City of London police who dealt with the Catherine Eddowes killing.

More junior Metropolitan police

Melville MacNaghten

Although not directly involved at the time of the ripper murders other than being the cause of James Monro's resignation as head of CID, **Sir Melville Leslie MacNaghten** will be most remembered for his February 1894 handwritten report naming three ripper suspects; this was the first time any police report named potential murderers for the case. His memorandum was not available, following the closure of the police files, until sixty-five years after it was first written; this being 1959, so we will come back again later to Sir Melville.

Donald Swanson

Donald Sutherland Swanson, who was born in Scotland, was in overall charge of the ripper murders. Robert Anderson, chief of the Criminal Investigation Department (CID) at Scotland Yard, placed Swanson in charge of the investigation into the Whitechapel Murders from 1st September 1888. Other ripperologists say Sir Charles Warren was the man who appointed him when Anderson went off on his sojourn to Europe. Swanson was freed of all other duties and given his own office at Scotland Yard from which to co-ordinate his inquiries. We will come across the chief inspector again later.

Frederick Abberline *Henry Moore* *Walter Andrews*

Frederick George Abberline [1] was one of three additional detective inspectors sent by Scotland Yard to investigate the Whitechapel killings and was therefore the best known detective at the time. He was assisted by Detective Inspector Henry Moore and Detective Inspector Walter Simon Andrews.

Edmund Reid

Other well-known men involved in the search for the ripper included Inspector **Edmund John James Reid**, who at the time of the ripper murders was the local Whitechapel Detective Inspector.

Thomas Arnold *William Thick*

Superintendent Thomas Arnold was the divisional superintendent for Whitechapel H Division during the ripper killings. Other men involved in Whitechapel that we will soon know included Chief Inspector **John West**, Divisional Inspector **Ernest Elliston**, Inspector **Walter**

Beck, Inspector **Joseph Chandler**, Inspector **Charles Pinhorn** and Detective Sergeant **William Thick**.

The City of London police

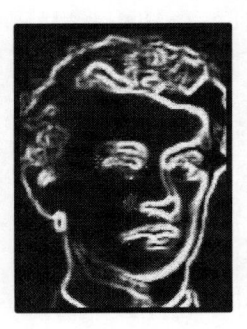

James Fraser

Sir James Fraser KCB, of whom little information can be found and no pictures seem to exist, was the retiring commissioner of the City of London police. He was on a two-month sabbatical at the time of the Eddowes murder on City of London police territory, although he returned quickly to duty. Meanwhile, during his absence Major Henry Smith was in command of the city police force.

Henry Smith

Major Henry Smith was acting commissioner of the City of London police during the Catherine Eddowes murder inquiry, and was on the scene when her body was found.

James McWilliams

City police Detective Inspector **James McWilliams** attended the scene of the Eddowes murder in Mitre Square. He was told by Detective Baxter Hunt of the discovery of the writing on the wall and a piece of bloody apron found in Goulston Street. McWilliams ordered that the writing be photographed; he was also present when Dr Brown matched the piece of bloody apron with that worn by Eddowes.

Daniel Halse

Detective Constable **Daniel Halse** was a City of London police officer who was quickly on the scene of the murder of Catherine Eddowes in Mitre Square. He was also at the Goulston Street building where the discarded apron portion was discovered, and objected to Sir Charles Warren removing the Graffiti on the wall before a photograph had been taken.

Other people

There were numerous civilian people involved in the ripper murders and the following will appear often in the investigation:

Wynne Baxter

Wynne Edwin Baxter, a lawyer, was the Whitechapel coroner during the ripper killings. He sat on three of the victim's cases and we shall come across him much more later.

George Phillips

George Bagster Phillips MBBS, MRCS Eng., L.M., LSA was H Division's police surgeon, and attended four ripper victim autopsies and three on site examinations of the murdered women.

Roderick Macdonald

Roderick Macdonald, MD, FRCS was a Scottish doctor and member of parliament; he was also the coroner who presided over the Mark Kelly inquest debacle, and closed the inquest in less than half a day!

Thomas Bond

Dr Thomas Bond FRCS, MB BS was a doctor who invented early offender profiling and was present at the Mary Kelly autopsy.

Henry Matthews

Henry Matthews, 1st Viscount Llandaff PC, QC was a lawyer and conservative politician; he was Home Secretary at the time of the ripper murders and did not get on well with Sir Charles Warren, conducting meetings with the head of Scotland Yard behind Warren's back.

2. THE FIRST VICTIM

Canonical victims

We have read of the policemen and others involved directly with the case, but now it is time to review the ripper victims. How many women died at the hands of the ripper? Well that depends upon who you ask or which ripper books you read. Thanks to Sir Melville Leslie MacNaghten's memorandum of 1894 (written six years after the events and not made public until 1959) the canonical (standard) number killed by Jack was five. The police also had three suspects, according to Sir Melville. Other ripperologists name between four and eleven victims, with three lesser savage killings before the first canonical victim and three after the last known victim. The five canonical victims are as follows:

Be aware that mortuary photographs follow

1/ Mary Ann Nichols (*aka* Polly Nichols) Bucks Row 31/8/1888

2/ Annie Chapman – rear yard of 29 Hanbury Street 8/9/1888

3/ Elizabeth Stride (*aka* Long Liz) Dutfields Yard, Berner Street 30/9/1888

and on the same night, about an hour later:

4/ Catherine Eddowes (*aka* Kate) Mitre Square, City of London 30/9/1888

5/ Mary Jane Kelly – room 13 Millers Court, Dorset Street 9/11/1888

There were other killings similar to but not attributed to the ripper both before and after the canonical five. Names such as Emma Smith, Martha Tabram, Alice Mackenzie and Frances Coles might soon be familiar to you. I and many others now believe that the canonical number of ripper victims should be reduced to four; that for reasons soon to be apparent, the third victim (Elizabeth Stride) was not a true ripper victim at all, but the result of an unfortunate attack incident that just happened to fall on the same night as a real ripper killing. This should not distract from the fact that in the space of an hour the police believed they had a double ripper attack when, in fact, it was not so.

First victim: Polly Nichols is found

The first canonical killing was that of prostitute Mary Ann Nichols, also known as Polly. At about 3:40 on the morning of 31st August 1888, Charles Cross (who was a Carman by trade – a driver of a wagon used to transport goods – his real name was Charles Allen Lechmere), turned from Brady Street into Buck's Row, which was then a dark road with terraced houses on the south side and warehouses on the north; it ended at a Board School where the Row joined Winthrop Street.

Cross walked on the north side of the street and just before he reached the end near the school, he noticed what he believed to be a tarpaulin lying in the gateway to Brown's Stable Yard. He walked across to take a closer look and found that what he had seen was actually a woman lying on the ground. Before he could investigate further he heard footsteps approaching from the direction of Brady Street where he had just come himself.

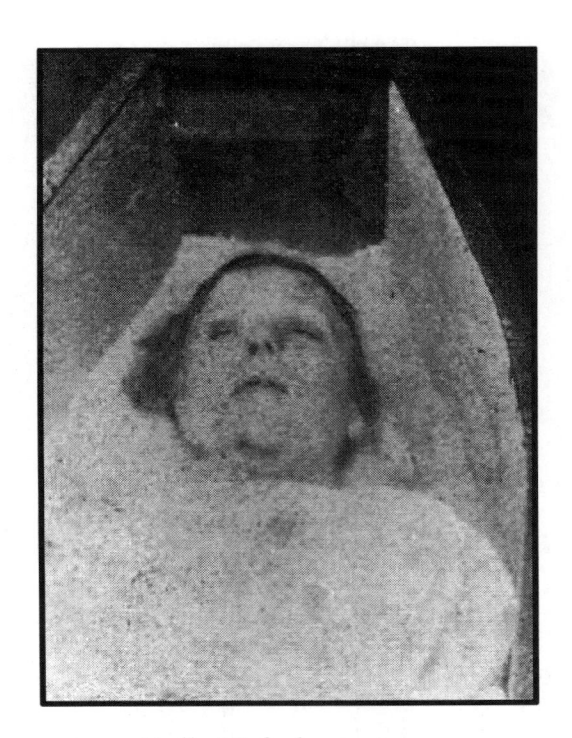

Polly Nichols mortuary

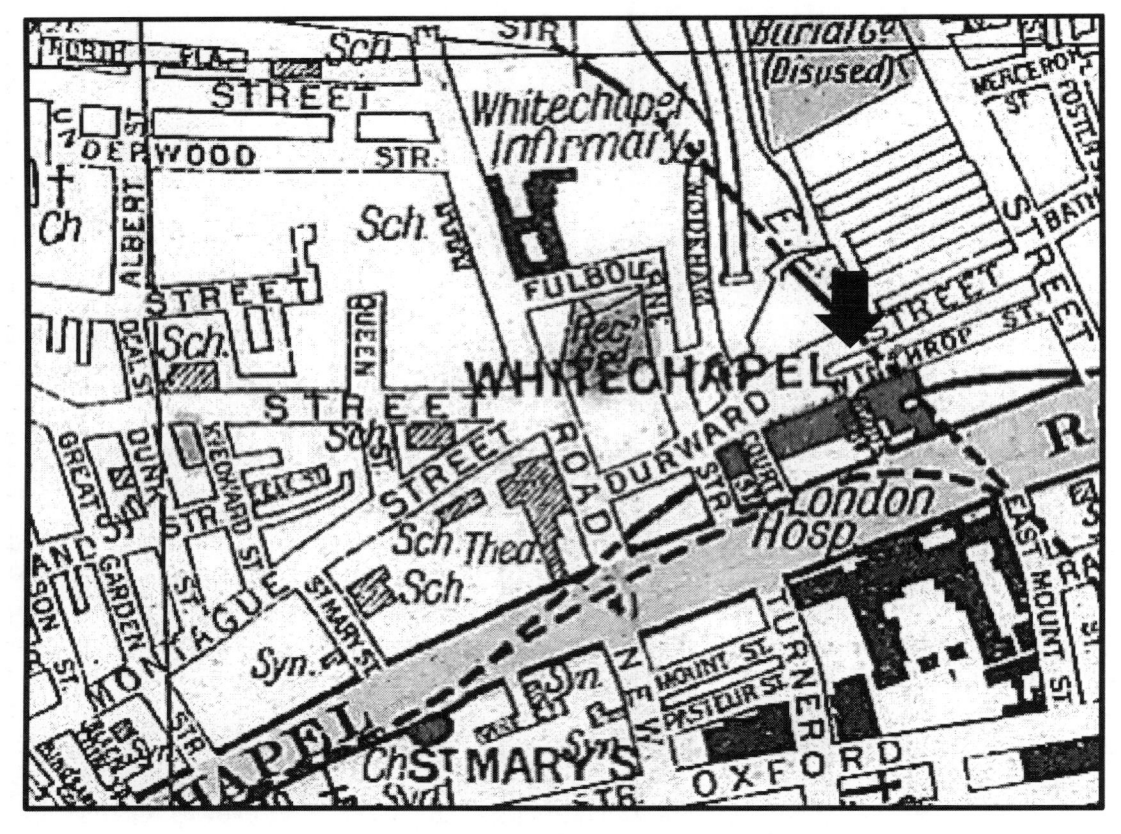

Bucks Row (now Durward Street) on the Mile End boundary (unknown general map).

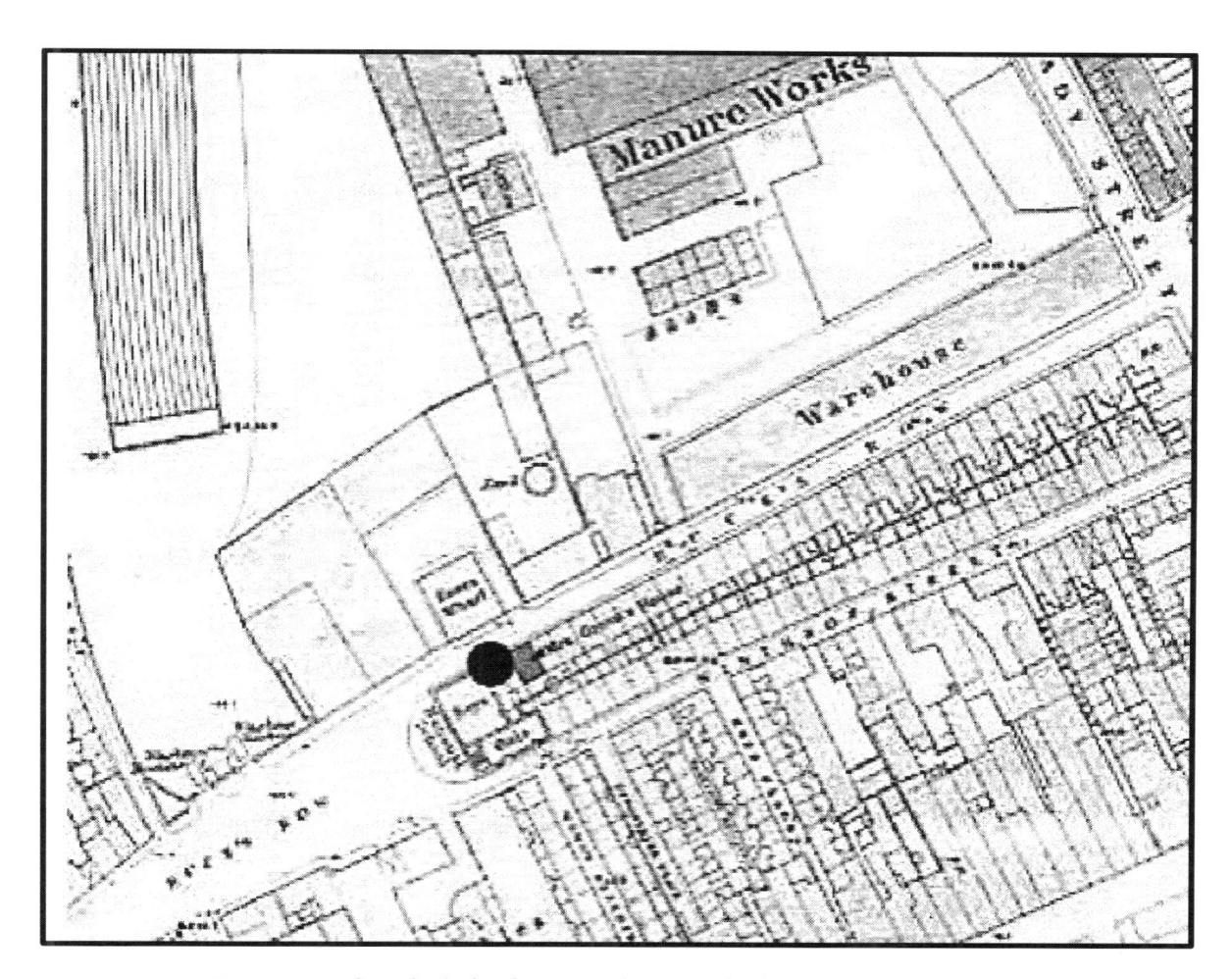

Location of Nichols body in Bucks Row (unknown general map).

Robert Paul was also a Carman and like Charles, was on his way to work. As he walked along Bucks Row, he saw movement close to the Board School. As he got closer a man came toward him, tapped him on the shoulder and said 'come and look over here; there's a woman lying on the pavement.' Drunks lying about in the streets were not an uncommon sight in the east end, and Robert didn't really want to get involved in things. Nevertheless, he and Charles drew closer to the woman. She was laying on her back with her head toward Brady Street; her hands were down by her sides, her legs straight out and slightly apart and her skirts raised. The two men probably thought that she wasn't drunk but had been the victim of some kind of attack or rape.

Charles Cross touched the woman's hand and felt that it was cold. He said to Robert 'I believe she's dead.' Robert also touched her face and hands and confirmed that the woman's flesh was cold. To be certain he crouched down and listened for any sounds of breathing; there were none, but as he brushed her breast he thought he noticed a slight movement. If she was breathing at all then it was very shallow. Standing up, Robert said 'I think she's breathing but very little if she is,' after which he suggested they prop her up but Charles would have none of this. Following a brief discussion, the two men decided that, since they were already going to be late for work the best thing would be to carry on to their respective places of work and to tell the first policeman they saw what they had found. The only thing they did on behalf of this woman was to pull her skirts down to preserve her modesty.

At the junction of Hanbury Street and Old Montague Street, the two men saw a constable, PC56H Jonas Mizen. As a result of what they said, disputed later at the inquest, the two men made their way to work whilst PC Mizen walked off toward Bucks Row. He was not the first policeman to find the woman, however, for Bucks Row was part of the beat of PC 97J John Neil, who had last walked down the street at around 3:15 that morning when he had noticed nothing unusual. At 3:45 he walked east along Bucks Row toward the Board School. He was on the south side of the street when he saw the shape laying in front of Brown's Stable Yard. Unlike Cross and Paul, John Neil had a lantern with him and he now shone its light on to the still figure. He could see what the other two men could not; that the woman had been attacked and her throat was cut. Blood still flowed slowly from the wound.

John Neil knew that another policeman, PC96J John Thain had a beat that took him along Brady Street at the top of Bucks Row. Seeing that Thain was just passing by, John flashed his lantern in order to summon assistance. Thain rushed down Bucks Row and heard John Neil call out that this woman had her throat cut, and he was to run at once for Dr Llewellyn. Thain ran off to fetch the doctor, leaving Neil alone with the body. Moments later PC Mizen arrived and Neil told him to fetch the ambulance and further assistance from Bethnal Green Police Station. Neil was alone with the woman and whilst waiting for assistance he took a look around to see if he could find any clues as to what might have happened.

The gates to Brown's Stable Yard were firmly shut and locked. Almost directly opposite the body was Essex Wharf and Neil rang the bell to determine whether the occupants might have seen or heard anything. His call was answered by Walter Purkiss, who appeared staring down from a second-floor window. Neil asked him if he had heard anything but Purkiss said he had not. Soon afterwards, Sergeant Kerby (sometimes spelt Kirby) arrived in Bucks Row, alerted by the other officers, and he proceeded to knock on the door of the first terraced house on the south side: 2 Bucks Row, right next to where the woman's body lay. This house was occupied by Emma Green and her family of two daughters and a son; like Walter Purkiss, Emma Green had heard nothing. Meanwhile, PC Neil was examining the roadway to see if he could find any marks of wheels where a cart might have dropped the woman. He found nothing.

The Board School – the person in black stands just a few feet from the spot where Polly Nichols was found (courtesy Google earth).

A sign painted on the wall commemorates Polly Nichols (courtesy Google earth).

At four o'clock that morning, Dr Rees Ralph Llewellyn of 152 Whitechapel Road had been awoken by PC Thain and arrived at Bucks Row. He made a quick examination of the woman and pronounced her dead. He too found that the woman's hands were cold but her legs were still warm and he determined that she had not been dead more than half an hour, so putting the time of death at around 3:30 a.m. By this time a small crowd of onlookers, including some men from Barber's Slaughter Yard in Winthrop Street, had gathered. Dr Llewellyn ordered the body moved to the mortuary, where he would make a more detailed examination later in the day.

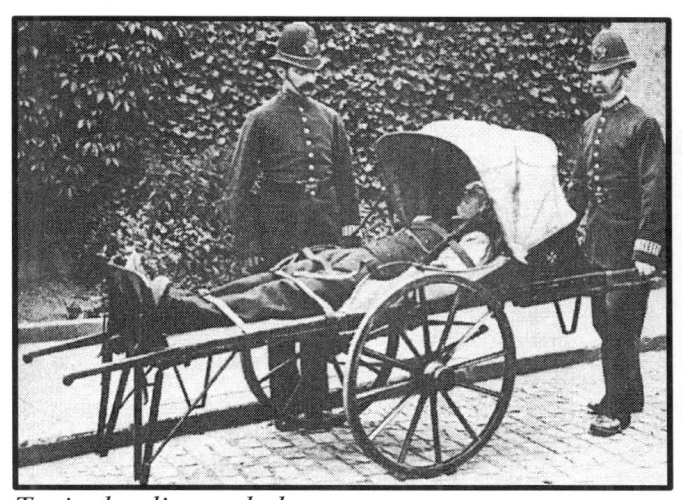

Typical police ambulance *Brown's Stable Yard*

The body was lifted on to a police ambulance (which was really a wooden cart with wheels) and Constables Neil and Mizen, accompanied by Sergeant Kerby, took the woman to the mortuary in Old Montague Street, whilst John Thain waited for senior officers to arrive in Bucks Row. In due course Inspector John Spratling arrived, and Thain pointed out to him where the body had been found. Apparently Mrs Emma Green's son had just washed away the last of the blood from the pavement, but small signs of it could still be seen between the paving stones in daylight. Satisfying himself that he could do no more in Bucks Row, Inspector Spratling went to the mortuary to view the body for himself and take down a description of her.

Body search and identification

The mortuary was locked at that time of day so the body still lay on the ambulance, which had been left in the yard. Inspector Spratling began to write down her description and while he was doing this Robert Mann, the mortuary keeper, arrived with the keys. The body was moved inside the mortuary and Spratling continued his notes. Looking for marks on the woman's clothing, he lifted her skirts and discovered that she had been mutilated. Her abdomen had been ripped open and her intestines were exposed. The inspector immediately sent for Dr Llewellyn again, who returned to make a second examination. The inspector noted down her possessions, looking all the time for things to identify her. She carried a comb, a white pocket handkerchief and a piece of looking glass, but these gave nothing away.

Her clothing appeared to consist of a reddish-brown ulster (coat) with seven large brass buttons, a brown linsey wool frock, a white chest flannel (in reality a cotton undergarment), two petticoats, a pair of stays, black ribbed woollen stockings, a pair of men's side-fastening boots and a black straw bonnet trimmed with black velvet. The inspector noticed that she wore a petticoat bearing the mark 'Lambeth Workhouse, P.R.', which indicated that at some time the victim had been a resident in that workhouse. Two women quickly came forward to identify the body. Reports of the murder spread throughout the district, leading to the news that a woman fitting the victim's description had been living at a lodging house at 18 Thrawl Street. Ellen Holland, who was a resident there, told police that she knew the dead woman as Polly.

A second witness, Mary Monk, an inmate from the workhouse, viewed the body at 7:30 on the evening of 31st August and stated that the victim was Mary Ann Nichols. Her identification enabled police to trace Mary Nichols' relatives. On 1st September Edward Walker, Mary's father and William Nichols, her estranged husband, both confirmed the identification. On that same morning, Dr Llewellyn carried out a full post mortem on the body of Polly. Later that same day, the inquest opened at the Working Lad's Institute in Whitechapel Road; the coroner was Wynne E. Baxter, coroner for the south east district of Middlesex. A jury, having been duly sworn, was taken to view the body which still lay in a coffin shell at the mortuary. Upon their return the first witnesses were called.

Public inquest

A summary follows now of the evidence presented to the inquest by the various witnesses. **Edward Walker**, father of the dead woman, stated his present address (Camberwell) and confirmed identification of Mary Ann Nichols, adding that he had not seen her for two years. The last occasion was Saturday 5th June 1886 at the funeral of his son, who had been burnt to death in an accident with a paraffin lamp. He went on to confirm the breakup of his daughter's marriage. According to the father, Mary's husband William Nichols had an affair with the nurse who attended Mary during her last confinement. As a result of this the couple separated. The eldest son went to live with his grandfather while the other four children of the marriage remained with their father, who had another child by this time with the nurse.

Although he had not seen his daughter in two years, Edward Walker had received a letter from her, which he showed the court, dated Easter that year, indicating that she was a domestic servant to a couple in Wandsworth. He replied to her letter but heard nothing more; he knew nothing of her whereabouts since that time. The next witness was Constable **John Neil**, who spoke of his discovery of Mary's body. He was walking on the right side of the street when he saw a figure lying in the street by a gateway. Having shone his lantern upon it, he saw a woman lying with her left hand touching the gates of the stable yard. Blood was still oozing from a wound in her throat.

Her eyes were wide open and her arm was quite warm from the joints upward. Her bonnet was off her head and lying by her side, close to her left hand. At that moment, Neil heard a fellow constable patrolling Brady Street and signalled him. Soon afterwards Constable Mizen arrived and was sent to fetch the police ambulance, which was no more than a handcart. PC Neil described awakening Walter Purkiss at Essex Wharf and the arrival on the scene of Sergeant Kerby. After Dr Llewellyn had said that the woman was dead, the constable helped lift the body on to the ambulance and afterward noticed a small patch of congealed blood where the body had been; it was no more than 6" in diameter.

Neil stayed at the mortuary with the body and was there when Inspector Spratling arrived. He saw the inspector writing a description of the woman and noticed the mutilations once her clothing was lifted. **Dr Llewellyn** said he was a surgeon practicing at 152 Whitechapel Road and that at about four o'clock in the morning of Friday 31st August he had been called to Bucks Row. Here he had found the dead woman lying on her back. She had severe injuries to her throat and although her hands and wrists were cold, her lower extremities were quite warm.

During this examination he noted that there was very little blood about the neck and no signs of a struggle having taken place. He estimated that she had been dead for no more than half an hour. Most ripperologists would now clear up the important point regarding the small amount of blood left at the scene of the murder. In a report to the press issued later the same day, the doctor stated that there was only a small pool of blood on the footway; he describes it as 'not more than would fill two wine glasses, or half a pint at the outside.' This comment led to speculation that Mary Nichols had been killed elsewhere and dumped in Bucks Row. In fact, witnesses, including Constables Neil, Mizen, and Thain, stated that a good deal of blood had been absorbed by Mary's clothing, and that her back appeared soaked in it.

PC Neil's hands had been smeared with blood when he helped lift the body on to the ambulance. There was little doubt, however, that Mary met her death at the spot where her body was found. Back to Llewellyn's evidence; he told of his being called out the second time by Inspector Spratling. He had gone immediately to the mortuary and there noted extensive abdominal mutilations. He then began to give details of his post mortem findings to the jurors. The body was that of a female 40 to 45 years of age, he said. Five of the teeth were missing and there was a slight laceration of the tongue. There was a bruise running along the lower part of the jaw on the right side of the face; that might have been caused by a blow from a fist or pressure from a thumb. There was a circular bruise on the left side of the face, which also might have been inflicted by the pressure of the fingers.

On the left side of the neck, about 1" below the jaw, there was an incision of about 4" in length, and ran from a point immediately below the ear. On the same side, but an inch below and commencing about 1" in front of it, was a circular incision, which terminated at a point about 3" below the right jaw. That incision completely severed all the tissues down to the vertebrae. The large vessels of the neck on both sides were severed. The incision was about 8" in length. The cuts must have been caused by a long-bladed knife, moderately sharp and used with great violence. No blood was found on the breast, neither of the body or clothes. There were no injuries about the body until just about the lower part of the abdomen. Two or three inches from the left side was a wound running in a jagged manner. The wound was a very deep one and the tissues were cut through.

There were several incisions running across the abdomen. There were also three or four similar cuts, running downwards, on the right side, all of which had been caused by a knife which had been used violently and downwards. The injuries were from left to right and might have been done by a left-handed person. All the injuries had been caused by the same instrument [2]. In response to questioning about the degree of medical knowledge exhibited by the killer, Dr Llewellyn replied that he 'must have had some rough anatomical knowledge, for he seemed to have attacked all the vital parts.'

He also stated that the crime could have been executed in four or five minutes. The doctor initially believed that the assailant had attacked Mary Nichols from in front, probably using his right hand to stifle her cries as he wielded the knife in his left hand and used it to cut her throat. Later, he came to doubt his own conjecture. There is little doubt that the victim's throat was not cut while she was standing, or there would almost certainly have been bloodstains on the front of her clothing. This was not the case. A more likely scenario is that she was either throttled or punched and placed on the ground by the murderer, who then knelt or crouched at her right side, probably facing Brady Street, whereby he cut her throat from left to right so that any blood spurted away from him. He then inflicted the other mutilations by drawing the knife downward and toward himself, indicating that he was right-handed after all.

There was corroborating evidence of throttling because the deceased woman's face was bruised and her tongue lacerated slightly. The doctor also confirmed that he had been to the mortuary a second time to examine the deceased. He found an old scar on the woman's forehead and also confirmed that no part of the viscera was missing. At this point the inquest was adjourned until Monday, 3rd September. It reopened then with Inspector **John Spratling**. He stated that he had arrived at Bucks Row at 4:30 in the morning of 31st August and by that time the body had been moved and two constables guarded the spot that was pointed out to him. At the time, the last of the blood was being washed away by one of Emma Green's sons. He then described his visit to the mortuary, his attempt to write down a description, his discovery of the abdominal mutilations and his call to Dr Llewellyn.

There followed some dispute about precisely what orders had been given regarding the body. The police said that instructions were given that the body was to be left alone, but two mortuary attendants, Robert Mann and James Hatfield, had stripped and cleaned the body before the post mortem! This point was confirmed by Detective Sergeant **Patrick Enright**, who swore that he had given express instructions that the body was not to be touched. Inspector Spratling gave details of the clothing the dead woman wore and mentioned that the stays she had worn were still fastened up. The inspector told the court that he and Sergeant George Godley had searched along the tracks of the East London and District Railway and had also searched the Great Eastern Railway yard, but had found nothing. There was a man on night duty at the gates of the Great Eastern yard, 50 yards from the spot where the body was found, but he heard nothing. Nobody heard anything within 150 yards of Bucks Row!

This was confirmed by the witness **Henry Tomkins**, from the Barber's Horse Slaughterer's yard. He testified that he and his fellow workmen, James Mumford and Charles Brittain, had started work between eight o'clock and nine o'clock in the evening of Thursday 30th August. At midnight he and Brittain had left the yard, not returning until around one o'clock in the morning. Throughout the night, the gates of the slaughter yard had been left open, and none of the men had heard anything until PC Thain came by to tell them about the body. Thain denied calling at the yard on his way to fetch Dr Llewellyn. Tomkins stated that he and Mumford were the first to leave the yard and go to look at the body at around 4:15 in the morning. They were followed a few minutes later by Charles Brittain.

Next to testify was police Inspector **Joseph Henry Helson**, the officer from Bethnal Green police station leading the Nichols inquiry. He said he had first heard of the murder at 6:45 on Friday 31st August and went to the mortuary where he saw the body, which was still fully clothed. He was present when the clothing was removed and noted that the bodice of the dress was buttoned down to the middle and the stays still fastened. The abdominal mutilations were visible while the stays were still on, the implication being that the stays had been in position while the injuries were inflicted. **PC Mizen** gave his testimony and told of the encounter with two men, Charles Cross and Robert Paul, placing this meeting at the junction of Baker's Row and Hanbury Street. Cross had told him that he was wanted by a policeman in Bucks Row, but had said nothing about having found a woman or about any murder.

Charles Cross stepped into the witness box to give his evidence; he told the court of his discovery of the body and his encounter with the other man, Robert Paul (although at this time, Paul had not been traced and Cross did not know his name). They had encountered PC Mizen, and Cross said he had told the officer that they had found a woman lying on the pavement and had touched her hands and found them cold. He said he had told Mizen that he thought she was either dead or drunk. The other man had expressed his belief that she was dead. Mizen walked off toward Bucks Row. Cross and the other man continued into Hanbury Street and he had seen his companion turn into Corbetts Court.

William Nichols, the dead woman's husband, next took the stand. He confirmed that he and Mary had been separated for eight years but denied that the separation had anything to do with an affair between him and the nurse. He claimed they had parted because of his wife's drinking. However, he never actually denied an affair had taken place. William confirmed that when he and Mary had first parted, he had paid her an allowance of 5s per week, but sometime in 1881 or 1882, he discovered that she was living with another man and stopped payments. The Guardians of the Parish of Lambeth had summoned Nichols to show why he should not contribute to his wife's support, but when he explained that she was living with another man the summons was withdrawn. He ended his evidence by saying that he had not seen his wife for three years.

Ellen Holland had seen Mary Nichols in the early hours of 31st August. She had gone to watch a large fire at the docks and on her way home had met Mary by accident at the corner of Osborn Street and Whitechapel Road. Ellen believed that Mary had been staying at the White House, where men and women were allowed to share accommodation – most lodging houses were very strict about separating sexes to discourage lewd behaviour. Mary was very drunk and Ellen tried to persuade her to come back with her to the lodging house at 18 Thrawl Street. Mary replied that she had no money for her bed, adding that she had earned it twice over that night but had drunk it away in the Frying Pan public house. Ellen was able to put the time of this meeting as 2:30 in the morning, because the clock at St. Mary's struck as they were talking. Soon afterwards, Ellen saw Mary staggering off eastwards along the Whitechapel Road.

The final witness on 3rd September was **Mary Ann Monk**, who merely confirmed that she had known Mary Nichols as an inmate of the Lambeth Workhouse, at which point Coroner Baxter adjourned the proceedings for two weeks. On Thursday 6th September 1888, Mary Ann Nichols was buried. That afternoon her body was transported in a polished elm coffin with the cortege consisting of a hearse and two mourning coaches, which carried William Nichols and their eldest son. Mary Nichols was buried at the City of London Cemetery (in Ilford) in public grave number 210752 on the edge of the present day Memorial Garden.

7th September 1888 police weekly reports

The police investigation proceeded as normal and the first suspects name came to light. A weekly report, signed by an acting Superintendent W. Davies dated 7th September, read 'a man named (John) Pizer alias Leather Apron, had been in the habit of ill-using prostitutes in various parts of the Metropolis for some time past, and careful enquiries have been made to trace him, but without success. There is no evidence against him at present. Enquiries are being continued.' Another report also dated 7th September and signed by Inspector Helson, confirmed that the police were convinced that Mary Nichols had met her death at the spot where her body was found.

It also confirmed that Mary had been seen in Whitechapel Road at about eleven o'clock on the evening of 30th August, and that she had been seen also leaving the Frying Pan public house on Brick Lane at 12:30. She had been seen again at 1:20 inside the lodging house at 18 Thrawl Street, where the deputy keeper asked her for the 4p for her bed. Mary had said that she had no money but was going back out to earn some. Her parting words were apparently 'I'll soon get my doss money; see what a jolly bonnet I've got now.' The final sighting was by Ellen Holland at 2:30. Helson's report also referred to John Pizer and repeated that there was no evidence against him at that time.

The inquest re-opens

The inquest on Mary Nichols reopened on Monday 17th September with **Dr Llewellyn** recalled to the stand (meanwhile, Annie Chapman, victim number two, had met her death and some of her internal organs had been removed and taken away by the killer). Dr Llewellyn had re-examined Mary's body before her burial and confirmed that no part of her viscera was missing. **Emma Green** of 2 Bucks Row, right next to where the body was found, was next witness. She said that she had retired for the night at eleven o'clock on Thursday 30th August. Both of her sons had already gone to bed, one at nine o'clock and the other at 9:45. Her daughter had retired at the same time as she had, and they both occupied the front room on the first floor. She heard nothing until the knock at the door at about four o'clock on 31st August. She had thrown open the window and seen three or four constables and two or three other men. She could also see the body of the victim, but it was too dark to see exactly what had taken place. Questioned by one of the jurymen, she confirmed that she was a light sleeper.

Walter Purkiss who lived in Essex Wharf almost opposite to where the body was found, said that he lived in that house with his wife, family and a servant. Purkiss and his wife slept in the front room on the second floor and they had both gone to bed at eleven o'clock or possibly 11:15. Purkiss had slept fitfully during the night and was awake between one and two o'clock. His wife had been awake most of the night, but neither of them had heard a sound. He described the street as unusually quiet that night. When the police officer had awakened him, Purkiss opened the window and looked out. He could see the body, the police, and some other men.

Patrick Mulshaw was a night watchman and on the night of Mary Nichols' death he had been guarding the sewage works in Winthrop Street at the rear of the Working Lad's Institute. He had gone on duty at 4:45 in the afternoon on Thursday and remained at his post until about 5:55 in the morning the following day. Mulshaw admitted that he had dozed during his watch but swore that he was not asleep between three and four o'clock. During that time, he had not seen or heard anything. Soon after that time, a man passed his position and said 'watchman, old man, I believe somebody is murdered down the street.' Patrick had then walked down to Bucks Row and seen the body. The man who had spoken to him had not been traced by police. Mulshaw was able to say that he had seen nobody after midnight but had seen two constables, one of whom was PC Neil.

PC Thain gave his testimony. His beat took him along Brady Street past the end of Bucks Row every thirty minutes. At 3:45 that morning he had seen a signal from Constable Neil and gone to offer assistance. After speaking to Neil, Thain went for Dr Llewellyn and accompanied him back to Bucks Row. By the time they arrived, there were a couple of workmen with PC Neil. After the body had been removed, Thain stayed to await Inspector Spratling. Thain said he did not tell the workmen at Barber's Horse Slaughterer's yard about the dead body. By this time **Robert Paul**, who had met Charles Cross in Bucks Row, had been found by police and was next to give evidence. He told of his walk down Bucks Row and of seeing a man standing in the middle of the road. As Paul drew nearer, the other man tapped him on the shoulder and said 'come and look at this woman here.'

After their cursory examination of the body, the two men went off to find a policeman and had found one at the junction of Old Montague Street and Hanbury Street. It was no more than four minutes since they had left the body in Bucks Row. **Robert Mann**, an inmate of the Whitechapel Workhouse, was next to give evidence. He was the man in charge of the mortuary and the key holder of that place. There was confusion over his evidence because Mann said he had received no instructions not to touch the body, which was the opposite of what the police said. However, he was not a good witness and Coroner Baxter informed the jury that Mann was subject to fits and hence 'neither his memory nor statements are reliable.'

James Hatfield, who was Mann's assistant at the mortuary, fared no better. He reported that Mary Nichols had not been wearing stays, but when questioned further he admitted that his memory was bad. It must be remembered that both he and Mann were giving evidence almost three weeks after the event. After further evidence of police searches given by Inspector Spratling, a juryman commented that if a substantial reward had been offered by the home secretary after the murder of Martha Tabram in George Yard, then the two later murders (Nichols and Chapman) might not have taken place. The inquiry was adjourned until Saturday 22nd September.

On the 22nd Coroner Baxter summed up the evidence that had been given. He started though, by complaining that there was no proper Coroner's Court in Whitechapel, and no proper public mortuary. He went on to describe Mary Nichols life and history. In the end Baxter linked the Mary Nichols death with that of Annie Chapman, suggesting that it was possible that in Mary Nichols case the killer might have sought to possess certain of the dead woman's organs but had been disturbed in his quest by the arrival of Charles Cross on the scene. The jury then returned the only verdict it could: 'murder by some person or persons unknown.'

Conclusions

Polly, or Mary Ann Nichols, was the first of the conical four (or five) ripper killings. There appeared to be no motive for her murder; the woman had no money and why would there be any sexual motive with a prostitute? The police, who operated a rigid beat policy with the officer only leaving his route to attend to an emergency summons from a colleague, saw and heard nothing unusual. The police were baffled, apparently, by the lack of a sound from the victim, and the small amount of blood on the pavement meant the killer probably had little blood on his person. Bruises and a cut to the tongue would seem to indicate some sort of punch or attack to the face, rendering the woman senseless and collapsed or laid on the ground, after which the throat was cut; alternatively, she may have gone down voluntarily expecting sex, only to find the man crushing her face with a hand to silence her whilst wielding the knife to deadly effect.

No anatomical knowledge was necessary for this attack, for as Polly Nichols bled to death the killer threw up her many skirts and attacked her lower stomach whilst squatting near her right shoulder or right chest – the attempt was probably to secure bodily organs for purposes unknown, only to see the shadowy figure of Charles Cross entering the Row from Brady Street at a distance of about 183 yards. Thus his effort to disembowel was cut short and the killer had to make good his escape. Just past the Board School and left towards Winthrop Street was an alleyway that led to Whitechapel Road, opposite the London Hospital. In all likelihood, this was the route the murderer took, for to go further along Bucks Row was asking for trouble from the beat policemen.

It's possible, of course, that the killer may have taken refuge amongst the many railway yards and sidings in the area, although these were searched and revealed nothing. There was talk of bloodstains seen in Brady Street leading into Bucks Row, but the police say they found nothing of the sort. There were so many people living in the Row and yet nobody heard anything! Perhaps the best clue could have come from Patrick Mulshaw, the night watchman guarding the sewage works in Winthrop Street at the rear of the Working Lad's Institute. During his night duty he had not seen or heard anything, but soon a man passed him at about 4:40 and said 'watchman, old man, I believe somebody is murdered down the street.'

Patrick had then walked down to Bucks Row; the man who had spoken to him had not been traced by police, nor was a description given. The coroner seemed to doubt Mulshaw's ability to stay awake at work! But he never asked for a description from this witness. It could well have been the murderer speaking to him whilst making good his escape via that narrow alley in Winthrop Street to Whitechapel Road. The man who spoke to Mulshaw has been regarded a sinister figure who has never been satisfactorily identified. This mysterious man spoke to Mulshaw in a manner that has been inferred suggesting he was a bit of a 'toff' with the remark 'I say, old man, a woman has been murdered down the street.' Exciting as it seems, Mulshaw was an old man at the time and this passer-by addressing him as 'old man' possibly intended it to be literal. Not many ripperologists or ripper books make much of this witness from the public inquiry, or the mystery man.

3 THE SECOND VICTIM

We go forward now eight days after the murder of Polly Nichols, to the morning of Saturday 8th September 1888, and the discovery of the second conical victim – Annie Chapman. Her body was found in the back yard of 29 Hanbury Street, Spitalfields.

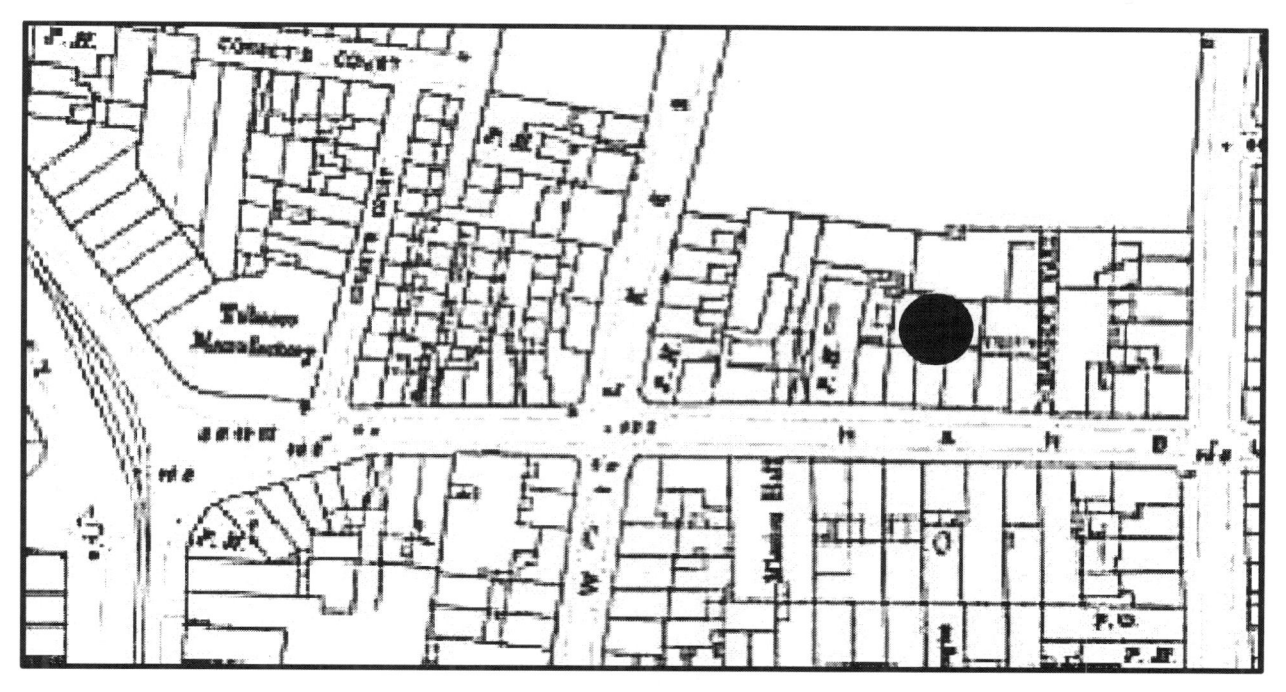

29 Hanbury Street, Spitalfields (unknown general map).

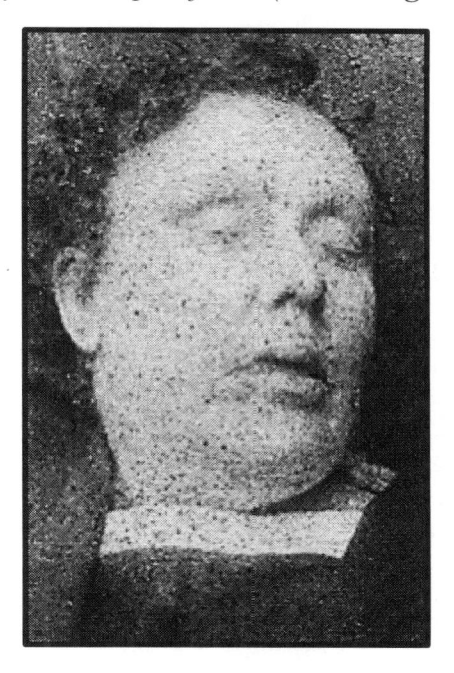

Annie Chapman

Front of no.29; there are two doors, the one on the right enters the front shop and the one on the left enters the rest of the building and the rear yard (unknown).

About 29 Hanbury Street

Today, a new building stands on the north side of Hanbury Street where no. 29 once stood – the buildings directly opposite still resemble in many ways those that once stood on the north side. No. 29 stood there in about 1976, when I visited it on my motorcycle. So, what do we know of what happened there? Well, seventeen people lived in the house for a start! Looking out on the street at the front was a cat's meat shop run by Harriet Hardiman, who slept in the shop with her son aged sixteen. There was one other room on the ground floor, at the back, which was used by Amelia Richardson to cook food and hold regular weekly prayer meetings; she and her grandson Thomas, aged fourteen, actually slept in the front room on the second floor, above the cat's meat shop. Amelia also used a cellar, access to which was through the backyard, from which she ran a packing case business. Also living on the second floor, at the rear, was a Mr Walker, a maker of tennis boots. He shared the room with his retarded adult son Alfred.

The front room on the third floor was occupied by a Mr Thompson, a Carman, his wife, and their adopted daughter. The third floor back room was home to a Mr and Mrs Copsey, who made cigars. The house also boasted an attic, at the front of which lived another Carman, John Davis, with his wife and three sons. Lastly, also in that same attic but at the rear of the house lived Mrs Sarah Cox, a widow. We can see here a good indication of the sort of overcrowding in the east end at the time of the ripper killings. The spooky and sinister events of what happened here began at around 3:30 in the morning of Saturday 8th September 1888. Mr

Thompson, the Carman, left the house to go to his work at Goodsons in Brick Lane. As he left the house, he was heard by Mrs Amelia Richardson, who called out 'good morning' as he passed her room; such was the thinness of the internal walls.

Rear yard of 29 Hanbury Street (unknown).

Just over an hour later and John Richardson, Amelia's son who lived in John Street, called in at no. 29. He was a porter at the Spitalfields Market but also helped his mother in her packing case business. It was about 4:45 or 4:50 when John came by; it was already getting light by that time. He checked the passageway that led from the street to the rear yard at the back, for occasionally people had been found sleeping rough there. On this occasion the passageway was clear of people. Whilst he was at no. 29 he noted that one of his boots was hurting so he opened the door that led into the backyard and sat on the top step, using his knife to trim some leather from the boot. He then left the house, having been there no more than three minutes or so.

The back door closed itself, and John Richardson later said that he closed the front door behind him, too. This house had two front doors, as we have seen in the photographs. The one on the right as we look at the building opened directly into the shop. The one on the left gave access to a passage (twenty to twenty-five feet long) that led to the rest of the house and then the rear yard. The occupants used its front door to come and go. At 5:45 John Davis rose from his bed and started to get ready for work. By six o'clock he was heading downstairs intending to go out into the yard.

Rear yard; the victim was found with her head at the foot of the bottom step, close to the wooden fence (unknown).

As he walked down the passageway he noticed that the front door that led out into Hanbury Street was wide open. John Richardson, the market porter, was to testify later that he had shut it when he left the house about an hour or so earlier, of course. There was nothing unusual about this, however, so John Davis pushed open the door that led into the rear yard.

Discovery

There were three stone steps leading down into the yard and a small recess lay between the steps and the fence to the left of the yard. Looking down, Davis saw the terribly mutilated body of a woman, with her head lying in that recess pointing toward the house. He stepped back, recovered his composure and ran out into Hanbury Street. As he stumbled out he saw two men – James Green and James Kent. They worked for Joseph and Thomas Bayley, packing case maker at 23a Hanbury Street, and were waiting outside their workshop. Henry John Holland, also a box maker, was walking along Hanbury Street on his way to work. Davis managed to gasp 'men, come here!' All three men, Kent, Green, and Holland, followed John Davis down the passageway to the back door, where they looked down at the body.

Only Henry Holland ventured down the three stone steps into the yard. He did not touch the body and went back up the steps seconds later. These men ran into Hanbury Street and off to find a policeman, all except James Kent, who felt in need of a stiff brandy to steady his nerves. It was by now about 6:10 in the morning, and Inspector Joseph Chandler was on duty in Commercial Street, close to the corner of Hanbury Street. He saw several men rushing toward him shouting, 'another woman has been murdered.' The inspector immediately rushed to no. 29 and later reported this: 'I at once proceeded to no. 29 Hanbury Street and in the back yard found a woman lying on her back, dead, left arm resting on left breast, legs drawn up, abducted, small intestines and flap of the abdomen lying on right side, above right shoulder, attached by a cord with the rest of the intestines inside the body; two flaps of skin from the lower part of the abdomen lying in a large quantity of blood above the left shoulder; throat cut deeply from left and back in a jagged manner right around throat.'

Chandler sent for Dr George Bagster Phillips, the divisional police surgeon and for further assistance from the police station. Dr Phillips arrived at 6:30 and later reported: 'I found the body of the deceased lying in the yard on her back, on the left hand of the steps that lead from the passage. The head was about 6" in front of the level of the bottom step and the feet were towards a shed at the end of the yard. The left arm was across the left breast and the legs were drawn up, the feet resting on the ground and the knees turned outwards. The face was swollen and turned on the right side, and the tongue protruded from the front teeth, but not beyond the lips; it was much swollen. The small intestines and other portions were lying on the right side of the body on the ground above the right shoulder, but attached. There was a large quantity of blood, with a part of the stomach above the left shoulder. The body was cold, except that there was a certain remaining heat, under the intestines, in the body. Stiffness of the limbs was not marked, but it was commencing. The throat was severed deeply. I noticed that the incision of the skin was jagged, and reached right around the neck.'

Dr Phillips believed that the woman had been dead for at least two hours, probably longer, thus putting his initial estimate of the time of death at 4:30 in the morning! The body was moved to the Whitechapel Mortuary, leaving Inspector Chandler to make a careful search of the yard. On the back wall of the house, close to where the woman's head had lain and about 18" from the ground, he found six patches of blood, varying in size from a pencil point to a sixpenny piece. There were also smears of blood about 14" from the ground on the wooden palings that divided no. 29 from the house next door. Close to where her feet had been, was a small piece of coarse muslin, a small toothed comb as worn in the hair and a pocket comb in a paper case. Near where her head had been lay a small portion of an envelope containing two pills.

The back of this envelope bore a seal and the words 'Sussex Regiment' embossed in blue; on the front was the letter 'M' and lower down the letters 'Sp', probably the remaining part of a name or address. There was no stamp but it was postmarked in red, 'London, Aug 23 1888.' Inspector Chandler's report was quite believable in that he was the first police officer on the scene and was experienced, with fifteen years in the force. His report makes no mention of any other items left at the murder scene, and therefore we must conclude that there were no coins, no rings and no other items other than those he mentions. After examining the yard, Inspector Chandler went to the mortuary and wrote down his description of the deceased.

This, together with the publicity of the case led to her rapid identification. Amelia Palmer from 30 Dorset Street had been a close friend of the victim, whom she named as Annie Chapman, stating that she had recently been living at Crossingham's lodging house at 35 Dorset Street. This was later confirmed by Timothy Donovan, the deputy at Crossingham's lodging house who said Annie had lodged there for the past four months. Annie Chapman was born Eliza Anne Smith in Paddington in 1841. She married John Chapman, a coachman, in 1869 at the All Saints Church in Knightsbridge, and soon afterward the couple lived in Bayswater. John and Annie Chapman had three children. Annie was too fond of drink apparently, and this led to a break-down of their marriage in 1884. Annie then moved to Spitalfields in London. In 1886 Annie lodged at 30 Dorset Street with a sieve maker, thus she earned the nickname of 'Annie Sivvy.'

After their separation, John Chapman allowed his wife an allowance of 10s a week, but this ended when he died in December 1886. Soon afterwards, Annie's relationship with the sieve maker ended. You might now remember the police report of 7th September regarding a man called John Pizer, or Leather Apron? At about eight o'clock in the morning of Monday 10th September, the long arm of the law, in the form of Sergeant William Thick, finally caught up with John, who had been staying at 22 Mulberry Street. When the house was searched, five long-bladed knives were found. These, along with Pizer, were taken to Leman Street Police Station.

Public inquest

Also that same day, the inquest on Annie Chapman opened before Coroner Wynne Edwin Baxter in the Working Lad's Institute in Whitechapel Road. **John Davis** spoke of finding the body on the morning of 8th September. The previous evening, he had gone to bed at eight o'clock. His son had got home at 10:45 and none of the family had gone out again. John was awake from three to five o'clock in the morning. He managed to fall asleep for half an hour but heard the clock at Spitalfields Church strike 5:45, when he and his wife got up.

Mrs Davis made a cup of tea and after drinking it, John went down to the yard just as the church bell was striking the hour. After finding the body and telling his story to the men outside, he ran off to find a policeman before returning to the house, although he did not enter it. He confirmed that he had not gone down into the yard and had not touched the body. He testified that he and his family had lived in the house for only two weeks! It should be noted that the back yard of no. 29 was often used by prostitutes for their pick-ups, although the tenants did not like to admit it.

Amelia Palmer spoke of her identification of the body. She stated that she had seen Annie in Dorset Street on Monday 3rd September, at which time Annie complained of feeling unwell. She had a bruise on one temple and said she had argued with another woman over a man known as Harry the Hawker. Amelia had seen Annie again the following day, this time near Spitalfields Church and Annie had again said that she felt ill and had added that she was thinking of going to the casual ward to see if the people there could help her. Amelia had kindly given her two pennies and warned her not to spend the money on drink. The last meeting between the two women was at five o'clock in the afternoon of Friday 7th September, again in Dorset Street. Annie said she felt too unwell to do anything but then countered with 'it's no good my giving way. I must pull myself together and go out and get some money or I shall have no lodgings.'

Timothy Donovan, the deputy at Crossingham's lodging house, testified that he had seen Annie in the kitchen at the lodging house on the Friday. She was still there at 1:45 in the morning on 8th September, eating a baked potato. He asked her for her doss money and she told him she had none but would be back soon. Annie then walked out into the street. **John Evans** was the night watchman at Crossingham's and he too saw Annie in the kitchen in the early hours of 8th September. She told him she had just had a pint of beer and had been to Vauxhall to see one of her sisters. After speaking to Donovan, Annie left the house and Evans saw her walk up Little Paternoster Row towards Brushfield Street. After hearing Evans' evidence, Baxter adjourned proceedings for two days. On the 11th September, John Pizer was released from police custody because no evidence against him had been found.

Coroner Baxter's inquest reopened again on Wednesday 12th September with **Fountain Smith**, a brother of the dead woman. He stated that his sister had been 47 years old and that he had seen her shortly before her death, when he gave her two shillings. **James Kent**, one of the men who worked for Bayley's in Hanbury Street, testified that he had left home at six o'clock on the day in question, getting to work about 6:10. His employer's gate was open, but while he was still waiting outside a man he now knew to be John Davis rushed up and appealed for assistance. Kent described how he and James Green had then gone to no. 29, walked down the passageway and stood at the top of the steps, from which they could plainly see the body. He said he noticed that the woman had a handkerchief of some kind around her throat and that her hands were bent with the palms upward. The sight distressed him so much that he had to leave the house and drink some brandy. Shortly afterward, he went to Bayley's to get a piece of canvas to cover the body.

James Green said he arrived at Bayley's about 5:50; he merely confirmed much of the evidence given by James Kent. **Amelia Richardson** told the court that at around six o'clock on 8th September she had heard some commotion and noise in the passage and her grandson, Thomas Richardson, had gone downstairs to investigate. He returned to say 'oh, grandmother, there is a woman murdered.' She went down herself and saw the body. At that time there were police and some other men in the passage, which was quite crowded. Mrs Richardson said she had retired the previous night at 9:30 p.m. She had been awake for most of the night and was certainly wide awake at three o'clock. After that she dozed fitfully and heard nothing apart from Mr Thompson leaving the house about 3:30. She was sure she would have heard anyone going through the passage, but she hadn't heard a thing.

Harriet Hardiman said she had gone to bed at 10:30 on 7th September and awoke at six o'clock when she heard footsteps in the passage. She too sent her son to investigate and he came back and told her a woman had been killed in the yard. **John Richardson** was described as a tall, stout man, with a very pale face, brown moustache and dark brown hair. He was shabbily dressed in a ragged coat and dark brown trousers. He swore he had seen nothing when he trimmed his boot in the yard. It was suggested at the time that the open back door might well have obscured Richardson's view; also, when questioned at 6:45 by Inspector Chandler, he did not even mention sitting on the steps to the back yard to trim his boot.

Inspector Chandler told the jury that Richardson had told him that 'he did not go down the steps and did not mention the fact that he sat down on the steps and cut his boot.' [3] Richardson had since changed his testimony for the inquiry! Dr Phillips had estimated the time of death at 4:30 in the morning and, if he was correct, then the body must have been lying in the yard when Richardson opened the door. In fact, it is highly unlikely that Annie was dead at this time – it is much more probable that the doctor was wrong in his calculations. John Richardson's testimony narrows the time of death to after 4:55 that morning. **John Pizer**, the man who had been suspected of the murder for a short time, was now called to show that he had been home at the time of the murder and had remained there until arrested by Sergeant Thick.

The final witness was **Henry John Holland**, who said that at 6:08 that morning he was passing down Hanbury Street on his way to his place of work in Chiswell Street. As he passed no. 29 an elderly man dashed out and cried 'come and look in the backyard.' Holland went through to the back door, saw the body and stepped down into the yard to get a clearer look. He then went in search of a policeman and found one on duty in Spitalfields Market. That officer was not able to assist because he was on fixed-point duty and unable to leave his post. This response so incensed Holland that later that day he made an official complaint at the police station in Commercial Street. On 13th September, the inquest began again with Inspector **Joseph Chandler** as first witness. He put the time he noticed the men in Hanbury Street as

6:02. By the time he arrived at no. 29 there were several people in the passage but none in the yard.

After giving his report of what he had found in the yard, Chandler said he sent for the doctor, the ambulance and further police assistance; this included sending a telegram to Detective Inspector Abberline at Scotland Yard, who had been called into assist with the murder inquiry of Polly Nichols. When other constables arrived, he ordered them to remove all the people from the passageway. After Chapman's body was removed, the inspector searched the yard and in addition to the items already mentioned, he found a leather apron, which was wet, about two feet away from a water tap. At the time this discovery was believed to be a possible clue, but the apron was soon shown to belong to John Richardson. His mother confirmed that she had found it in the cellar, rather green and mouldy, and had washed it out before leaving it in the yard to dry.

The final part of Chandler's evidence confirmed that there was no sign of a struggle in the yard and that the back door opened outward, into the yard, on the left-hand side – the same side where the body was found, so it was possible that John Richardson could have missed seeing it when he opened the door. The door could have blocked his view to the left where the body lay. Sergeant **Edward Badham** was one of the officers sent to assist Inspector Chandler, but his only real contribution was to convey Annie Chapman's body to the mortuary on the police ambulance. Dr **Bagster Phillips** outlined the medical evidence. He described the scene upon his arrival and then spoke of his initial examination. There was a bruise on Annie's right temple, another on her upper eyelid and two more on the top of her chest, but these appeared to not be fresh.

There were more recent marks on Annie's face and jaw, from which Phillips deduced that the killer had seized her by the chin before her throat was cut. This, and the protruding swollen tongue, indicated that she had been partially strangled before the wounds were inflicted. There were also the marks of one or more rings on Annie's ring finger, but an abrasion there suggested that the killer had wrenched these items from her. The immediate cause of death, Phillips said, had been the loss of blood from the throat. This had been cut from left to right and an attempt made to cut off Annie's head. Although the details of the injuries were not revealed by the press, an article in the Lancet of 29th September gave more detail: 'the abdomen had been entirely laid open; the intestines, severed from their mesenteric attachments, had been lifted out of the body and placed by the shoulder of the corpse; whilst from the pelvis the uterus and its appendages, with the upper portion of the vagina and the posterior two-thirds of the bladder had been entirely removed.'

The article went on to say that 'the incisions were cleanly cut, avoiding the rectum and dividing the vagina low enough to avoid injury to the cervix uteri.' Other parts of the doctor's testimony were deemed controversial. He deduced that the killer was a medical expert, or at least one who 'had such knowledge of anatomical or pathological examinations as to be enabled to secure the pelvic organs with one sweep of a knife.' However, as will become clearer when future crimes are looked at, the killer need not have had much medical knowledge. Many ripperologists believe that the killer was just a trophy collector and it is possible all he sought was some organ from his victims. **Mary Elizabeth Simonds**, a nurse at Whitechapel Infirmary, gave evidence that she and another woman named Frances Wright had undressed and washed the body at the mortuary. After this, the inquest was adjourned again until 19th September.

Police investigations

The police, meanwhile, were following up the possible lead of the envelope found next to Annie's body. The crest they traced to the 1st battalion the Sussex Regiment at Farnborough, and this identification was confirmed by Captain Young of that regiment. He told the police that the men used this stationery to write letters home and that the envelopes could be purchased in the canteen. However, no men could be found who had written to any address in Spitalfields and none of the men's handwriting matched the writing on the front of the envelope. The trail was confused still further when it was discovered that the stationery could also be bought over the counter in the local Post Office.

On 14th September, **Ted Stanley**, also known as 'the Pensioner,' called at Commercial Street Police Station. He had been mentioned at the inquest as a close friend of the dead woman, but up to this point the police had been unable to trace him. Stanley gave a satisfactory account of his movements and said he had last seen Annie on the corner of Brushfield Street on 2nd September, at which time she was wearing two rings (brass, not gold) on one of her fingers.

On the same day another suspect, **Edward McKenna**, was arrested. He had been seen at Heath Street carrying a knife and was taken to the police station in Commercial Street. However, he was able to prove that he was at a lodging house in Brick Lane at the time Annie had met her death. Also on 14th September, Annie Chapman was laid to rest in Manor Park Cemetery (Forest Gate); the ceremony was deliberately kept quiet and only members of her family attended. The next day, the mystery clue of the torn envelope was revealed; what the police failed to do with the Sussex Regiment in Farnborough was sorted when **William Stevens**, a painter lodging at Crossingham's who had known Annie, said that on Friday 7th September she come into the house and told him she had been to the hospital. She had with her a bottle of medicine, a bottle of lotion and a box containing two pills.

As she was showing him the box, it fell to pieces in her hands so she took out the pills, picked up a piece of envelope from the floor and wrapped the pills in it. On 19th September, Coroner Baxter opened his inquest again. Details had been given in the press of an argument Annie was supposed to have had in Crossingham's lodging house before her death. **Eliza Cooper**, who had lodged at that same address for the past five months, said she had argued with Annie on the Tuesday 4th September before the latter died. According to Eliza, the argument was about a piece of soap, borrowed from the man known as 'the Pensioner' which had not been returned to him by Annie. Things cooled and they all went for a drink at Britannia public house on the corner of Commercial and Dorset Streets. Here the argument flared up again and Annie lashed out and slapped Eliza's face. She in turn retaliated by striking Annie's left eye and on her chest.

Dr **Bagster Phillips** was recalled to discuss the various bruises on Annie's body in the light of Eliza Cooper's testimony. He confirmed that he had seen the old bruises but stated that there were scratches of recent origin about 2" below the lobe of one ear. He stated again his belief that Annie had been seized by the throat and that her killer seemed to display some anatomical knowledge. Also on that day at the inquest appeared **Elizabeth Darrell**, also referred to in the press coverage as **Durrell** or **Elizabeth Long**. She lived at 32 Church Street but on the morning of 8th September, at 5:30 in the morning, she was walking along Hanbury Street on the same side as no. 29 on her way to Spitalfields Market. Close to the shutters of that house she saw a man and a woman talking. The man had his back towards Brick Lane and the woman was facing Mrs Darrell.

She had seen the dead woman since and was sure that the woman she saw was the same person. As she passed, Mrs Darrell heard the man say 'will you?' and the woman replied 'Yes.' Although she never saw the man's face, Mrs. Darrell was able to give a partial description. He was dark, wore a brown deerstalker hat and looked to be aged over forty. He had a shabby genteel appearance, was a little taller than Annie and appeared to be a foreigner. Since Annie Chapman had been only five feet tall, this would put her companion at about 5 feet 2". Many ripperologists suggest Elizabeth had her timing wrong here, and that the clock bell she thought she heard ring 5:30 when she saw Chapman with this man was in fact the quarter bell – 5:15. This would give time for the murderer to go about his work.

The other useful witness that day was **Albert Cadoche** (or **Cadosch**) who lived next door to the murder site at 27 Hanbury Street. On the morning that Annie's body was found, Albert got up at 5:15 and soon afterwards went out into his yard. As he returned to his house he heard a voice say 'no' from behind the dividing wooden fence, although he was not absolutely certain it came from that yard. Three or four minutes later, he was again in his yard and heard a sound as if something was falling against the dividing fence. He did not attempt, however, to look over to see what was going on. Since he heard no further noises he soon left his house to go to work.

He passed Spitalfields Church about 5:32. He does not describe whether the voice was male or female. Allowing for slight errors in the timings given, if these two new witnesses were telling the truth then this information pins down the time of the attack upon Annie Chapman to around 5:30 in the morning. The time frame, if correct, was contrary to the estimation of Dr Bagster Phillips; also, it indicates that the man seen outside no.29 by Mrs Darrell could only be the murderer of Annie. On 26th September the coroner summed up the evidence: he said that 'the wretch must have then seized the deceased, perhaps with Judas-like approaches. He seized her by the chin. He pressed her throat and while thus preventing the slightest cry, he at the same time produced insensibility and suffocation.

There was no evidence of any struggle. The clothes were not torn. The deceased was then lowered to the ground and laid on her back; and although in doing so she may have fallen slightly against the fence, the movement was probably effected with care. Her throat was then cut in two places with savage determination.' Regarding the clothes not being torn, the pocket of Annie's underskirt had been cut open at the front and side. The jury then returned the verdict of 'murder by some person or persons unknown.' At this time the press was linking together four murders in Whitechapel: Emma Smith, Martha Tabram, Mary Ann Nichols (Polly) and now Annie Chapman.

Conclusions

An air of mystery and fear began to pervade the east-end of London when the verdict was returned, and the press made four the recent number of unsolved murders in Whitechapel. The police, bolstered perhaps by the supplement of Detective Inspectors Abberline, Henry Moore and Walter Andrews, continued to follow the reports of the divisional surgeon, George Bagster Phillips. His opinion that Annie Chapman had died sometime between two and 4:30 in the morning, deduced by her body coldness at the time of examination on the ground, brought forward a prime suspect; he who had a knife upon him and mended his boot on the steps of the rear yard – John Richardson.

'There is doubtful evidence (*which*) points to something between 5:30 and six – but medical evidence says about four o'clock.' This is in the Home Office file. [4] Perhaps we should take time now to consider for a moment where all the paperwork, statements and meagre photographs ended up? There are two ripper files in fact: the Metropolitan police file at the Public Records Office, and the Home Office file, for which written permission from the Home Office was usually required to view it at the PRO. Technically, it is 'closed' for one hundred years. Detective Chief Inspector Swanson, the man commanding the ripper murder investigation, wrote a report dated 19th October in which he tells us that the police, rather than seeing John Richardson as a crucial witness, saw him as a very real suspect.

'If the evidence of Dr Phillips is correct as to time of death, it is difficult to understand how it was that Richardson did not see the body when he went into the yard at 4:45; but as his clothes were examined, the house searched and his statement taken in which there was not a shred of evidence, suspicion could not rest upon him, although police specially directed their attention to him.'

Thus, the detectives working on the Chapman case, by accepting that Dr Phillips' estimated time of death was correct, so made Elizabeth Darrell and Alfred Cadoche's statements irrelevant. Swanson was forced to admit that 'up to the present the combined result of those inquiries did not supply the police with the slightest clue to the murderer.' And also 'again if the evidence of Mrs Long (*Darrell*) is correct that she saw the deceased at 5:30, then the evidence of Dr Phillips as to probable time of death is incorrect. He was called and saw the body at 6:20 and he then gives it as his opinion that death occurred about two hours earlier, viz: 4:20. Hence the evidence of Mrs Long, which appeared to be so important to the coroner, must be looked upon with some amount of doubt, which is to be regretted.'

By the end of the year, Inspector Walter Andrews stated that 'the police are perfectly powerless, no one ever having seen the murderer except the victims.' Dr Phillips' error was most likely due to the chilly September morning, and the deceased having lost so much blood. However, the doctor did not revise his estimation as he could have done, and the investigation into Annie Chapman was hampered almost from the moment her body was found.

4 THIRD (NON-CONICAL) VICTIM

Nothing was heard from the murderer for about twenty-two days, and many people in the east end of London started to believe that the killer of Polly Nichols and Annie Chapman had put away his disembowelling knife for good. But it was not so. Just about all ripperologists term the stormy night of 30th September 1888 the 'double event,' for the ripper struck twice within an hour. Much more progressive or maverick ripperologists, myself included, term the first killing that night, that of Elizabeth Stride, as not included in the ripper repertoire of murders. Nevertheless, for more than 129 years Elizabeth Stride was always counted as a ripper victim, and it is fitting perhaps that we examine, like the others, the details of why police thought she was murder victim number three.

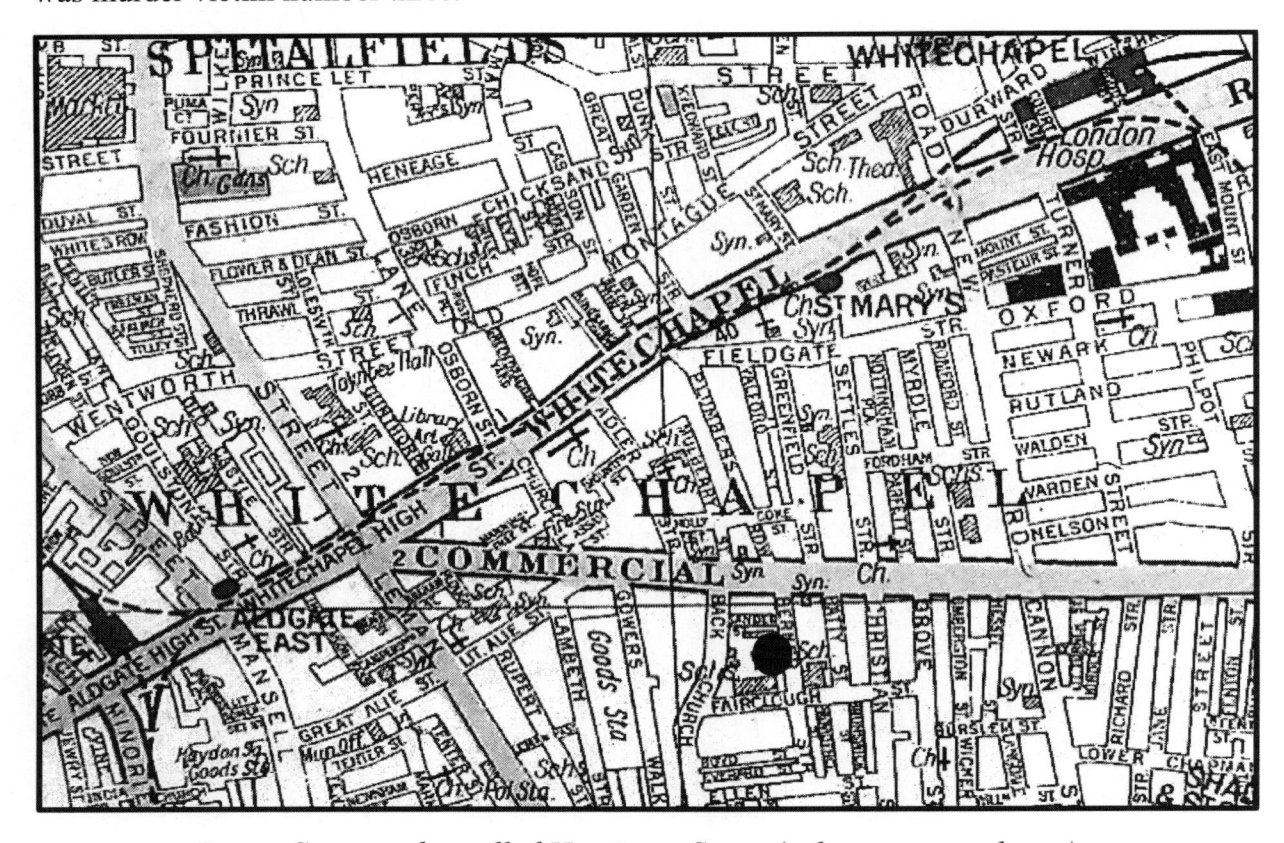

Berner Street, today called Henriques Street (unknown general map).

Louis Diemschutz was a peddler in cheap jewellery and had spent most of Saturday 29th September selling his stuff at the Westow Hill Market near Crystal Palace. He was returning home in the early hours of Sunday 30th September with his remaining unsold stock. In addition to sales, Louis was also a steward at the International Workingmen's Educational Club at 40 Berner Street, which runs south from Commercial Road, and he lived at that address with his wife who helped in the running of the place. When he had returned his stock to the club buildings, Diemschutz planned to climb back on to his cart and drive the pony to his stables in George Yard.

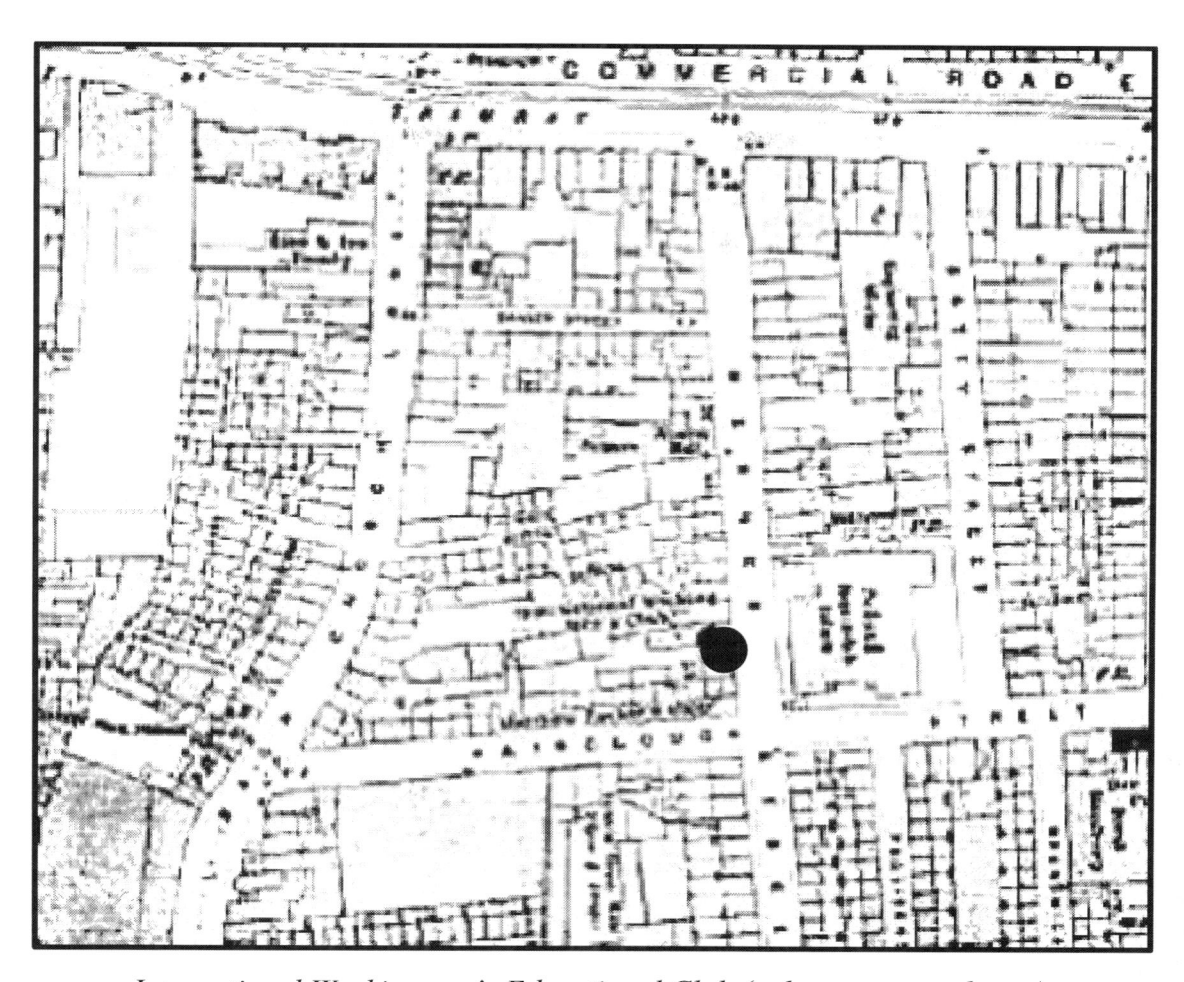

International Workingmen's Educational Club (unknown general map).

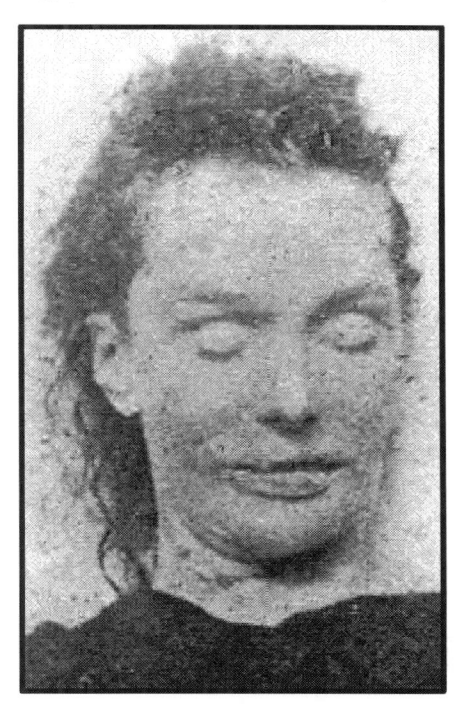

Elizabeth Stride

He turned his pony and cart from Commercial Road into Berner Street, noticing as he passed a tobacco shop that a clock in the window showed the time was about one o'clock in the morning. A few seconds later, he turned his cart toward the yard that divided the club from no. 42. At the entrance were two large wooden gates with the names 'W. Hindley, sack manufacturer and A. Dutfield, van and cart builder' painted on them. Only Hindley now operated from the yard after Arthur Dutfield moved away to Pinchin Street, but it was the latter business that gave the yard its then current name: Dutfield's Yard. The wooden gates opened into the yard, and there was also a wicket doorway in the northern most gate for access when the main gates were shut. That night, as was normal, the gates were thrown back against the side walls of the club building and no. 42. There was little light in the yard, except that from the upper windows of the club.

As the cart turned into the yard, the pony shied towards the left. Looking down, Diemschutz saw a dark shape lying on the ground close to the wall of the club. It was much too dark to see what it was and Diemschutz's first instinct was to prod it and try to lift it with the handle of his whip. When this method didn't work, he jumped down and struck a match to see clearer. The flame flickered and died quickly in the wind, but burnt long enough for him to see that there was a person lying on the ground; the fact that it wore a dress told him it was a woman. Diemschutz thought that the woman might be his wife, so he quickly entered the club by the side door to look for her. When he saw that she was safe, he told her and some club members who were standing nearby 'there's a woman lying in the yard, but I cannot say whether she's drunk or dead.'

He took a candle outside to get a better look, accompanied by a friend named **Isaac Kozebrodsky**. When they took a closer look, both men could plainly see that there was a good deal of blood around. It had flowed from where the woman lay almost to the side door of the club. Mrs Diemschutz, standing at the door saw this too, and let out a scream, bringing more club members rushing outside. Louis and Isaac ran for the police. They turned right at the gates and headed south down Berner Street until they reached Fairclough Street, where they turned left and dashed past Providence Street, Brunswick Street, Christian Street and ran as far as Grove Street. All the time they were shouting loudly for the police. They saw no officer, so at Grove Street they turned and began to retrace their steps.

Passing the Bee Hive public house on the corner of Fairclough and Christian Streets, they ran past a young man, **Edward Spooner** and his lady friend. Spooner stopped them and asked what the matter was. Once they told him they had found a woman's body, he ran with them back to Dutfield's Yard. There were a number of people now gathered there and one of them struck a match. Spooner bent down and lifted the woman's chin, finding it slightly warm to the touch. He noticed that the woman's throat was cut and blood still flowed from the wound. Five minutes later and two police constables arrived on the scene.

When Diemschutz and Kozebrodsky had turned right out of the gates, another member of the club, **Morris Eagle**, had also run for help but he had turned left instead and run to the junction of Berner Street and the Commercial Road. Turning right, he found Constable **Henry Lamb** with Reserve Constable **Albert Collins** between Batty Street and Christian Street. Those two officers dashed back with Eagle. When they arrived at Dutfield's Yard, Lamb told Collins to fetch the doctor whilst Morris Eagle ran for help to the police station in Leman Street. As they left, Lamb placed his hand against the woman's face and found that she was slightly warm. He also held her wrist to see if he could detect a pulse but found nothing.

PC Collins arrived at the surgery of Dr **Frederick William Blackwell** of 100 Commercial Road between 1:05 and 1:10 that morning. Whilst Blackwell dressed and collected his things, he sent his assistant, **Edward Johnston**, back to the scene with Collins. They arrived at Dutfield's Yard at about 1:13 and Johnston's initial examination showed that the woman had an incision in her throat, which by now had stopped bleeding. Her body felt warm, with the exception of her hands, and so Johnston unfastened her blouse to see if her chest was also warm. He saw that her knees were closer to the club wall than her head and that her bonnet was lying on the ground three or four inches from her head. The gates to the yard were then closed. Dr Blackwell arrived at the yard three minutes later, checking his watch to confirm the time.

He noted that the woman lay on her left side, close to and facing the right side of the passage, which was the club wall. Her feet were some nine feet from the actual gates and almost touched the wall. Blackwell also found her neck and chest quite warm and her legs and face slightly less so. Only her hands were cold. The woman's right hand lay on her chest and was smeared inside and out with blood. This hand was open but her left hand, lying on the ground, was partially closed. Upon examination, Dr Blackwell found that it held a small packet of cachous (Parma violet sweets) wrapped in tissue paper, and some had spilled out on to the ground.

The woman's face was placid with the mouth slightly open and she wore a checked silk scarf around her neck. The bow was turned around to the left side and pulled very tight, indicating that her killer had grabbed it to pull her down to the ground. There was a large incision in her neck that corresponded with the lower border of the scarf. Although Dr Blackwell originally thought that the bottom edge of this scarf was frayed, he later concluded that it had been cut when the killer drew his knife across the woman's throat. The single incision started on the left side of the neck and did not quite divide the vessels on that side. It then cut the windpipe in two and stopped at the right side, where the vessels were not cut. In Blackwell's opinion, the woman had been dead for about twenty to thirty minutes, putting the time of death between 12:46 and 12:56 that morning.

About half an hour after Blackwell's arrival, divisional police surgeon George Bagster Phillips attended, and after making his own examination estimated that the woman would have bled to death relatively slowly, taking about a minute and a half to die. This calculation would put the time of the actual attack somewhere between 12:44 and 12:54 that morning. This detail would prove to be important later. Meanwhile, Dr Phillips examined the hands and clothing for blood of everyone in Dutfield's Yard; later, the residents had to endure a thorough police search of their homes. This was concluded at about five o'clock in the morning, when news had already circulated of a second body found in the City of London.

Whilst the dead woman carried no identification, the police soon had a name for her; when the inquest opened in the Vestry Hall, Cable Street on Monday 1st October before the usual coroner, Wynne E. Baxter, the victim was identified as Elizabeth Stride. Stride was Swedish and had been born Elisabeth Gustafsdotter in 1843 near Gothenburg. At the age of seventeen she entered domestic service, but by 1865 had been registered by police as a prostitute. She then moved to London in February 1866 and in March 1869 married John Thomas Stride; her name given on the marriage certificate was Elizabeth Gustifson. The following year, John Stride was running a coffee house in Poplar, but in due course their marriage broke down. John Stride died at the Poplar Union Workhouse in October 1884 and from 1885 onwards, Elizabeth Stride lived with a man named Michael Kidney.

Public inquest

The first witness at the inquest on 1st October was **William West**, who described the layout of the workingmen's club and the adjacent yard. According to West, there was a front door to the club in Berner Street itself that led to a passage through the rest of the building. At the midpoint of this passage, was a staircase that led to the second floor. There was also a window facing Berner Street. The front room on the ground floor of the club was used as a dining room and behind this was the kitchen, from which a door led directly into Dutfield's Yard. On the second floor of the club was a large room used for entertainment. It had three windows facing the yard and on the Saturday night there had been a lively discussion titled 'why Jews should be socialists.'

Ninety plus people had attended, and the meeting had broken up between 11:30 and midnight; most people then left the club via the Berner Street door but between twenty and thirty remained in the large room with another dozen or so downstairs. Regarding Dutfield's Yard, William West said that directly opposite the doorway of the kitchen were two water closets. To the left of the wooden gates was a house occupied by two or three tenants that had three separate doors, all of which led into the yard. Opposite the gates were the workshops occupied by Messrs. Hindley and Co. and next to these was a stable. There were only two exits from the yard: through the gates or through the door that led into the club's kitchen. On that Saturday, William West had been in the club until nine in the evening, when he popped out briefly.

He was back at 10:30 and at 12:30 on that Sunday morning and took some literature to a printing office on the site. He went into the yard via the kitchen door and returned to the club the same way. As he walked back to the club he saw that the wooden gates were wide open and pushed against the walls. Although he admitted he was near-sighted, West was sure he would have noticed anyone standing inside the gates, or the body of Elizabeth Stride had it been there then. Soon afterwards he, his brother and another club member called **Louis Stanley** left the club by the street door and went home, turning right into Berner Street and walking past the gates.

The discussion at the club on Saturday 29th September that West had referred to was chaired by the next witness, **Morris Eagle**, who said that after the discussion broke up he left the club by the front door to escort his young lady home. It was by then 11:45 in the evening. Eagle returned to the club at 12:35 and found the Berner Street door closed, so he had to walk through the gateway and into the club through the kitchen door. It was rather dark and he was unable to swear that there was anything on the ground, although he doubted it. When he went inside he heard a friend singing in Russian. Eagle went upstairs and joined his friend and had been there about twenty minutes when he heard that a woman had been found in the yard.

Going outside, he struck a match and saw her near the gates, lying in a pool of blood. He saw two men run for the police, going in the direction of Fairclough Street, so he went the other way, heading for Commercial Road where, at the corner of Grove Street, he found the two constables. He described how one of them later sent him to the police station to tell the inspector what had taken place. The next witness was **Joseph Lave**, who had only recently arrived in London from America and was actually living, temporarily, at the Workingmen's Club. He testified that he had walked out into Berner Street to get some fresh air about 12:30 in the morning and had then walked into Dutfield's Yard itself.

The yard was very dark and Lave had to find his way by groping along the club wall. He swore that there was no body lying on the ground at that time and estimated that it was around 12:40 when he went back inside the club. The next witness was **Louis Diemschutz**, who told of his discovery of Stride's body when he returned at one o'clock on the 30th September. He told of his search for a policeman and of meeting Edward Spooner in Fairclough Street. Soon after the pair returned to Dutfield's Yard, Morris Eagle had appeared with the two police constables. After Diemschutz had finished the coroner adjourned the inquest until the next day.

On Tuesday 2nd October PC **Henry Lamb** gave his evidence. He estimated that he had been at the scene about ten minutes before Dr Blackwell arrived, putting the time of his own arrival at around 1:06 in the morning. It was Lamb who closed the gates and he said that he had been able to do so without disturbing the position of Elizabeth Stride's body. It was likely done to prevent curious on-lookers. Once the gates were shut, PC Lamb saw that there were men still in the yard and he warned them to stay away in case they got blood on themselves. This might draw suspicion. Later, he went into the club and checked every room, finding another fifteen or twenty people still inside.

He also examined the water closets and the houses whose front doors opened into Dutfield's Yard. He found nothing and confirmed that all the occupants of the cottages were in bed when he knocked on their doors. Finally, Lamb outlined details of his beat, stating that the closest it brought him to the murder scene was when he walked across the top of Berner Street on the Commercial Road. He had passed that spot six to seven minutes before he was called to the scene. The next witness was **Edward Spooner**, the man who had been standing outside the Bee Hive public house in Fairclough Street. He said he had arrived at Dutfield's Yard five minutes before the two policemen, which puts the time of his arrival, according to his own estimate, at just one minute past 1 o'clock. Spooner had helped PC Lamb close the gates.

Penultimate witness was **Mary Malcolm**, who lived at 50 Eagle Street, Red Lion Square, and had viewed the body lying in the mortuary and swore that it was that of her sister, Elizabeth Stokes, whom she said she recognized by a black mark on her leg. She went on to then assassinate her own sister's character, and had wasted a good deal of police time until the real Elizabeth Stokes appeared, alive and well! Mary had got it wrong. Last witness that day was Dr **Frederick Blackwell**, who gave details of the injury to Stride's throat, the position of her body in the yard, and the cachous found in her left hand. The last item would be mentioned again in further hearings because there was a great deal of supposition about Stride having had grapes or a grape stalk in her hand.

The hearing was adjourned until the following day and on 3rd October more evidence of the victim's correct identity was given. First witness was **Elizabeth Tanner,** the deputy keeper of the common lodging house at 32 Flower and Dean Street. She had viewed the dead woman's body and said that it was a woman she had known as Long Liz for about six years. She knew Long Liz was Swedish and had been told a story of her husband and children going down with the sinking of the ship *Princess Alice* (an unfounded story). Tanner had last seen Stride alive at 6:30 in the evening of Saturday 29th September in the Queen's Head public house on Commercial Street, and again at seven o'clock in the kitchen of her lodging house. The dead woman had been at the lodging house on both Thursday and Friday nights and on Saturday had cleaned Tanner's private rooms, for which she had been paid sixpence.

Catherine Lane was a fellow lodger at the same lodging house. She and her husband, Patrick, had lived there since February and had known Long Liz for six or seven years. Catherine had spoken to her on Thursday night sometime between ten and eleven o'clock and Elizabeth had told her that she had argued with her man and left him. Catherine also saw her on Saturday, when the latter had cleaned Tanner's rooms and the two women last met between seven and eight o'clock that same evening in the kitchen of the lodging house. Another resident at that lodging house was **Charles Preston**. He had lived there for eighteen months and knew the dead woman as Long Liz. He had last seen her between six and seven o'clock in the evening of Saturday 29th September, in the kitchen. He too had heard the story of the *Princess Alice* from the victim, but he also knew that her surname was Stride; that her husband had once run a coffee stall in Poplar.

Next to give evidence was the man in Stride's life: **Michael Kidney**. He said he was a waterside labourer who had lived with Stride for three years. He denied that there had been any quarrel between them and said he had last seen her on Tuesday 25th September in Commercial Street as he was going to work. There had been no bad words between them and he fully expected her to be there when he got home from work that night. He also said that she had left him from time to time in the past, but it had always been because of drink. They had been apart a total of about five months in their three years together.

Kidney was obviously deeply upset at Stride's death. He said that if he had a force of detectives at his command he could catch the killer himself, but when pressed as to whether he had any concrete information that might lead to the apprehension of the murderer, Kidney had to admit he knew nothing. **Thomas Coram** was called to the stand; he lived at Mile End but had been visiting friends near Brady Street and was walking home along the Whitechapel Road at around 12:30 in the morning of 30th September. As he drew near no. 253, he noticed a knife on the doorstep. There was a bloodstained handkerchief wrapped around the handle, but Coram did not touch it. Instead he pointed out the knife to a constable who was walking toward him.

This policeman was PC **Joseph Drage**, who picked up the knife and saw that it was smothered in dried blood. He and Coram took the knife to Leman Street Police Station and it was later handed over to Dr Phillips for examination. Dr **Bagster Phillips** was then called to give his testimony both on that knife and on the death of Stride. Dr Phillips and Dr Blackwell had performed the post-mortem on Monday 1st October. In addition to the throat wound the two doctors had found mud on the left side of the dead woman's face and a bluish discoloration over both her shoulders, under her collarbone and on her chest.

They inferred from this that the marks had been caused by the assailant seizing her and forcing her down on to the ground, where he then cut her throat. Dr Phillips also referred to the cachous that Elizabeth had held in her hand – he had also found some in the gutter that presumably had fallen from the tissue paper as her hand relaxed after the attack. Finally, he stated that although the knife found in Whitechapel Road might have caused the injuries, it was unlikely because it would have proved too unwieldy. Also, the evidence showed that Elizabeth Stride had been attacked later than the time the knife was discovered by Thomas Coram. The inquest was adjourned again until Friday 5th October.

Both doctor's **Phillips** and **Blackwell** were recalled. Dr Phillips stated that he had examined Stride's body again and found no old injury to her mouth (claimed by the victim before her death) thus laying to rest the story of the *Princess Alice* disaster. Phillips had also examined two handkerchiefs found in her possession and said that he believed the marks on the larger one were possibly fruit stains. He was certain that she had not swallowed either the skin or seeds of grapes within many hours of her death. This point was confirmed by Dr Blackwell. The debate over the possibility of Stride having eaten grapes was fuelled by a man who was not called to the inquest. **Matthew Packer** ran a greengrocer and fruiterer's shop from 44 Berner Street; these premises were just south of the murder site, separated from Dutfield's Yard only by house no. 42.

Routinely the police had spoken to every householder living in Berner Street. At nine o'clock in the morning of the 30th September, Sergeant Stephen White had spoken to Matthew Packer, who said he had closed his shop at 12:30 early that morning. He was asked by the sergeant whether he had seen anything unusual and replied 'no, I saw no one standing about, neither did I see anyone go up the yard. I never saw anything suspicious or heard the slightest noise and knew nothing about the murder until I heard of it this morning.' Also living in the same house were Mrs. Packer, Sarah Harrison, and Harry Douglas. When Sergeant White spoke to them, they also said they had seen or heard nothing. Matthew Packer, however, changed his story, for on 2nd October two private detectives named Grand and Batchelor (working for Whitechapel Vigilance Committee) spoke to Packer, who now swore that at 11:45 in the evening of 29th September he sold half a pound of black grapes to a man and a woman who were standing outside his shop.

He said the couple continued to loiter about the street for another half hour or so. Packer described the man as being middle-aged, but then qualified the estimate to age twenty-five to thirty. He described him as about 5'7" tall, stout, squarely built and wearing a 'wide-awake' hat and dark clothing. The man had the appearance of a clerk. Further inquiries by detectives Grand and Batchelor led to Mrs Rosenfield and Miss Eva Harstein of 14 Berner Street. These women claimed that on Sunday morning, after the body had been moved, they noticed some white flower petals and a bloodstained grape stalk in Dutfield's Yard. The two detectives visited the yard for themselves and amongst the rubbish there found a grape stalk. They decided to test the veracity of Packer's story by taking him to the mortuary in Golden Lane, where the body of Catherine Eddowes (whose murder is described next chapter) had been taken and asking if this was the woman he had seen in Berner Street.

Packer replied that he had never seen her before. They then went to St. George's-in-the-East mortuary, where Elizabeth Stride was. The story of the grapes was made public by the *Evening News* on 4th October, causing Chief Inspector Henry Moore to ask Sergeant Stephen White to interview Packer again. The sergeant found that Packer was not there; his wife said two detectives had taken him to the mortuary to view the body. Sergeant White immediately went to St. George's-in-the-East and found Packer there with one of the private detectives. Packer confirmed that he had sold grapes to a man at around midnight. As he was speaking the other detective came up and asked Packer to leave with them. At four o'clock that afternoon, Sergeant White again visited 44 Berner Street in time to see a hansom cab appear and take Packer to Scotland Yard to supposedly see Sir Charles Warren, commissioner of the Metropolitan Police.

Packer was not called, however, to the inquest, for it appears true that he changed his tale to fit the facts of the case. He also managed to incorporate some errors from the case too; he stated that Stride had a white flower pinned to her dress, when in fact it was a red one. It is possible that during his statement to Sergeant White, Packer forgot the grape-buying customer and only realized the significance of it later. This surely must be very unlikely; that so vital a piece of information was forgotten about until later? Nevertheless, the police believed Packer's testimony unreliable and so he was not called. There were others too who could not be relied upon and who were probably making things up for their own self-aggrandizement.

If Packer could be relied upon, then his testimony and description of the potential murder was crucial to the police inquiry – his mistake was not getting the description of Stride correct and having no corroborating evidence. Other witnesses who could have given crucial evidence were not called: the first was **Fanny Mortimer** who lived at 36 Berner Street. When interviewed by police during their door-to-door inquiries, Mrs. Mortimer said she had been standing at her front door for most of the half hour from 12:30 until one in the morning. She stated that she first went outside after hearing the measured tread of a policeman passing her house; later testimony from the officer on the Berner Street beat put this time at 12:30.

While at her door Mrs. Mortimer saw no one except a man with a shiny black bag in his hand. Although some ripperologists believe this sighting was of a typical Jack the Ripper killer, the man she had seen was in fact **Leon Goldstein** of 22 Christian Street, who reported to Leman Street police station after the murder to say that he had passed down Berner Street after leaving a coffee house in Spectacle Alley. Goldstein's shiny black bag contained just empty cigarette boxes. The other witness was **Israel Schwartz** of 22 Ellen Street; he made a statement to police as early as 30th September indicating that he might have seen the murderer attack Stride and that the killer might have had an accomplice.

Schwartz's police statement said he turned into Berner Street from Commercial Road at 12:45 in the morning of 30th September. As he drew closer to the entrance to Dutfield's Yard he saw a man stop and speak to a woman who was standing in the gateway. Schwartz could not hear what was said but the man tried to pull the woman out into the street, turned her around and threw her down to the pavement. She screamed three times and in order to avoid this domestic dispute, Schwartz crossed to the other side of the road. As he passed them he saw a second man lighting a pipe. The first man called out 'Lipski', apparently addressing the man with the pipe. Schwartz found himself being followed by the second man, so he ran as far as the railway arch, by which time the man with the pipe had vanished.

Schwartz was taken to view the body of Elizabeth Stride and swore that she was the woman he had seen in Berner Street. He went on to describe both men; the first, the violent man, was aged about thirty, was 5'5" tall with a fair complexion, dark hair and a small brown moustache. He had a full face, was broad-shouldered and wore a dark jacket and trousers. He also wore a black peaked cap and carried nothing in his hands. The second (the follower) was a little older, about thirty-five. He was tall at 5'11" with a fresh complexion, light brown hair and also a brown moustache. He wore a dark overcoat and an old black hard felt hat, with a wide brim and, of course, a pipe in his hand.

There was much discussion between police officers as to why the first man had called out 'Lipski'. Apparently, Israel Lipski was a Polish man who had lived in the attic room of 16 Batty Street, which runs parallel to Berner Street. The room below Lipski's was home to a married couple, Isaac and Miriam Angel, and on 28th June 1887 Miriam Angel and Israel Lipski were found in the house, both having been poisoned with nitric acid. Miriam Angel died, but Lipski recovered and was subsequently charged with her murder. He was tried at the Old Bailey and hanged at Newgate Prison in August 1887. The police considered that one interpretation was that the man had called out in the sense of 'I am going to Lipski this woman,' although most widely accepted was the notion that the man with the pipe was simply called Lipski. A search for a man with that name was launched but without success; thus Israel Schwartz was not called to give evidence either.

Inspector Abberline himself gave a most likely explanation; he knew that the term 'Lipski' was used as a derogatory label for Jews and Israel Schwartz had a Jewish appearance. Abberline believed that the man who called out had noticed Schwartz and was using the word to warn him off. Back to the 5th October inquest, the next witness was **Sven Olsson**, who was clerk to the Swedish Church in Princes Square. He had known the dead woman for seventeen years but added little to the evidence beyond saying that she had registered with the church in July 1868.

Next was **William Marshall**, who lived at 64 Berner Street and he too had viewed the body in the mortuary. He was sure it was a woman he had seen at 11:45 in the evening of 29th September. He had gone to his front door at 11:30 and about fifteen minutes later noticed a man and a woman on the pavement between his house and the club, but on the other side of the road. The couple was kissing and he heard the man say 'you would say anything but your prayers.' After that the couple walked up the street toward Matthew Packer's shop and Dutfield's Yard. Marshall described the man as middle aged, about 5'6" tall, rather stout and looking like a clerk.

He wore a small black coat, dark trousers and a round cap with a small peak (a typical description for the times, it appears – we shall examine the various witness descriptions of suspects later in volume II and see if there is a common denominator between them). Next witness was **James Brown** of 35 Fairclough Street. At 12:45 in the morning he left home to go to a chandler's shop for his supper. The shop was at the corner of Berner Street and Fairclough Street, and as he was crossing the road he saw a man and a woman standing together by the wall at the school opposite Dutfield's Yard.

Brown was sure that the woman was Elizabeth Stride. He heard her say to the man 'no, not tonight, some other night.' The man was described as stout and about 5'7" tall, wearing a long coat almost reaching to his heels. Another sighting of a man and a woman was made by PC **William Smith**; the officer whose beat took in Berner Street. Smith began his testimony by giving details of his beat. It began at the corner of Jower's Walk and went down Commercial Road as far as Christian Street. From there he went down Christian Street and Fairclough Street as far as Grove Street, then back along Fairclough Street as far as Back Church Lane. From there, he passed along Back Church Lane as far as the Commercial Road, taking in all the interior streets such as Berner Street and Batty Street.

Smith said he had last been in Berner Street at 12:30 or 12:35 that morning. This statement helped fix the time that Mrs Mortimer had gone to her front door. On his 12:30 visit to Berner Street, Constable Smith had seen a man and a woman standing in the street across from Dutfield's Yard. The woman had a flower on her jacket, which indicated that she was Stride. The man had a newspaper parcel in his hand about eighteen inches long and six or eight inches broad. He was 5'7" tall and wore a hard felt deerstalker hat and dark clothes; he was about twenty-eight years old and had no whiskers.

After the murder, PC Smith was on his normal beat and as he turned into Berner Street at about one o'clock he saw a crowd of people outside the gates of Dutfield's Yard. Two policemen were already there and after speaking to them Smith went to fetch the police ambulance. As he was leaving, Dr Blackwell's assistant, Edward Johnston, was just arriving at the scene. **Philip Kranz** was editor of '*Der Arbeter Fraint*', a foreign newspaper. He said he had been in the back room of the printing offices from nine o'clock until he was told that a body had been found in the yard. During that time, he heard no cry for help, but there was a good deal of singing coming from upstairs in the club and it was possible that he simply didn't hear any sounds made by the victim or her killer.

Detective Inspector **Edmund Reid** arrived at Dutfield's Yard at 1:45 in the morning, by which time Chief Inspector West, Inspector Pinhorn and several other police officers were already attending. Dr Blackwell and Dr Phillips were also there, as were a number of bystanders. Reid ordered that everyone's name and address be taken and that they all be examined for bloodstains. Twenty-eight people were seen, questioned and searched, but nothing related to the crime was found. At 4:30 that morning Sunday 30th September, Elizabeth Stride's body was moved to the mortuary in Cable Street, and Edmund Reid followed it there to take a description. According to his notes, the dead woman was about forty-two years old, 5'2" tall with curly dark-brown hair. Her complexion was pale, her eyes were light grey and her upper front teeth were missing.

She wore a long black jacket trimmed with black fur, an old black skirt, a dark-brown velvet bodice, two light serge petticoats, a white chemise, a pair of white stockings, a black crepe bonnet and a pair of side-sprung boots. Her jacket was decorated by a single red rose backed by a maidenhair fern. The only possessions found in her pockets were two handkerchiefs, a thimble and a piece of wool on a card. The inquest was now adjourned until the 23rd October, when the usual verdict of 'murder by some person or persons unknown' was announced. Earlier, on the 6th October, the body of Elizabeth Stride was laid to rest in a pauper's grave in the East London Cemetery.

Conclusions

We can see from all this evidence just how poor the ripper victims actually were. Most carried all their worldly goods on their persons, including clothing, washing items and so on; they must have worn the same clothes for long periods of time without ever washing. Most were potential, if not already, alcoholics. Stride, for example, had been before magistrates eight times in the two years prior to her death. Later, we shall look at why Elizabeth Stride cannot any longer be counted as a canonical ripper victim, but for now we have looked at the circumstances of her murder. It ties us in nicely for the actual third ripper victim, discovered about an hour after Stride's body was found. The victim, Kate Eddowes, was found two-thirds of a mile from Berner Street (as the current roads go) and within the City of London police force boundary; the investigation now fell into their hands and not those of the Metropolitan police, although events immediately following the killing also involved the Met.

5 THE THIRD VICTIM

Just a short time after the discovery of Elizabeth Stride's body, a second victim was discovered by police in the City of London. At 1:30 in the morning of Sunday 30th September 1888, PC Edward Watkins was on his beat and this took him into Mitre Square. Although close to busy roads, the square was quiet at night and very dimly lit. There were in fact only two lamps: one outside the big Kearley and Tongue warehouse in the northwest corner near to a narrow passage that led into St. James's Place, and the other on the wall at the entrance to Church Passage leading to Duke Street. There was a third lamp outside the square on the corner of Mitre Street, but it threw very little light into the Square itself because much of its glow was obstructed by a Taylor's shop on the corner.

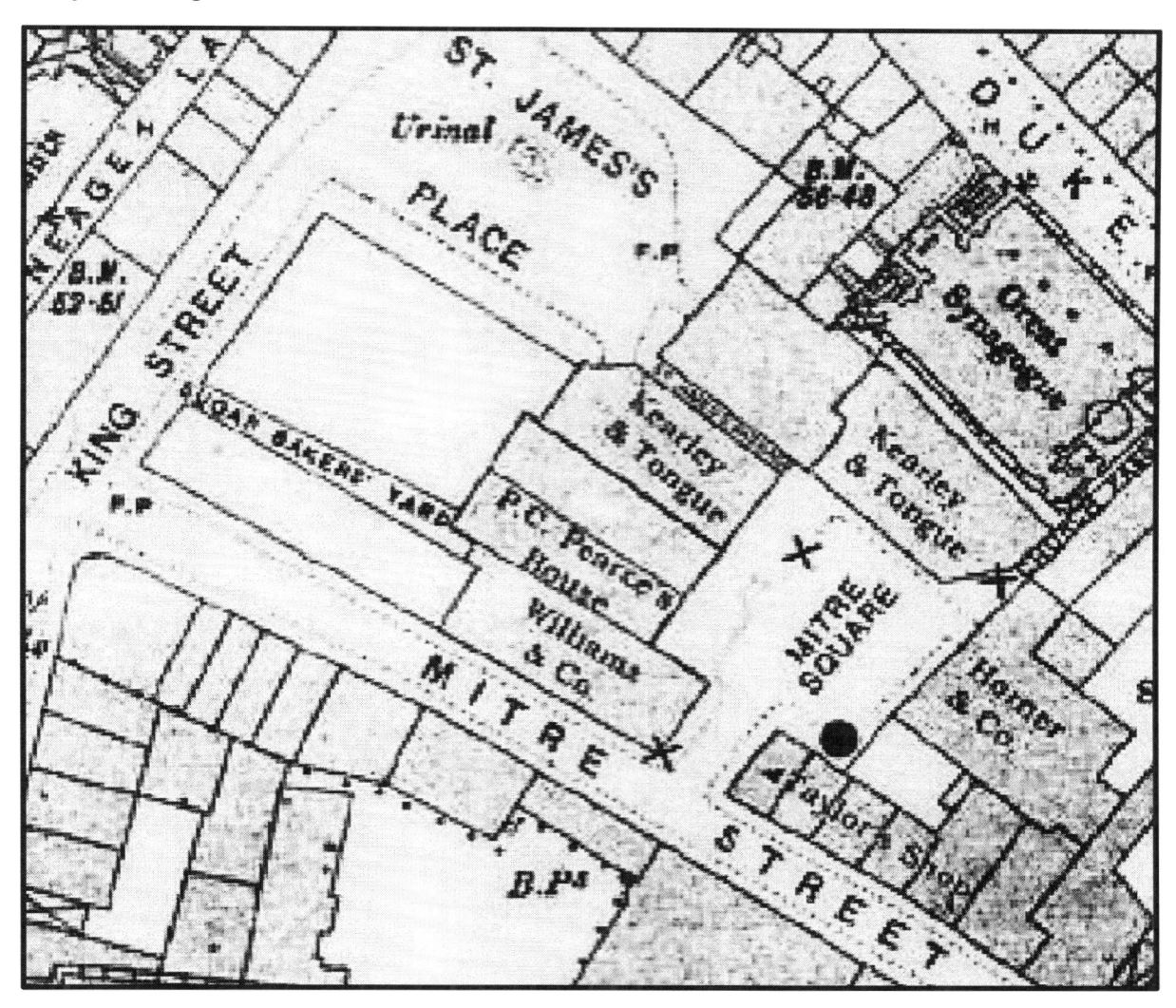

Mitre Square; black dot is where body was found, X are street lamps, note the urinal in St James's Place!

Ripper's corner Mitre Square

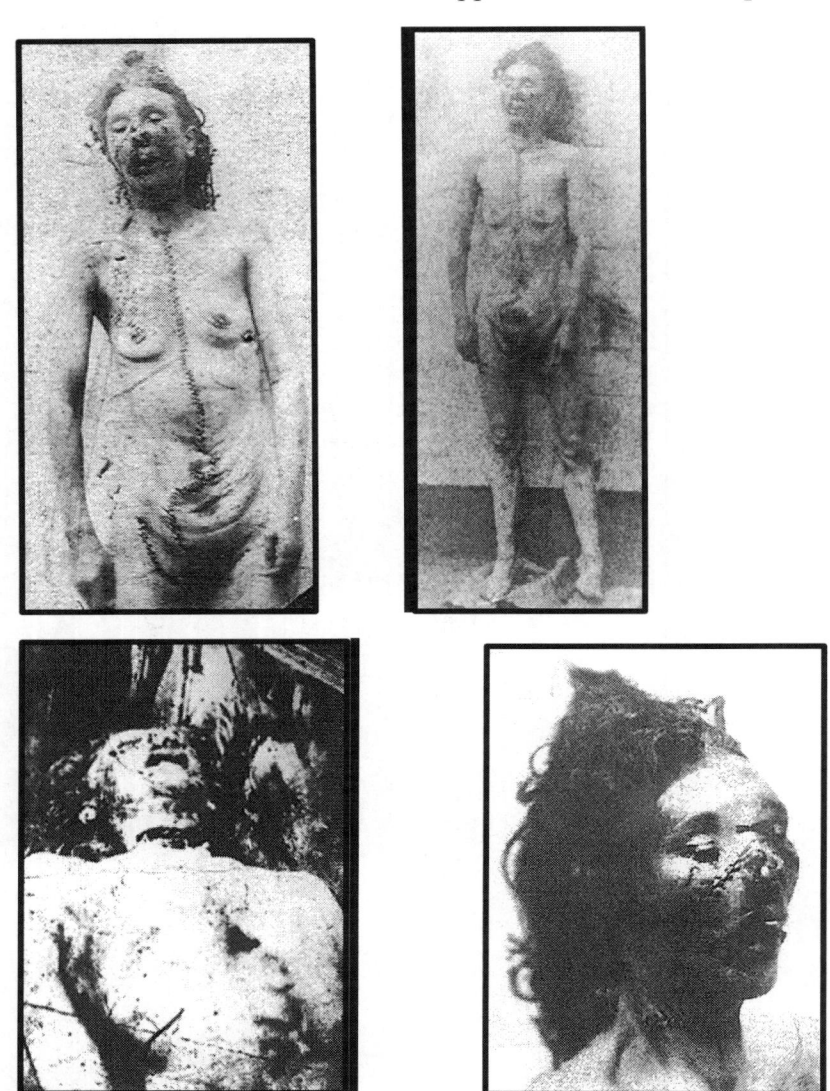

Eddowes in coffin & mortuary photos

    Very few people lived or worked in Mitre Square. There was only one family living there at no. 3; that of a PC Pearce on the immediate left on entry to the square. Next to him was an empty house and then the north bit of the Kearley and Tongue warehouse; on the other side

49

of no. 3 was the warehouse of Williams and Co. There were also three houses next to a Taylor's shop at the entrance to the square from Mitre Street, but these were all empty and the Taylor's shop itself was locked up and deserted at night. The rest of the square consisted of further Kearley and Tongue warehouses that should have had night watchmen. This was how PC Watkins found it at 1:30 in the morning.

After walking through Mitre Square and checking it carefully, PC Watkins left via the St. James's Place passageway. Turning right, he passed up Duke Street. He continued along Duke Street and turned back toward St. James's Square again, then down King Street and Creechurch Place before passing St. Katharine's Church into Leadenhall Street. He then passed around into Mitre Street and back into Mitre Square. This small, unexciting beat took about fourteen minutes to complete, so that about 1:44 in the morning, assuming the constable maintained his walk and vigilance, PC Watkins turned back into Mitre Square again.

This time, in the south most, darkest part of the square, lay the body of a woman who had been savagely mutilated. Watkins ran over to the Kearley and Tongue warehouse, where he knew the night watchman, George James Morris. The night watchman was a retired police officer himself. Watkins found the door to the warehouse open a little so he pushed it and found Morris sweeping the steps.

'For God's sake, mate, come to my assistance,' Watkins cried.

'What's the matter?' Morris asked.

'Oh, dear, there's another woman cut to pieces!'

Morris collected his own lamp and followed Watkins out into the square, where they looked at the woman's body. Whilst Watkins stood guard, Morris ran through Mitre Street and left into Aldgate; blowing a whistle to attract attention. He quickly found two police constables, PC James Holland and PC James Harvey, who had adjacent beats to PC Watkins. Appraised of the situation, PC Holland ran for medical assistance; the nearest surgery was that of Dr George William Sequeira at 34 Jewry Street, Aldgate. By the time Holland had called on him it was 1:55 in the morning. Dr Sequeira reached Mitre Square soon afterward but didn't touch the body. It was plain that the poor woman was beyond all human aid and Sequeira believed it would be better if a detailed examination was made by the official police surgeon.

That man was Dr Frederick Gordon Brown, who arrived at Mitre Square at 2:18. Before his arrival, at about 2:03, Inspector Edward Collard had arrived after being alerted at Bishopsgate police station. Once he had made a quick examination, Dr Brown ordered the body be moved to the city mortuary in Golden Lane. More officers arrived at the scene. At 1:58 three plain-clothes officers (Detective Sergeant Robert Outram, Detective Constable Daniel Halse and Detective Constable Edward Marriott) had been on duty by the corner of Houndsditch and Aldgate High Street, at the St. Boltolph Church, having been searching passageways and houses as part of the police effort to trace the Berner Street killer in Whitechapel.

They were only 150 yards from the body of Eddowes! Alerted to the fact that there had been a murder in Mitre Square they ran there and set out in different directions to see if they could find the killer. Only Daniel Halse would later be called to give testimony at the inquest. He left Mitre Square and walked through Middlesex Street then on to Wentworth Street. Here he saw two men and stopped them; satisfied with their explanation as to what they were doing at that time of the morning, he allowed them to go. From Wentworth Street, Halse walked into

Goulston Street, by which time it was about 2:15. Having found nothing he returned to Mitre Square to report and receive further instructions.

Halse received news that a discovery had been made so he and Detective Constable Baxter Hunt went immediately to Leman Street police station to find out more. Here they were directed to Goulston Street, where they spoke to PC Alfred Long. His beat took him through 108-119 Wentworth Model Dwellings, close to the junction of Goulston Street and Wentworth Street, every half hour. At 2:20 he had seen nothing out of the ordinary, but at 2:55 he had spotted a piece of apron on the right-hand side of the open doorway. Just above the apron, written in white chalk on the black brick fascia, was a message. This read as written: 'The Juwes are The men That Will not be Blamed for nothing.'

PC Long had left a fellow constable from a nearby beat to guard this graffito whilst he took the piece of apron to the Commercial Street police station. The Leman Street station was also notified of the find. Daniel Halse stayed with the writing whilst Detective Hunt returned to Mitre Square to report to Inspector James McWilliam. The inspector ordered the writing be photographed and sent Hunt back to Goulston Street with instructions that he and Halse should carry out a thorough search of the premises. Their search revealed nothing, however, and this important clue was never photographed. Its eventual erasure might have proved to be crucial; Sir Charles Warren, commissioner of the Metropolitan Police and Superintendent Thomas Arnold, head of H Division, agreed that the writing should be washed from the wall and their decision was carried out at 5:30 that morning, despite Halse's objections.

The piece of apron, meantime, was handed over to Dr Brown, who took it to the Golden Lane mortuary to compare it with the clothing of the dead woman. Inspector McWilliam was present when the garment was compared to a cut apron worn by the victim. The match was exact, even down to a seam that corresponded in both pieces. There was no doubt that the killer had cut the apron from the dead woman, probably used it to wipe his hands and knife on, and later discarded it in Goulston Street. If PC Long was correct when he stated that he had not seen the apron at 2:20, then the murderer must have dropped it after that time, which indicates that he was on the streets somewhere from 1:44 in the morning.

108-119 Wentworth Model Dwellings Goulston Street: the entrance, and the stairs

Identifying the dead woman was relatively easy, for a mustard tin found near her body contained two pawn tickets for items pledged to a shop at 31 Church Street, Spitalfields. The items turned out to be a man's flannel shirt pledged on 31st August in the name of Emily Birrell of 52 Whites Row, and a pair of men's boots, pledged on 28th September in the name of Jane

Kelly of 6 Dorset Street. Police checks showed that both names and addresses were false, but the reports of the two items and the fact that the dead woman had the letters 'TC' tattooed in blue on her left forearm soon brought John Kelly, a labourer, to Bishopsgate police station on 2nd October.

He told police that he believed the Mitre Square victim was a woman he had been living with for seven years, mostly at Cooney's lodging house at 55 Flower and Dean Street. Viewing the body, he confirmed the identification and said the woman was called Kate Conway, who sometimes called herself by his surname Kelly. From this the police were able to establish that in fact the dead woman's real name was Catherine or Kate Eddowes. Eddowes had been born in Wolverhampton on 14th April 1842. In December 1844 the family moved to London and by 1851 lived in Bermondsey. In November 1855, Catherine's mother died and her large family dispersed; Catherine was sent to live with an aunt called Elizabeth Eddowes, in Wolverhampton.

Kate, however, was not happy living with her aunt and later she ran away to Birmingham, where she moved in with an uncle, Thomas Eddowes. Not long afterwards she met Thomas Conway, the man whose initials were tattooed on her arm. Conway and Catherine never married but they stayed together until 1881; she bore him three children: a daughter and two sons. The family came back to London and it was there that the couple separated. Catherine next met John Kelly at the Flower and Dean Street lodging house. She kept in touch with her daughter, Annie Phillips (married name) for some time but Catherine's constant demands for money created friction between them both. When Annie moved in 1886 she didn't bother to give her mother her new address. By 1888 mother and daughter had not met for two years.

John Kelly gave police further information about Catherine Eddowes; she had three sisters living in London. Two of them (Eliza Gold and Emma Jones) hadn't been friendly toward Catherine, possibly owing to her habit of trying to borrow money – the third sister, Elizabeth Fisher, had seen Catherine from time to time. Regarding the events of the past days, Kelly told police that he and Catherine had spent much of the autumn in Hunton near Maidstone, hop-picking. They made some money and Kelly bought himself a new pair of boots. However, by Thursday 27th September, they were back in London and had no money again, meaning they could not afford their usual lodging house and had to sleep at the Casual Ward in Mile End.

On Friday 28th September, Kelly earned sixpence doing some labouring work; he generously gave four pence to Catherine so she could have a single bed at Cooney's whilst Kelly himself had the intention of going back to Mile End. Catherine wouldn't hear of it and she insisted that he should have the bed and she would go to the Casual Ward. Kelly agreed rather reluctantly. On Saturday, Catherine Eddowes and Kelly met again, still without much money. Kelly announced that he would pawn his new boots. This he did and the boots were exchanged at the pawnbroker's shop for 2s and sixpence. The couple then had breakfast at the Flower and Dean lodging house, bought some tea and sugar, and at two o'clock in the afternoon parted in Houndsditch with Catherine announcing that she intended to visit her daughter Annie.

One of the last things Kelly said to her was a warning about the killer stalking the streets of Whitechapel. Catherine is said to have replied 'don't you fear for me. I'll take care of myself and I shan't fall into his hands.' When Catherine and Kelly parted for the final time in Houndsditch, she had no money; she must have earned some in the next few hours, however, for at 8:30 that Saturday evening she was drunk and incapable. PC Louis Robinson noticed a small crowd of people around 29 Aldgate High Street and pushing through found Catherine lying on the pavement. He picked her up and leaned her back against some shutters but she slid sideways. Robinson called over a fellow officer, PC George Simmons, and together they took her to Bishopsgate police station. At this time neither officer knew the identity of the woman they had just arrested. Upon arrival at the station at 8:45, Catherine was asked her name but did not reply, so she was placed in a cell to recover.

An hour later at 9:45, PC George Hutt came on duty and visited the cells several times during the next few hours to check on his prisoners. At 11:45 Catherine was awake and singing softly to herself and at about 12:30 on 30th September she was asking when she would be allowed to leave. Hutt told her shortly, to which she replied 'I am capable of taking care of myself now.' Half an hour later the desk officer, Sergeant James George Byfield, told PC Hutt to see if any of the prisoners were fit to be discharged. Hutt unlocked Catherine's cell and took her up to the office where she asked him what time it was.

'Too late for you to get any more drink,' replied Hutt. Catherine persisted in asking the time and was told one o'clock. Catherine replied 'I shall get a damned fine hiding when I get home, then.' Hutt responded 'and serve you right. You have no right to get drunk.' Asked again for her name and address, she said she was Mary Ann Kelly and lived at 6 Fashion Street. After this information was noted she was formally discharged without charge, and PC Hutt held the door open for her as she left. He watched her walk down the passage that led to the main street doors and asked her to pull them closed behind her. She shouted back 'all right. Good night, old cock.' Hutt noticed that she turned left toward Houndsditch. Mitre Square was just an eight-minute walk away; about 675 yards by road – she could have arrived there as early as 1:10.

There is then a period of about 34 minutes unaccounted for in the last moments of Eddowes' life. It also appears that despite the late hour of the night, she was seen close to Mitre Square. House-to-house inquiries brought three witnesses to the attention of the police: Joseph Lawende, Joseph Levy and Harry Harris. These men had spent the night of 29th September at the Imperial Club at 16-17 Duke's Street (renamed Duke's Place in 1939 – which was then about 100 yards away from Church Passage in 1888). The men left the club at about 1:30 on the Sunday morning and as they came into the street, Joseph Lawende noticed a man and a woman standing at the corner of Church Passage leading into Mitre Square.

Joseph Levy seemed disturbed by them and remarked to his companions that he didn't like walking home alone when there were such people around. However, he did not take particular notice of them and he was unable to offer any description of the man and woman. Neither could Harris. Lawende, however, did take a look and noticed that the woman, who had her back to him, was wearing a black jacket and bonnet and was quite small. She was resting one hand on the man's chest and their conversation was hushed. Her companion was facing Lawende so his description was quite detailed.

According to newspaper reports of the time, he was about thirty years old, 5'7" or 5'8" tall and of medium build, with a fair complexion and moustache. He wore a pepper-and-salt loose jacket, a grey cloth cap with a peak and a reddish neckerchief tied in a knot. Lawende thought he looked like a sailor. Lawende had not seen the woman's face, however, but was later shown Catherine Eddowes's clothing and believed them to be the same. If true, then we know that Eddowes was alive with a man at the top of Church Passage at 1:35 that morning, twenty-five minutes after she first arrived near Mitre Square and but nine minutes before her body was found by PC Watkins.

This means that Lawende almost certainly must have seen her killer. The time of the murder can be narrowed even further; PC James Harvey's beat took him down Duke Street and along Church Passage. He did not go into Mitre Square but, having reached its junction with the Church Passage, he turned and retraced his steps back into Duke Street. Harvey reckoned he walked down Church Passage at 1:41 or 1:42 and looked into the square, seeing nothing. Harvey's timings are approximate, as most timings are. He must have guessed the time and looked into Mitre Square when he was passing the post office clock, then reading about 1:28 or 1:29.

If Harvey's timing was accurate, then when he looked into Mitre Square, Eddowes's body must surely have been lying in that darkened far corner? Jack could have still been there, panting from his exertions and hiding in the shadows, perhaps behind those gates in ripper corner? Alternatively, Catherine's body was already lying in the dark and her killer had made good his escape. The minimum time required to inflict the mutilations, according to the medical evidence, was three minutes. Harvey, however, was dismissed from the police in July 1889 for reasons unknown, perhaps suggesting he was not an ideal police officer and skipped part of his beat in order to save time? Had he paid more attention to his patrol duties then it may well have been PC Harvey who would be honoured for all time as the man who caught the ripper in the act of murder!

What did the killer do, or where did he go immediately after killing Kate Eddowes? We know from the apron that he was stained with blood and faecal matter, so cleaning up would be a priority. Some ripperologists think that Jack likely returned home, cleaned himself up, changed clothing and then left home again, carrying nothing but that piece of apron which he discarded in the doorway in Goulston Street; possibly writing the message on the wall as well. This would have been between 2:20 and 2:55 that morning. His sole reason for doing this would have been to throw the police off his scent; making them think that his home was to the northeast near Brick Lane/Dorset Street. Other ripperologists, such as Donald Rumbelow, suggest that the killer washed his hands in a water sink in Dorset Street. [5]

The police thus followed him from Mitre Square, to Goulston Street and then north to Dorset Street. Another oddity of this case was that, when discharged from Bishopsgate police station, Eddowes gave her name as Mary Ann Kelly – similar to the Mary Jane Kelly who was the final ripper victim and who happened to live in Dorset Street, where Eddowes' killer was supposed to have washed his hands after leaving Goulston Street.

Public inquiry

The inquest on Catherine Eddowes opened before a new man, Coroner **Samuel Frederick Langham** at Golden Lane mortuary on 4th October. There was only one adjournment and proceedings were concluded quickly on 11th October. The medical and police evidence was good compared to that of the Met; the post-mortem was conducted by Dr Brown on Sunday 30th September – also present were Dr Sequeira, Dr William Sedgwick Saunders and Dr Bagster Phillips. The first witness was **Eliza Gold**, who lived at 6 Thrawl-street, Spitalfields. She recognized the deceased as her poor sister (and then commenced to weep very much such that, for a few moments, she was unable to proceed further with her story). Her sister was named Catherine Eddowes but Eliza could not exactly tell where she was living; Catherine was staying with a gentleman, but was not married to him. Her age last birthday was aged about forty-three years.

She has been living for some years with Kelly, who was in court. Witness last saw her alive about four or five months ago. She used to go out hawking for a living, and was a woman of sober habits. Before she went to live with Kelly, she had lived with a man named Conway for several years, and had two children by him. Witness could not tell how many years she lived with Conway; she did not know if Conway was still living. He was a pensioner from the army and used to go out hawking. Eliza Gold was quite certain that the body seen was her sister. The Coroner asked if deceased was on friendly terms with the man Kelly, to which the witness could not say. Apparently, the deceased was seen with Kelly three or four weeks ago by the witness, together, and they were then on happy terms. They were then living at 55 Flower and Dean Street, a lodging-house. A Juryman then pointed out that the witness previously said she had not seen her sister for three or four months, whilst later on she spoke of three or four weeks. The Coroner said 'you said your sister came to see you when you were ill, and that you had not seen her since. Was that three or four weeks ago?' The witness replied in the affirmative. The Coroner replied 'so that you are saying three or four months was a mistake?' which the witness confirmed because she was so upset and confused – then she commenced crying again. Since she could not write, she had to affix her mark on her deposition.

Next witness was **John Kelly**, a labourer. He said: 'I live at a lodging house, 55 Flower and Dean Street. Have seen the deceased and recognize her as Catherine Conway. I have been living with her for seven years. She hawked a few things about the streets and lived with me at a common lodging house in Flower and Dean Street. The lodging house is known as Cooney's. I last saw her alive about two o'clock in the afternoon of Saturday in Houndsditch. We parted on very good terms. She told me she was going over to Bermondsey to try and find her daughter, Annie. Those were the last words she spoke to me. Annie was a daughter whom I believe she had had by Conway. She promised me before we parted that she would be back by four o'clock, and no later. She did not return.'

The Coroner asked: 'did you make any inquiry after her?' The witness replied 'I heard she had been locked up at Bishopsgate Street on Saturday afternoon. An old woman who works in the lane told me she saw her in the hands of the police.' The Coroner then asked: 'did you make any inquiry into the truth of this?' Kelly replied: 'I made no further inquiries. I knew that she would be out on Sunday morning, being in the City.' The Coroner said: 'did you know why she was locked up?' The witness replied: 'yes, for drink; she had had a drop of drink, so I was told. I never knew she went out for any immoral purpose. She occasionally drank, but not to excess. When I left her she had no money about her. She went to see and find her daughter to get a trifle, so that I shouldn't see her walk about the streets at night.'

The Coroner queried with: 'what do you mean by walking the streets?' Kelly said: 'I mean that if we had no money to pay for our lodgings, we would have to walk about all night. I was without money to pay for our lodgings at the time. I do not know that she was at variance with any one – not in the least. She had not seen Conway recently – not that I know of. I never saw him in my existence. I cannot say whether Conway is living. I know of no one who would be likely to injure her.' The Foreman of the Jury asked: 'you say you heard the deceased was taken into custody. Did you ascertain, as a matter of fact, when she was discharged?' Kelly replied: 'no, I do not know when she was discharged.'

The Coroner continued: 'what time was she in the habit of returning to her lodgings?' Kelly said early, to which the Coroner asked what was early? About eight or nine o'clock, was the reply. The Coroner had it in for Kelly, it seems. 'When she did not return on this particular evening, did it not occur to you that it would be right to inquire whether she had been discharged or not?'

'No,' the witness replied. 'I did not inquire. I expected she would turn up on the Sunday morning.' The Coroner said: 'have you any idea where her daughter lives?' Kelly said: 'she told me in King Street, Bermondsey, and that her name was Annie.' Had she been previously there for money was the next question. Yes, once last year. How long have Kelly been living in the lodging house together with Eddowes? Seven years was the answer, in the same house. Kelly was able to explain a bit of their life together up until Kate's murder. 'On Monday, Tuesday, and Wednesday, we were down at the hop-picking, and came back to London on Thursday. We had been unfortunate at the hop-picking and had no money.'

'On Thursday night, we both slept in the casual ward. On the Friday I earned 6d at a job, and I said, 'here, Kate, you take 4d and go to the lodging-house and I will go to Mile-end,' but she said, 'No, you go and have a bed and I will go to the casual ward,' and she went. I saw her again on Saturday morning, early.' The Coroner asked: 'at what time did you quit one another on Friday?' Kelly could not tell, but thought it would be about three or four in the afternoon. Why did the victim leave him? 'To go to Mile End (to get a night's shelter in the casual ward). 'When did you see her next morning?' the Coroner asked.

'About eight o'clock. I was surprised to see her so early. I know there was some tea and sugar found on her body. She bought that out of some boots we pawned at Jones's for 2s 6d. I think it was on Saturday morning that we pawned the boots. She was sober when she left me. We had been drinking together out of the 2s 6d. All of it was spent on drink and food. She left me quite sober to go to her daughter's. We parted without an angry word. I do not know why she left Conway. In the past seven years, she only lived with me. I did not know of her going out for immoral purposes at night. She never brought me money in the morning after being out at night.'

Next witness was **Frederick William Wilkinson** a deputy of the lodging house at Flower and Dean Street. He had known the deceased and John Kelly during the last seven years. They passed as man and wife and lived on very good terms. They had a quarrel now and then, but not violent. They sometimes had a few words when Kate was in drink, but they were not serious. He believed Kate got her living by hawking about the streets and cleaning amongst the Jews in Whitechapel. Kelly paid him pretty regularly. Kate was not often in drink. She was a very jolly woman, always singing. Kelly was not in the habit of drinking, and was never seen the worse for drink. During the week, the first time Wilkinson saw the deceased at his lodging house was on Friday afternoon. Kelly was not with her then. She went out and did not return until Saturday morning, when he saw her and Kelly in the kitchen together, having breakfast. He did not see her go out, and did not know whether Kelly went with her. He never saw her again.

The Coroner asked if he knew she was in the habit of walking the streets at night? No, Wilkinson replied, she generally used to return between nine and ten o'clock. He never knew her to be intimate with any particular individual except Kelly. She use to say she was married to Conway; that her name was bought and paid for, meaning that she was married. She was not at variance with any one that he knew of. When he saw her last, on Saturday morning, between ten and eleven, she was quite sober. He first heard from Kelly on Saturday night that Kate was locked up, and he said he wanted a single bed. That was about 7:30 in the evening. A single bed is 4d, and a double 8d.

A Juryman asked about his lodgers. Wilkinson said: 'I don't take the names of the lodgers, but I know my regulars. If a man comes and takes a bed, I put the number of the bed down in my book, but not his name. Of course, I know the names of my regular customers.' Mr. Crawford, solicitor representing the City of London asked: 'when was the last time Kelly and the deceased had slept together in your house previous to last week?' The reply was: 'the last time the two slept at the lodging-house was five or six weeks ago, before they went to the hop-picking. Kelly slept there on Friday and Saturday, but not Kate.

I did not make any inquiry about her not being there on Friday. I could not say whether Kate went out with Kelly on Saturday, but I saw them having their breakfast together. I saw Kelly in the house about ten o'clock on Saturday night. I am positive he did not go out again. I cannot tell when he got up on Sunday. I saw him about dinner time. I believe on Saturday morning Kate was wearing an apron. Nothing unusual struck me about her dress.'

Mr. Crawford said: 'did anyone come into your lodging-house and take a bed between one and two o'clock on the Sunday morning?' The reply was that no stranger came in then. Crawford then asked if anyone come into the lodging house about that hour? No was the reply; two detectives came about three and asked if any women were out. Crawford asked: 'did anyone come into your lodging house about two o'clock on Sunday morning whom you did not recognize?' Wilkinson replied: 'I cannot say; I could tell by my book, which can soon be produced.' The deputy was dispatched for his book, with which after an interval he returned. It merely showed, however, that there were fifty-two beds occupied in the house on Saturday night. There were only six strangers. Wilkinson could not say whether any one took a bed about two o'clock on Sunday morning. He had sometimes over 100 persons sleeping in the house at once. They paid for their beds, and were asked no questions.

Edward Watkins, PC 881 of the City Police, said: 'I was on duty at Mitre Square on Saturday night. I have been in the force seventeen years. I went on duty at 9:45 upon my regular beat. That extends from Duke Street, Aldgate, through Heneage Lane, a portion of Bury-street, through Cree-lane into Leadenhall Street, along eastward into Mitre Street, then into Mitre Square, around the square again into Mitre Street, then into King Street to St. James's Place, around the place, then into Duke Street, where I started from. That beat takes twelve or fourteen minutes. I had been patrolling the beat continually from ten o'clock at night until one o'clock (*sic*) on Sunday morning.'

Had anything excited his attention during those hours, the Coroner asked. No was the reply. Or any person? 'No, I passed through Mitre Square at 1:30 on the Sunday morning. I had my lantern alight and on - fixed to my belt. According to my usual practice, I looked at the different passages and corners.'

'At half-past one did anything excite your attention?' No was Watkins reply. Did he see anyone about? No again was the reply. 'Could any people have been about that portion of the square without your seeing them?' the Coroner asked.

'No. I next came into Mitre Square at 1:44, when I discovered the body lying on the right as I entered the square. The woman was on her back, with her feet towards the square. Her clothes were thrown up. I saw her throat was cut and the stomach ripped open. She was lying in a pool of blood. I did not touch the body. I ran across to Kearley and Long's warehouse.

The door was ajar, and I pushed it open, and called on the watchman Morris, who was inside. He came out. I remained with the body until the arrival of Police Constable Holland. No one else was there before that but myself. Holland was followed by Dr. Sequeira. Inspector Collard arrived about two o'clock, and also Dr. Brown, surgeon to the police force.'

The Coroner asked: 'when you first saw the body did you hear any footsteps as if anybody were running away?' No, was the response. 'The door of the warehouse to which I went was ajar, because the watchman was working about. It was no unusual thing for the door to be ajar at that hour of the morning. I was continually patrolling my beat from ten o'clock up to half-past one. I noticed nothing unusual up till 1:44, when I saw the body.'

The Coroner asked by what means he summoned assistance? 'I did not sound an alarm. We do not carry whistles. My beat is not a double but a single beat. No other policeman comes into Mitre Street.'

Frederick William Foster, an architect and surveyor, produced a plan which he had made of the place where the body was found, and the district. From Berners Street to Mitre Street is three-quarters of a mile, he said, and a man could walk the distance in twelve minutes (*actually about 2/3rd of a mile – my italics*).

Inspector Edward Collard of the City Police, said 'at five minutes before two o'clock on Sunday morning last, I received information at Bishopsgate Street Police Station that a woman had been murdered in Mitre Square. Information was at once telegraphed to headquarters. I dispatched a constable to Dr. Gordon Brown, informing him, and proceeded myself to Mitre Square, arriving there about two or three minutes past two.'

'I there found Dr. Sequeira, two or three police officers, and the deceased person lying in the south-west corner of the square, in the position described by Constable Watkins. The body was not touched until the arrival shortly afterwards of Dr. Brown. The medical gentlemen examined the body, and in my presence Sergeant Jones picked up from the foot way by the left side of the deceased three small black buttons, such as are generally used for boots, a small metal button, a common metal thimble, and a small penny mustard tin containing two pawn-tickets.'

'They were handed to me. The doctors remained until the arrival of the ambulance, and saw the body placed in the conveyance. It was then taken to the mortuary and stripped by Mr. Davis, the mortuary keeper, in the presence of the two doctors and myself. I have a list of articles of clothing more or less stained with blood and cut.'

'Was there any money about her?' the Coroner asked. 'No; no money whatever was found. A piece of cloth was found in Goulston Street, corresponding with the apron worn by the deceased. When I got to the square I took immediate steps to have the neighbourhood searched for the person who committed the murder. Mr. McWilliams, chief of the detective department, on arriving shortly afterwards sent men to search in all directions in Spitalfields, both in streets and lodging houses.'

'Several men were stopped and searched in the streets, without any good result. I have had a house-to-house inquiry made in the vicinity of Mitre Square as to any noises or whether persons were seen in the place; but I have not been able to find any beyond the witnesses who saw a man and woman talking together.'

Mr Crawford asked 'when you arrived, was the deceased in a pool of blood?' The reply was 'the head, neck, and, I imagine, the shoulders were lying in a pool of blood when she was first found, but there was no blood in front. I did not touch the body myself, but the doctor said it was warm.'

Was there any sign of a struggle having taken place? No, none whatever. The inspector made a careful inspection of the ground all around; there was no trace whatever of any struggle. There was nothing in the appearance of the woman, or of the clothes, to lead to the idea that there had been any struggle.

From the fact that the blood was in a liquid state, he conjectured that the murder had not been long previously committed. In his opinion, the body had not been there more than a quarter of an hour. He endeavored to trace footsteps, but could find no trace whatever. The backs of the empty houses adjoining were searched, but nothing was found.

The medical evidence was heard when the inquest re-opened on 11th October. No effort was spared to get the details by the city police. **Dr Brown** entered Mitre Square at about 2:18 that morning. According to his notes taken at the time, the body was on its back: the head turned to the left shoulder, the arms by the sides of the body as if they had fallen there, both palms upwards, the fingers slightly bent – a thimble was lying off the finger on the right side.

The clothes were drawn up above the abdomen: the thighs were naked with the left leg extended in a line with the body, the abdomen was exposed. The right leg was bent at the thigh and knee, the bonnet was at the back of the head and there was great disfigurement of the face with the throat cut across.

Below the cut was a neckerchief, the upper part of the dress was pulled open a little way with the abdomen all exposed and the intestines drawn out a large extent and placed over the right shoulder. These were smeared over with feculent matter and a piece of about two feet long was quite detached from the body and placed between the body and the left arm, apparently by design.

The lobe and auricle of the right ear was cut obliquely through and there was a quantity of clotted blood on the pavement on the left side of the neck, around the shoulder and upper part of the arm, with fluid blood serum under the neck to the right shoulder – due to the pavement sloping in that direction.

The body was quite warm and death had occurred within the half hour. The doctors looked for superficial bruises and saw none; there was no blood on the skin of the abdomen nor secretion of any kind on the thighs – no spurting of blood on the bricks or pavement and no marks of blood below the middle of the body.

Several buttons were found in the clotted blood after the body was lifted and removed; there was no blood on the front of the clothes and no traces of recent connection (*sexual intercourse* – my italics). Dr Brown continued to describe his findings from the post-mortem. Eddowes' throat was cut across to the extent of about six or seven inches.

A superficial cut commenced about 1½" below the lobe and about 2½" below and behind the left ear and extended across the throat to about 3" below the lobe of the right ear. The big muscle across the throat was divided through on the left side. The large vessels on the left side of the neck were severed. The larynx was severed below the vocal cord.

All the deep structures were severed to the bone, the knife marking intervertebral cartilages. The sheath of the vessels on the right side was just opened. The carotid artery had a fine opening. The internal jugular vein was opened 1½" but not divided. The blood vessels contained clot. All these injuries were performed by a sharp instrument like a pointed knife.

Dr Brown examined the abdomen. The front walls were laid open from the breast bone to the pubes. The cut commenced opposite the ensiform cartilage. The incision went upwards, not penetrating the skin that was over the sternum. It then divided the ensiform cartilage.

The knife must have cut obliquely at the expense of the front surface of that cartilage. Behind this the liver was stabbed as if by the point of a sharp instrument. Below this was another incision into the liver of about 2½" and below this the left lobe of the liver was slit through by a vertical cut.

Two cuts were shown by a jagging of the skin on the left side. The abdominal walls were divided in the middle line to within quarter of an inch of the navel. The cut then took a horizontal course for 2½" towards the right side. It then divided around the navel on the left side and made a parallel incision to the former horizontal incision, leaving the navel on a tongue of skin.

Attached to the navel was 2½" of the lower part of the rectus muscle on the left side of the abdomen. The incision then took an oblique direction to the right and was shelving. The incision went down the right side of the vagina and rectum for ½" behind the rectum. There was a stab of about one inch on the left groin. This was done by a pointed instrument. Below this was a cut of three inches going through all the tissues making a wound of the perineum about the same extent.

An inch below the crease of the thigh was a cut extending from the anterior spine of the ilium obliquely down the inner side of the left thigh and separating the left labium, forming a flap of skin up to the groin. The left rectus muscle was not detached. There was a flap of skin formed from the right thigh attaching the right labium and extending up the spine of the ilium.

The muscles on the right side inserted into the Poupart's ligament were cut through. The skin was retracted through the whole of the cut in the abdomen, but the vessels were not clotted. Nor had there been any appreciable bleeding from the vessel. Dr Brown concluded that the cut was made after death and there would not be much blood on the murderer.

The cut was made by someone on the right side of body, kneeling below the middle of the body. The doctor had removed the contents of the stomach and placed it in a jar for further examination. There was little in it in the way of food or fluid, but from the cut end partly digested farinaceous food escaped (*that is, food rich in starch: probably bread, macaroni or potato* – my italics).

The intestines had been detached to a large extent from the mesentery with about two feet of colon cut away. The sigmoid flexure was invaginated into the rectum very tightly (*meaning folded or drawn back within itself* – my italics). The right kidney was pale, bloodless, with slight congestion of the base of the pyramids (*if Eddowes had Bright's disease, then the remaining kidney would have it too; this was not the case* – my italics).

There was a cut from the upper part of the slit on the under surface of the liver to the left side and another cut at right angles to this, which were about 1½" deep and 2½" long. The liver itself appeared healthy. The gall bladder contained bile. The pancreas was cut but not through on the left side of the spinal column. 3½" of the lower border of the spleen by ½" was attached only to the peritoneum.

The peritoneal lining was cut through on the left side and the left kidney carefully taken out and removed! The left renal artery was cut through. Dr Brown thought that someone who knew the position of the kidney must have done it. The lining membrane over the uterus was cut through and the womb was cut through horizontally, leaving a stump of ¾". The rest of the womb had been taken away along with some of the ligaments.

The vagina and cervix of the womb was uninjured. The bladder was healthy and uninjured and contained three or four ounces of water. There was a tongue-like cut through the anterior wall of the abdominal aorta. The other organs were healthy.

The face of the victim was very much mutilated. There was a cut about ¼" through the lower left eyelid dividing the structures completely through. The upper eyelid on that side had a scratch through the skin near to the angle of the nose. The right eyelid was cut through to about ½".

There was a deep cut over the bridge of the nose extending from the left border of the nasal bone down near to the angle of the jaw on the right side across the cheek. This cut went into the bone and divided all the structures of the cheek except the mucous membrane of the mouth.

The tip of the nose was quite detached from the nose by an oblique cut from the bottom of the nasal bone to where the wings of the nose join on to the face. A cut from this divided the upper lip and extended through the substance of the gum over the right upper lateral incisor tooth. About ½" from the top of the nose was another oblique cut.

There was a cut on the right angle of the mouth, as if by the cut of a point of a knife. The cut extended 1½" parallel with the lower lip. There was on each side of the cheek a cut which peeled up the skin forming a triangular flap of about 1½".

On the left cheek there were also two abrasions of the epithelium (*tissues lining the cavities, surfaces of blood vessels and organs – my italics*). There was a little mud on the left cheek of the victim and two slight abrasions of the epithelium under the left ear.

Some further questions were put to Dr Brown to which he replied that in his opinion, the killer had inflicted the throat wound first, while Eddowes was lying on the ground. The knife used was sharp and pointed and at least 6" long.

Referring to the degree of anatomical knowledge exhibited by the murderer, Dr Brown said the killer showed considerable knowledge of the position of the various organs and how they might be removed, but that someone used to cutting up animals could have this level of skill.

He believed that the killer must have taken about five minutes over the murder and mutilations. Finally, turning to the piece of apron found in Goulston Street, Dr Brown stated that it certainly had been cut from the apron Catherine Eddowes was wearing when she died.

Dr Sequeira, the first doctor on the scene, agreed with Dr Brown's findings, but when asked about the murderer's surgical expertise stated that he saw no evidence of surgical skill whatsoever! Furthermore, he did not believe the killer was searching for any particular organ to remove but had merely happened to take away the kidney and part of the uterus.

Dr Saunders also gave evidence at the inquest and he too believed that there was no evidence of surgical skill. He had examined Eddowes's stomach contents for traces of any narcotic or drug that might have been used to render her senseless, but had found nothing.

Dr Bagster Phillips, the last of the four doctors who had been at the post-mortem, did not give evidence at the inquest, but a report from Chief Inspector Swanson gave Phillips' opinion. He too saw no degree of particular anatomical knowledge, but he believed that the killer might just as likely be a hunter, butcher, or slaughterman, as a student of surgery.

Other witnesses were called before the inquest was finished. **Annie Phillips** from Dilston Road, Southwark Park Road, said 'I am the daughter of the deceased, who formerly lived with my father. She always told me that she was married to him, but I have never seen the marriage lines. My father's name was Thomas Conway.'

She confirmed that her father had left her mother, not on very good terms, because of her drinking habits. Annie confirmed that she had not seen her father (Conway), mother (Eddowes) or two brothers for about eighteen months.

City of London Constable Lewis Robinson, PC 931, said 'at half-past eight, on the night of Saturday, September 29th, while on duty in High Street, Aldgate, I saw a crowd of persons outside number 29, surrounding a woman whom I have since recognized as the deceased.'

The Coroner asked what state was she in? The officer replied drunk. 'Lying on the footway?' Yes, the officer replied. 'I asked the crowd if any of them knew her or where she lived, but got no answer. I then picked her up and sat her against the shutters, but she fell down sideways. With the aid of a fellow-constable I took her to Bishopsgate Police Station. There she was asked her name and she replied 'Nothing.' She was then put into a cell.'

Did anyone appear to be in her company when the officer found her? No one in particular was the reply. Mr Crawford asked 'did anyone appear to know her?' The officer replied 'no.' The apron was produced, torn and discoloured with blood, and the witness said that to the best of his knowledge, it was the apron the deceased was wearing.

Sergeant James Byfield, of the City Police said 'I remember the deceased being brought to the Bishopsgate Station at a quarter to nine o'clock on the night of Saturday, September 29th.' The Coroner asked in what condition she was in? Very drunk, was the response. She was brought in supported by two constables and placed in a cell, where she remained until one o'clock the next morning, when she was sober. He then discharged her, after she had given her name and address. This was Mary Ann Kelly, 6 Fashion Street, Spitalfields. Did she say where she had been, or what she had been doing, the sergeant was asked? 'She stated that she had been hopping.'

Constable George Henry Hutt, 968 of the City Police, said 'I am gaoler at Bishopsgate Station. On the night of Saturday, September 29th, at a quarter to ten o'clock, I took over our prisoners, among them the deceased. I visited her several times until five minutes to one on Sunday morning. The inspector, being out visiting, I was directed by Sergeant Byfield to see if any of the prisoners were fit to be discharged.

I found the deceased sober, and after she had given her name and address, she was allowed to leave. I pushed open the swing-door leading to the passage, and said 'this way, missus.' She passed along the passage to the outer door. I said to her, 'Please, pull it to.' She replied, 'all right. Good night, old cock.' She pulled the door to within a foot of being closed, and I saw her turn to the left.'

That was leading towards Houndsditch, the Coroner asked? Yes, was the reply. The Foreman then asked 'is it left to you to decide when a prisoner is sober enough to be released or not?' The answer was no; but this was down to the inspector or acting inspector on duty.

Was it usual to discharge prisoners who have been locked up for being drunk at all hours of the night? Certainly, was the reply. The Coroner asked 'how often did you visit the prisoners?' The answer was about every half-hour. At first the deceased remained asleep; but at a quarter to twelve she was awake and singing a song to herself. PC Hutt went to her again at half-past twelve, and she then asked when she would be able to get out. He replied shortly. She said she was capable of taking care of herself.

Mr Crawford asked 'did she tell you where she was going?' Hutt replied no. About two minutes to one o'clock, when he was taking her out of the cell, she asked what time it was. 'I answered 'too late for you to get any more drink.' She said 'well, what time is it?' I replied, 'Just on one.' Thereupon she said 'I shall get a fine hiding when I get home, then.''

The Coroner asked if that was her parting remark? PC Hutt replied 'that was in the station yard. I said 'serve you right; you have no right to get drunk.'' The Coroner added 'you supposed she was going home?' I did, was the reply.

'In your opinion,' the Coroner continued, 'is that the apron the deceased was wearing?' To the best of PC Hutt's belief, it was.

A Juror then asked 'do you search persons who are brought in for drunkenness?' No was the reply, 'but we take from them anything that might be dangerous. I loosened the things around the deceased's neck, and I then saw a white wrapper and a red silk handkerchief.'

George James Morris, night watchman at Kearley and Tonge's tea warehouse, Mitre Square, said 'on Saturday, September 29th, I went on duty at seven o'clock in the evening. I occupied most of my time in cleaning the offices and looking about the warehouse.'

The Coroner asked what happened about a quarter to two in the morning? The watchman replied 'Constable Watkins, who was on the Mitre Square beat, knocked at my door, which was slightly ajar at the time. I was then sweeping the steps down towards the door. The door was pushed when I was about two yards off. I turned around and opened the door wide.

The constable said 'for God's sake, mate, come to my assistance.' I said 'stop till I get my lamp. What is the matter?' 'Oh, dear,' he exclaimed, 'here is another woman cut to pieces.' I asked where, and he replied 'in the corner.' I went into the corner of the square and turned my light on the body. I agree with the previous witnesses as to the position of the body. I ran up Mitre Street into Aldgate, blowing my whistle all the while.'

'Did you see any suspicious persons about?' the Coroner asked. 'No. Two constables came up and asked what was the matter. I told them to go down to Mitre Square, as there was another terrible murder. They went, and I followed and took charge of my own premises again.'

Joseph Lawende said 'I reside at 45, Norfolk Road, Dalston, and am a commercial traveler. On the night of September 29th, I was at the Imperial Club, Duke Street, together with Mr Joseph Levy and Mr Harry Harris. It was raining, and we sat in the club till half-past one o'clock, when we left. I observed a man and woman together at the corner of Church Passage,

Duke Street, leading to Mitre Square.

The woman was standing with her face towards the man, and I only saw her back. She had one hand on his breast. He was the taller. She had on a black jacket and bonnet. I have seen the articles at the police station, and believe them to be those the deceased was wearing. He had on a cloth cap with a peak of the same.'

Mr Crawford said 'unless the jury wish it, I do not think further particulars should be given as to the appearance of this man.' The Foreman replied 'the jury do not desire it.' Mr. Crawford (to witness): 'you have given a description of the man to the police?' Yes, was the reply. Asked if he would know this man again, Lawende said 'I doubt it. The man and woman were about nine or ten feet away from me. I have no doubt it was half-past one o'clock when we rose to leave the club, so that it would be twenty-five minutes to two o'clock when we passed the man and woman.'

The witness did not overhear anything that either said, neither did either appear in an angry mood. Did anything about their movements attract his attention? 'No. The man looked rather rough and shabby.'

Police Constable Alfred Long, 254 A, Metropolitan police 'I was on duty in Goulston Street, Whitechapel, on Sunday morning, September 30th, and about five minutes to three o'clock I found a portion of a white apron (item produced). There were recent stains of blood on it. The apron was lying in the passage leading to the staircase of numbers 106 to 119, a model dwelling-house.

Above on the wall was written in chalk, 'The Jews are the men that will not be blamed for nothing.' I at once searched the staircase and areas of the building, but did not find anything else. I took the apron to Commercial Road Police Station and reported to the inspector on duty.'

The Coroner asked 'had you been past that spot previously to your discovering the apron?' PC Long replied 'I passed about twenty minutes past two o'clock.' Was he able to say whether the apron was there then? 'It was not.'

Mr. Crawford asked 'as to the writing on the wall, have you not put a 'not' in the wrong place? Where not the words 'The Jews are not the men that will be blamed for nothing?' PC Long replied that he believed the words were as he had stated.

The Coroner said 'was not the word 'Jews' spelt 'Juwes?' It may have been, was PC Long's reply. The Coroner said 'yet you did not tell us that in the first place. Did you make an entry of the words at the time?' Yes, was the reply, 'in my pocket book.' Was it possible that he had put the 'not' in the wrong place? 'It is possible, but I do not think that I have.'

What did he notice first - the piece of apron or the writing on the wall? 'The piece of apron, one corner of which was wet with blood.' How did he come to observe the writing on the wall? 'I saw it while trying to discover whether there were any marks of blood about.'

The Coroner said 'did the writing appear to have been recently done?' PC Long could not form an opinion on that. Regarding searching the buildings, he went into the stair cases. He did not make inquiries in the houses. At the request of the jury, PC Long's pocket book was to be fetched.

Daniel Halse, detective officer, City police said 'on Saturday, September 29th, pursuant to instructions received at the central office in Old Jewry, I directed a number of police in plain clothes to patrol the streets of the City all night. At two minutes to two o'clock on the Sunday morning, when near Aldgate Church, in company with Detectives Outram and Marriott, I heard that a woman had been found murdered in Mitre Square. We ran to the spot, and I at once gave instructions for the neighbourhood to be searched and every man stopped and examined. I myself went by way of Middlesex Street into Wentworth Street, where I stopped two men, who, however, gave a satisfactory account of themselves. I came through Goulston Street about twenty minutes past two, and then returned to Mitre Square, subsequently going to the mortuary. I saw the deceased, and noticed that a portion of her apron was missing. I accompanied Major Smith back to Mitre Square, when we heard that a piece of apron had been found in Goulston Street. After visiting Leman Street police station, I proceeded to Goulston Street, where I saw some chalk-writing on the black facia of the wall. Instructions were given to have the writing photographed, but before it could be done the Metropolitan police stated that they thought the writing might cause a riot or outbreak against the Jews, and it was decided to have it rubbed out, as the people were already bringing out their stalls into the street. When Detective Hunt returned, inquiry was made at every door of every tenement of the model dwelling house, but we gained no tidings of anyone who was likely to have been the murderer.'

The Coroner said 'as to the writing on the wall, did you hear anybody suggest that the word 'Jews' should be rubbed out and the other words left?' Halse replied: 'I did. The fear on the part of the Metropolitan police that the writing might cause riot was the sole reason why it was rubbed out. I took a copy of it, and what I wrote down was as follows: 'The Juwes are not the men who will be blamed for nothing.'

Did the writing have the appearance of having been recently done, the Coroner said? Yes, was the reply; it was written with white chalk on a black facia. The jury Foreman asked 'why was the writing really rubbed out?' Detective Halse replied 'the Metropolitan Police said it might create a riot, and it was their ground.'

Mr Crawford asked 'I am obliged to ask this question. Did you protest against the writing being rubbed out?' Halse replied 'I did. I asked that it might, at all events, be allowed to remain until Major Smith had seen it.'

Why did he say that it seemed to have been recently written? 'It looked fresh, and if it had been done long before it would have been rubbed out by the people passing. I did not notice whether there was any powdered chalk on the ground, although I did look about to see if a knife could be found.

There were three lines of writing in a good schoolboy's 'round' hand. The size of the capital letters would be about 3/4 of an inch, and the other letters were in proportion. The writing was on the black bricks, which formed a kind of dado, the bricks above being white.'
A Juror said 'it seems surprising that a policeman should have found the piece of apron in the passage of the buildings, and yet made no inquiries in the buildings themselves. There was a clue up to that point, and then it was altogether lost.'

Mr Crawford replied 'as to the premises being searched, I have in court members of the City police who did make diligent search in every part of the tenements the moment the matter came to their knowledge. But unfortunately, it did not come to their knowledge until two hours after. There was thus delay, and the man who discovered the piece of apron is a member of the Metropolitan police.'

The Juror added 'it is the man belonging to the Metropolitan police that I am complaining of.' Here, PC Alfred Long returned with his pocket note book. The City solicitor, Mr Crawford, asked what was the entry. Constable Long replied 'the words are 'the Jews are the men that will not be blamed for nothing.''

The Coroner said 'both here and in your inspector's report the word 'Jews' is spelt correctly?' The officer replied 'yes; but the inspector remarked that the word was spelt 'Juwes.'' So, why did PC Long write 'Jews' then? The officer made his entry before the inspector made the remark. From the Coroner 'but why did the inspector write 'Jews?' PC Long could not say. At all events, the Coroner continued, there is a discrepancy? 'It would seem so,' Long replied.
'What did you do when you found the piece of apron?' the Coroner asked.
'I at once searched the staircases leading to the buildings.'
He did not search the tenements of the buildings, but did search the staircases, of which there were six or seven of them. He confirmed that he searched every staircase up to the top, but found no trace of blood or footmarks. This was completed by three o'clock, when he proceeded back to the station.

The Coroner then said 'before going, did you hear that a murder had been committed?' Yes, PC Long had heard that. 'It is common knowledge,' he said, 'that two murders have been perpetrated.'
Which did he hear of, the Coroner asked?
'I heard of the murder in the City. There were rumours of another, but not certain.'

The Coroner asked when did he return to the building? This was about five o'clock. The writing on the wall was rubbed out in his presence at half-past five. He did not hear of any objections to it being rubbed out. This concluded his evidence. So, according to the best medical evidence, the ripper appeared to have shown no special skills in his butchery of Catherine Eddowes. On 8th October 1888, Catherine Eddowes was laid to rest in the City of London Cemetery at Ilford. Crowds lined the streets and hundreds gathered about the grave to see her body committed to the ground. The Coroner's inquest could only return the one usual verdict: 'murder by some person or persons unknown.'

Conclusion

The savagery of the ripper attacks was increasing, from the first victim Polly Nichols to that of Catherine Eddowes (excluding Elizabeth Stride, who I and others do not believe was really a ripper victim). For now, there was a long period of silence from Jack, thirty-nine days to be exact. There was one unusual 'incident' occurring on the 16th October, when half a kidney purporting to have come from Catherine Eddowes arrived for Mr George Lusk, head of the Whitechapel Vigilance Committee. We shall look at this incident, plus further inquiries into Catherine Eddowes's cut apron and shawl, in volume II. But for now, we can skip forward to Friday 9th November 1888, and the last ripper victim.

6 FOURTH CANONICAL VICTIM

By November, many believed that the ripper's reign of terror was finally over. October had been relatively quiet, with only the horror of that piece of kidney sent to George Lusk of Whitechapel Vigilance Committee. Therefore, at 10:45 on the morning of 9th November 1888, John McCarthy was at his chandler's shop at 27 Dorset Street, checking his accounts. He also owned 26 Dorset Street, which had been divided off into separate rooms and a number of properties in Millers Court, which ran between numbers 26 and 27. Most of his tenants paid their rent on time, but Mary Jane Kelly (aged 25, the youngest victim) had run up arrears of 29s. McCarthy sent his assistant, Thomas Bowyer, to call on her and see whether he could get any rent. **(Gory pictures follow below)**

Millers Court entrance   *Room 13 door (enhanced picture)*

Mary Kelly lived at 13 Millers Court. This small, partitioned room was the back room of 26 Dorset Street, and was entered by the second door on the right as you walked down the arched court passage. Thomas Bowyer walked down this narrow passageway and stopped at Mary's door; knocking to get her attention. There was no reply, which was not unusual, so he knocked a second time, but again there was no sound from inside. It was also the day of the Lord Mayor's show in London, and Bowyer knew that Mary had expressed an interest in going to watch the parade. Perhaps that was where she had gone? Nevertheless, to be sure Bowyer thought he would investigate and went further into the court, turning right where there were two windows from room 13 looking directly into the court. The windows were different sizes, as you can see from the photographs. The smallest one was very close to the edge of the wall and had two panes of glass broken. Bowyer reached in through one of them and pulled the curtain aside.

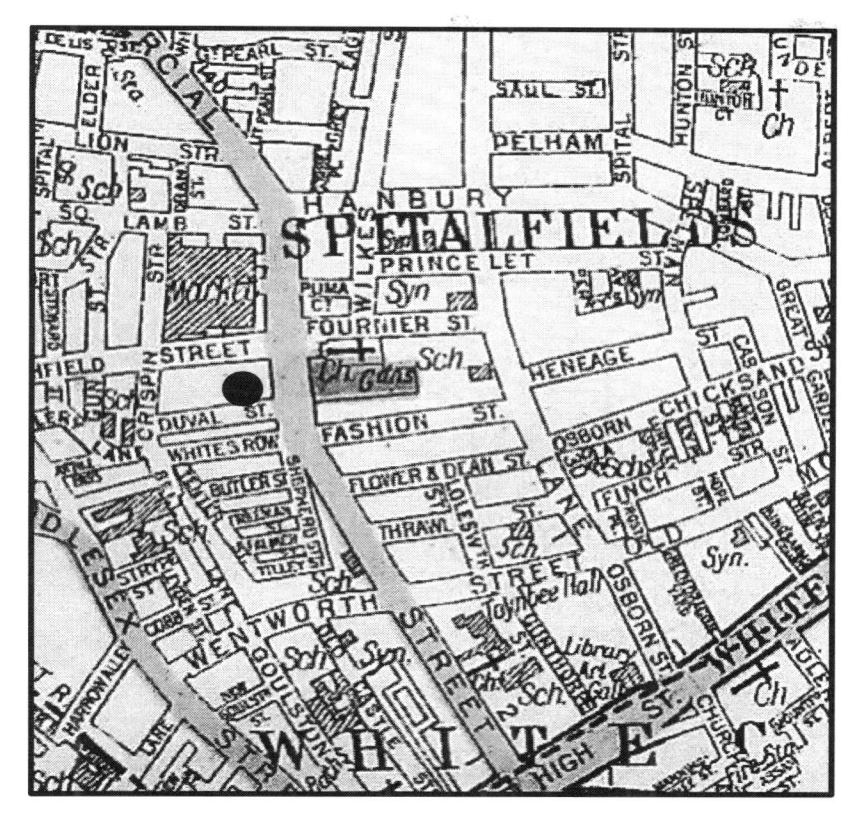

Dorset Street (renamed Duval Street) (unknown general map).

Arched Millers Court entrance from Dorset Street (left) and room 13 (right), entrance door (at side) and victim's windows through which her body was first seen (unknown)

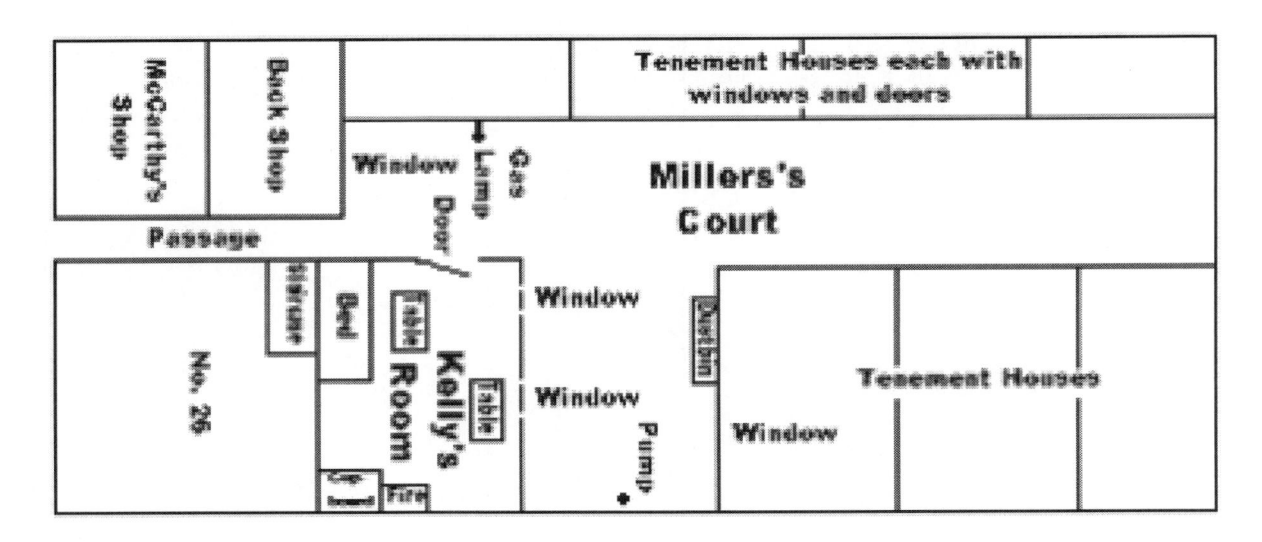

Millers Court layout (unknown).

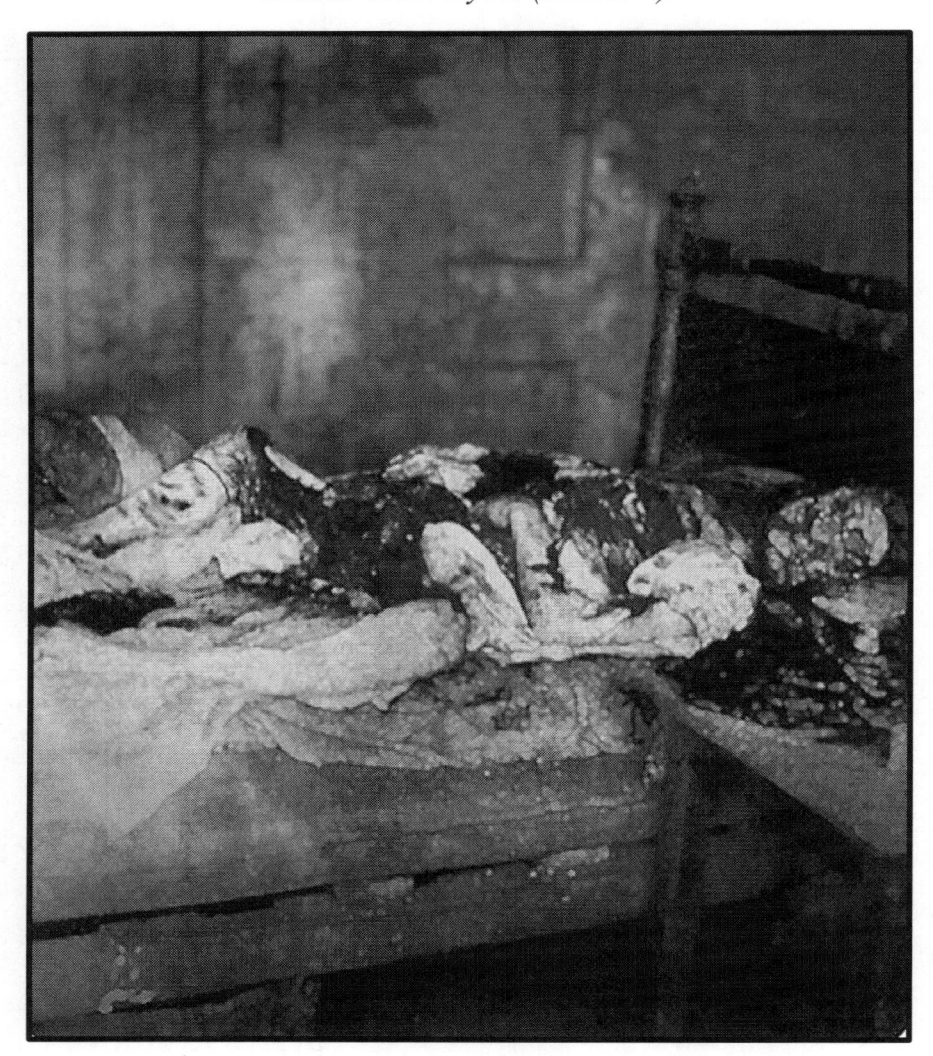

Computer enhanced picture of Mary Kelly as found (police).

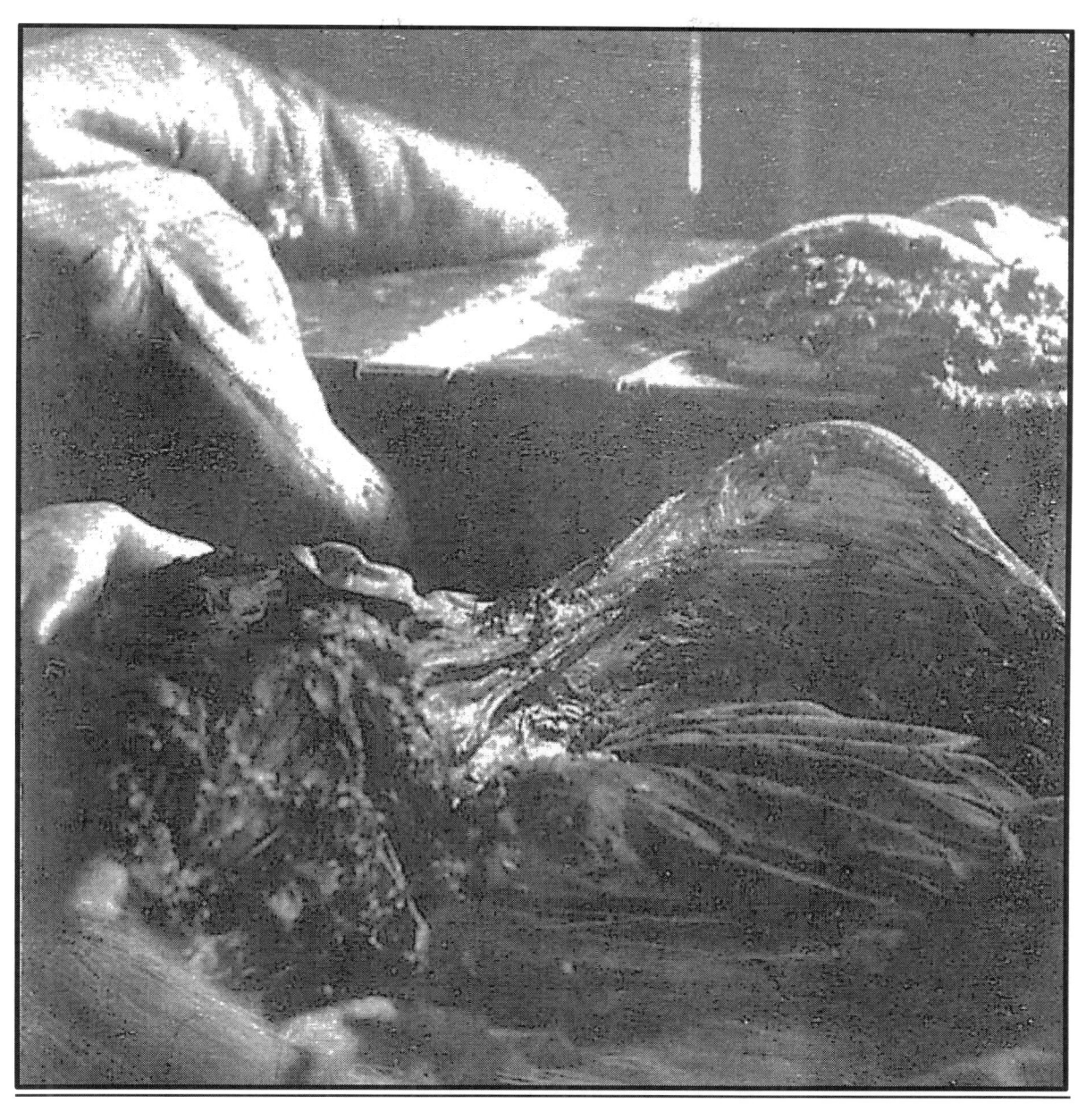

The only known second photo of Kelly's body, taken from the partition side of the room, looking towards the entrance door in background and bedside table, upon which a pillow sits and bits of her body was left by the murderer (police)

Coroner R Macdonald

The first thing he saw was what looked like two lumps of flesh piled on the bedside table. Then, as his eyes grew accustomed to the darkness, he also saw a body lying on the bed, and a great deal of blood. He turned and ran back up the court to his employer's shop, where he gasped out 'governor, I knocked at the door and could not make anyone answer. I looked through the window and saw a lot of blood.' McCarthy went to see for himself, taking Bowyer with him. Looking through the window, McCarthy told his assistant to run to the police station and fetch someone. Bowyer ran to Commercial Street police station, which was closest, and blurted out his story to Inspector Walter Beck and Detective Constable Walter Dew.

As he did so, his employer, McCarthy, also came in and told the two officers what he and Bowyer had just seen at Millers Court. All four men were soon hurrying back to the narrow court, and it was just after eleven o'clock in the morning when they arrived. Once the two police officers had taken their turn at the window and seen the carnage inside, they sent for further assistance. At 11:15 Dr Bagster Phillips arrived and confirmed, after his own view through the broken window, that the body on the bed was in such a state to be beyond any medical aid. At 11:30 Detective Inspector Abberline arrived, but the door to 13 Millers Court was still firmly locked.

The police had sent for some Bloodhounds tested recently as trackers by Sir Charles Warren himself, so they decided not to force entry until the dogs arrived. What they did not know was that Warren had resigned the day before! Nevertheless, the police and other people living in the court merely stood around, waiting for something to happen. At 1:30 that afternoon Superintendent Thomas Arnold arrived and announced that the Bloodhounds were not coming; also, that the door should be forced open immediately. John McCarthy took a pickaxe and smashed it open himself.

Dr Phillips was the first man to enter the room, banging the door against a table that stood next to the bed. The scene inside the small, dingy room was beyond belief, and it was clear that the ripper had struck again, this time indoors where he could be secure in the knowledge that he would not be disturbed. The body on the bed was unrecognizable and could only be identified as Mary Kelly by her eyes and hair. The body was eventually moved to the

Shoreditch Mortuary at four o'clock that afternoon, after which the windows of Room 13 were boarded up and the front door padlocked. Two police officers stood guard at the entrance to the court to stop the curious from trying to crowd the court to look at the scene.

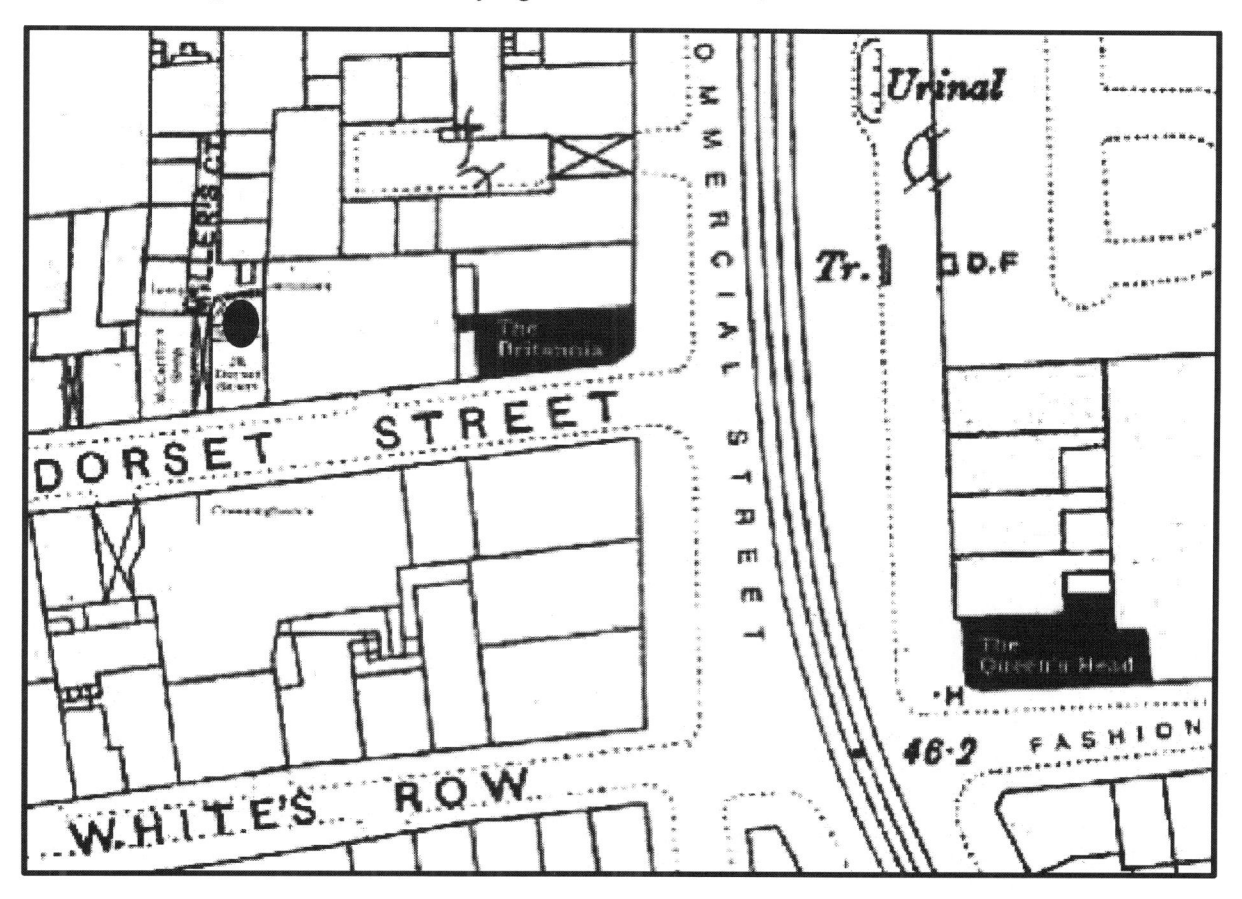

Dorset Street, showing Millers Court and local pubs 'The Britannia' (middle top) and 'The Queen's Head' (bottom right) (unknown general map)

Next day, being Saturday 10th November, Detective Inspector Abberline returned to Millers Court and made a careful search of the room. He paid particular attention to the ashes in the fire grate, which appeared to have been the scene of a recent very fierce blaze. The spout of a kettle had dropped off after the solder had melted. Abberline found that clothing had been burned, possibly in order to give the killer light with which to see. That same day, the post-mortem was carried out by Dr Phillips, Dr Thomas Bond and Dr Frederick Gordon Brown. Later that day, Dr Phillips and Dr Roderick Macdonald (the coroner) also visited Millers Court to sift through the grate ashes themselves, seeking out any burnt human remains. Their search seems to contradict later press reports stating that no bodily organs were missing.

Still here today; The Queen's Head – but no longer a pub. The original facia can just be seen just behind the lamp post, above the boarding.

Public inquest

The inquest on Mary Jane Kelly opened at Shoreditch town hall at eleven o'clock on Monday 12th November before Dr Roderick Macdonald. Some jurors objected, stating Wynne E Baxter was their coroner, but Macdonald would not have it. Where the body lay determined, in his opinion, who the coroner was. Inspector Abberline began by escorting the jury to the mortuary to view the body and then to Millers Court to see the scene of the murder. The jurors then returned to the town hall.

First witness was **Joseph Barnett**, an unemployed market porter who had previously worked at Billingsgate and who had been Mary Kelly's companion. He explained that he and Mary had first met in Commercial Street on Good Friday in April 1887, at which time she was living at Cooley's lodging house in Thrawl Street. From the first moment they had gotten on well together and had agreed to meet again the following day. Once again they had enjoyed each other's company and had agreed to live together. They first shared a home in George Street, then lived in Little Paternoster Row just off Dorset Street. After that, they lived in Brick Lane before moving to Millers Court in early 1888.

Dr Thomas Bond   *Dr Phillips (sketch)*   *Joseph Barnett (sketch)*

They continued to live together in Millers Court until 30th October, when they argued. According to Barnett, this came about because Mary allowed a homeless prostitute to move in with them. He accepted this situation for a few days, but then they argued and he moved into a lodging house at New Street, Bishopsgate. He and Mary remained on good terms, however, and he visited her most days, usually giving her some money when he had some. On the evening of 8th November, Barnett visited Kelly at about 7:30 or 7:45 and stayed until about eight o'clock. When he first arrived a friend of Kelly's, Lizzie Albrook, was there, but she soon left him alone with Mary. He apologized that he had no money to give her and said they were on good terms when they parted.

Barnett's visit was confirmed by **Maria Harvey**, another close friend of Mary's. Maria Harvey testified that she had slept at 13 Millers Court on the nights of 5th and 6th November, after which she found lodgings for herself at New Court, also off Dorset Street. According to Harvey, she spent the afternoon of 8th November with Mary and was in her room when Barnett called by. Harvey then left so the couple could be alone and confirmed that the two seemed friendly. The only discrepancy here was that Harvey put the time of Barnett's arrival as about 6:55 in the evening. She also said that she had left some clothing with Mary and that most of it was now missing. This implies that her garments were amongst those burned in the fire grate.

There is some confusion here, for press reports of the time state that the woman who was in Mary's room when Barnett called was in fact Lizzie Albrook. According to Maria Harvey, she actually spent the entire afternoon of the 8th November with Mary Kelly. The victim had called to visit Maria at her room in New Court and they had gone out drinking. They parted company at about 7:30 and Harvey believed that Kelly was heading off toward Thrawl Street. In fact, Mary Kelly then went home to Millers Court, where she was joined later by Lizzie Albrook with Joe Barnett calling soon afterwards.

Thomas Bowyer and **John McCarthy** both told of their discovery of the body and with Joe Barnett, were also able to fill in details of Mary Kelly's background. None of this story could be confirmed, however. She had said that she had been born in Limerick, Ireland, but her family had moved to Wales while she was still young. When she was sixteen, Mary had married a collier named Davies, but soon afterward he had been killed in the coal mines. She said she had first come to London in 1884 and had begun working as a prostitute in a brothel in the west end. One of her clients had taken her to France, after which she began to call herself Marie 'Jeanette' Kelly.

After returning to London, she took up with a man named Morganstone, who lived in Stepney. After that relationship ended, she began living with a Joe Fleming in Bethnal Green. Eventually, she moved to the East End, living first with a Mrs Buki and later at Mrs Carthy's at Pennington Street. The only true facts so far that can be corroborated is a hotel in Merthyr Tydfil that lists, amongst its guests in the 1881 census, a widow aged sixteen years named Mary Davies. [6] We will shortly look into Kelly's background again, (see volume II) since new evidence has started to appear suggesting she was divorced and that an ex-husband was the person responsible for her murder! [7]

So, the last sighting of Mary Kelly was by Joe Barnett at around eight o'clock in the evening of 8th November. Other witnesses were now called by the coroner who would testify to Mary's movements later that night. The first of these was **Mary Ann Cox**, a widow and unfortunate (usually meaning a prostitute) who lived at 5 Millers Court and had known the dead woman for nine months. Cox had been out soliciting in Commercial Street and returned to her room to warm herself about 11:45 that night.

As she turned into Dorset Street, she saw Mary Kelly walking in front of her in the company of a man. At that time, Kelly seemed to be much the worse for drink and as Mrs Cox watched, the couple turned into Millers Court. By the time Cox reached the archway, Mary and her male friend were just going inside no.13. As she passed by, Mrs Cox called out 'good night, Mary Jane,' and Mary replied in kind, although with some difficulty owing to the drink. She added that she intended to have a song. Cox got a good look at the man because there was a light almost directly opposite the door to no.13. She described him as about thirty-six years old and 5'5" tall.

He was stout with a fresh complexion but had blotches on his face. He had a thick, carroty moustache and was dressed in rather shabby dark clothes, with a dark overcoat and a black billycock hat (a derby, similar to a bowler hat). He carried a quart can of beer and Cox heard Mary Kelly singing inside her room. The song was reported to be 'only a violet I plucked from my mother's grave when a boy,' actually 'A Violet from Mother's Grave,' written in 1881 by J. W. Pepper. At midnight, Mary Ann Cox went back out again, returning to Millers Court at one in the morning. She heard Mary Kelly still singing inside her room!

That is, seventy-five minutes of singing – perhaps Mary only sang that tune when doing prostitute things with men? But when Cox returned for the last time at three o'clock, there was no light from the windows of Room 13 and all was quiet. Cox slept fitfully after this; she heard several men entering and leaving the court and finally heard someone leave at about 5:45 in the morning, although she could not say from which room. The next witness was **Elizabeth Prater**, living at 20 Millers Court, which was the room immediately above Mary Kelly's. Prater returned to the court at about one o'clock on the 9th November and stood for a time in the archway in Dorset Street, waiting for the man she was living with. When he did not appear, she went up to her room and finally retired for the night at about 1:30. She slept for a few hours until awakened by her kitten walking over her.

Soon afterwards, she heard a cry of 'murder,' but such cries were a daily occurrence in Whitechapel and people rarely took any notice. If only she had. She had no idea what time it was but, because a lodging house light was out, assumed it was sometime after four in the morning. At 5:30 Prater went to the Ten Bells public house for a tot of rum, and then went back to her room and slept until eleven o'clock. **Sarah Lewis** lived at 29 Great Pearl Street but very early on the 9th November she had argued with her husband and walked out of the house. She decided she would stay with some friends, the Keylers, living at 2 Millers Court. It was 2:30

when Lewis passed Christ Church; soon after she was in Dorset Street, approaching the entrance arch to Millers Court.

Here she saw a man standing by a lodging house that was directly opposite the court; she described him as not tall but stout, and stated he was wearing a black wide-awake hat. As she looked at him, another young man with a woman passed along the street. The man near the lodging house appeared to be looking up Millers Court, as if waiting for someone to come out (more on this man in volume II).

Wide-awake hat style   *Billycock hat style*

In the Keylers' room, Sarah Lewis slept in a chair until about 3:30 in the morning, then she sat there awake until five o'clock. Just before four o'clock she heard a single loud scream of 'murder,' so confirming Elizabeth Prater's story. This cry must have been Mary Kelly's last word, placing the time of her murder at about four o'clock on the 9th November. More contentious was the testimony of **Caroline Maxwell,** however, who also lived in Dorset Street. The general consensus was that Mary Kelly had been killed sometime in the early hours of the 9th November; however, Mrs Maxwell claims to have seen Mary Kelly after this time. She had known Mary Kelly for only four months and had spoken to her only twice, but Maxwell stated that between eight and 8:30 on the morning of the 9th she had seen Kelly standing on the corner of Millers Court.

The two women spoke and Kelly admitted that she was feeling the worse for drink; she pointed out some vomit in the gutter that she said was hers. One hour after this, at about 9:30, Maxwell saw Kelly again, talking to a stout man in dark clothes outside the Britannia public house. Many ripperologists seized upon this as being some sort of Masonic conspiracy and that someone other than Mary Kelly died in Millers Court (more in volume II). The most likely explanation is that Maxwell was mistaken about the date (some ripperologists have suggested that this vomiting was an indication that Mary Kelly was pregnant).

After Maxwell's dubious sighting of Kelly, Dr **Bagster Phillips** started the medical evidence, but the onlookers and reporters of the press were to be sadly disappointed – for Phillips reported that the immediate cause of death was the severance of Mary's right carotid artery. Beyond that, he would say only that he deduced that she had been attacked while lying at the far right side of the bed and that her body had subsequently been pulled from that side after death, probably so that her killer could more easily inflict the other injuries.

Phillips placed the time of death somewhere between 4:45 and 5:45 in the morning, which does not agree with the testimony of the two women who had heard the cry of 'murder.' Although Phillips did not reveal all of his testimony, and the coroner accepted it, we do have Dr Bond's written report on the autopsy to go by (more later). Bagster Phillips, the senior police doctor involved in the murder investigations, said 'I was called by the police on Friday morning at eleven o'clock, and on proceeding to Millers Court, which I entered at 11.15, I found a room, the door of which led out of the passage at the side of 26 Dorset Street, photographs of which I produce.

It had two windows in the court. Two panes in the lesser window were broken, and as the door was locked I looked through the lower of the broken panes and satisfied myself that the mutilated corpse lying on the bed was not in need of any immediate attention from me, and I also came to the conclusion that there was nobody else upon the bed, or within view, to whom I could render any professional assistance. Having ascertained that probably it was advisable that no entrance should be made into the room at that time, I remained until about 1:30 p.m., when the door was broken open by McCarthy, under the direction of Superintendent Arnold.

On the door being opened it knocked against a table which was close to the left-hand side of the bedstead, and the bedstead was close against the wooden partition. The mutilated remains of a woman were lying two-thirds over, towards the edge of the bedstead, nearest the door. Deceased had only an under-linen garment upon her, and by subsequent examination I am sure the body had been removed, after the injury which caused death, from that side of the bedstead which was nearest to the wooden partition previously mentioned. The large quantity of blood under the bedstead, the saturated condition of the paillasse, pillow, and sheet at the top corner of the bedstead nearest to the partition leads me to the conclusion that the severance of the right carotid artery, which was the immediate cause of death, was inflicted while the deceased was lying at the right side of the bedstead and her head and neck in the top right-hand corner.'

Coroner Dr Roderick Macdonald then told the inquest jury that they would hear Dr Phillips' full post mortem report at an adjourned inquest – clearly indicating that there would be a further session, as had happened with previous victims. However, after hearing a few more witnesses, he said that if the jury wished to bring in a verdict – all they had to go was agree on a cause of death, and leave other matters in the hands of the police; there was no point in continually going over the same matters, so the jury conferred quickly and then said that they wished to bring in a verdict of 'willful murder against a person or persons unknown.'

Macdonald then closed the inquest after the final two witnesses had given evidence. Penultimate witness was **Inspector Beck**, one of the first officers on the scene. Beck said he gave orders to prevent any persons leaving the court. He had directed officers to make a search. He was not aware that the deceased was also known to the police. The final witness was **Inspector Abberline**, who had an intimation from Inspector Beck that the Bloodhounds had been sent for, and the reply had been received that they were on the way.

'Dr. Phillips was unwilling to force the door, as it would be very much better to test the dogs, if they were coming. We remained until about 1:30 p.m., when Superintendent Arnold arrived, and he informed me that the order in regard to the dogs had been countermanded, and he gave orders for the door to be forced. I agree with the medical evidence as to the condition of the room. I subsequently took an inventory of the contents of the room. There were traces of a large fire having been kept up in the grate, so much so that it had melted the spout of a kettle off. We have since gone through the ashes in the fireplace; there were remnants of clothing, a portion of a brim of a hat, and a skirt, and it appeared as if a large quantity of women's clothing had been burnt.'

Maria Harvey had testified that she left Mary Kelly when Joseph Barnett turned up at 6:55 P.M. and left with her two men's dirty shirts, a little boy's shirt, a black overcoat, a black crepe bonnet with black satin strings, a pawn-ticket for a grey shawl upon which 2s had been lent, and a little girl's white petticoat. These were found burnt in Kelly's fire grate when sifted through by Detective Inspector Abberline. All except the black overcoat, which was recovered by police.

The coroner asked if he could give any reason why the clothing was burnt? 'I can only imagine that it was to make a light for the man to see what he was doing. There was only one small candle in the room, on the top of a broken wine-glass. An impression has gone abroad that the murderer took away the key of the room. (Joseph) Barnett informs me that it has been missing some time, and since it has been lost they have put their hand through the broken window, and moved back the catch. It is quite easy. There was a man's clay pipe in the room, and Barnett informed me that he smoked it.'

The missing key business will be discussed in volume II, when we also consider how the murderer exited 13 Millers Court without detection, how the photos *in situ* were taken, and why Sir Charles Warren had just resigned as Met police commissioner. Mary Kelly was the only victim photographed by police where she died; all the other victim's pictures were mortuary photos and not from the death sites. Because of the suppression of Phillips' evidence, the coroner had not complied with the legal requisite that the length, breadth and depths of all wounds to the deceased must be recorded and, with conflicting evidence having been given, the time of death had not been firmly established either.

Phillips conferred in private with the coroner before the hearing opened, something he had wanted to do at a previous inquest but had been refused. Thus Bagster Phillips' vital medical report was never heard in full. Because of the coroner's attitude in wanting to rush things and close the case, much vital evidence could well have been lost. However, **Dr Bond's** post-mortem notes on Mary Kelly were long lost, until 1987, when they were returned anonymously to Scotland Yard. His report provides the best view into the mutilations performed on Mary Kelly in Millers Court:

'Position of body – the body was lying naked in the middle of the bed (not quite true; she was wearing some sort of chemise), the shoulders flat, but the axis of the body inclined to the left side of the bed. The head was turned on the left cheek. The left arm was close to the body with the forearm flexed at a right angle and lying across the abdomen. the right arm was slightly abducted from the body and rested on the mattress, the elbow bent and the forearm supine with the fingers clenched.'

'The legs were wide apart, the left thigh at right angles to the trunk and the right forming an obtuse angle with the pubes. The whole of the surface of the abdomen and thighs was removed and the abdominal cavity emptied of its viscera. The breasts were cut off, the arms mutilated by several jagged wounds and the face hacked beyond recognition of the features. The tissues of the neck were severed all round down to the bone.'

'The viscera were found in various parts (places): the uterus and kidneys with one breast under the head, the other breast by the right foot, the liver between the feet, the intestines by the right side and the spleen by the left side of the body. The flaps removed from the abdomen and thighs were on a table.'

'The bed clothing at the right corner was saturated with blood, and on the floor beneath (the bed) was a pool of blood covering about two feet square. The wall by the right side of the bed and in a line with the neck was marked by blood which had struck it in a number of separate splashes.'

'Postmortem examination – The face was gashed in all directions, the nose, cheeks, eyebrows and ears being partly removed. The lips were blanched and cut by several incisions running obliquely down to the chin. There were also numerous cuts extending irregularly across all the features.'

'The neck was cut through the skin and other tissues right down to the vertebrae, the 5th and 6th being deeply notched. The skin cuts in the front of the neck showed distinct ecchymosis (hemorrhagic spots). The air passage was cut at the lower part of the larynx through the cricoid cartilage.'

'Both breasts were removed by more or less circular incisions, the muscles down to the ribs being attached to the breasts. The intercostals between the 4th, 5th and 6th ribs were cut through and the contents of the thorax visible through the openings.'

'The skin and tissues of the abdomen from the costal arch to the pubes were removed in three large flaps. The right thigh was denuded in front to the bone, the flap of skin included the external organs of generation and part of the right buttock. The left thigh was stripped of skin, fascia and muscles as far as the knee.'

'The left calf showed a long gash through skin and tissues to the deep muscles and reaching from the knee to five inches above the ankle. Both arms and forearms had extensive and jagged wounds. The right thumb showed a small superficial incision about one-inch long, with extravasation of blood in the skin and there were several abrasions on the back of the hand, moreover showing the same condition.'

'On opening the thorax, it was found that the right lung was minimally adherent by old firm adhesions. The lower part of the lung was broken and torn away. The left lung was intact: it was adherent at the apex and there were a few adhesions over the side. In the substances of the lung were several nodules of consolidation. The pericardium was open below and the heart absent.'

'In the abdominal cavity was some partially digested food of fish and potatoes, and similar food was found in the remains of the stomach attached to the intestines.'

Some newspaper reports

The **Croydon Times** of the 14th November 1888 described how the 'door was forced open and the police officers entered the room. The sight, in truth, was enough to un-nerve strong men. The pieces of flesh which had been dimly seen through the grimy window proved inexpressibly more ghastly at a close view. Large pieces of the thighs had been cut off and thrown about with brutal carelessness.'

'Both breasts of the unhappy victim had been removed, and one of them lay on the table alongside a confused and horrible mass of intestines (*incorrect* – my italics). The throat had been cut with such ferocious and appalling thoroughness that the head was almost severed from the trunk. The body, which was almost naked, had been ripped up and literally disemboweled.'

'The chief organs had been entirely removed; some were thrown upon the floor, and others placed on the table. It is stated upon authority which should be reliable that the uterus, as in the case of the Mitre Square victim, had been removed and taken away by the fiend, (*incorrect* – my italics) but upon this important point the police officers and surgeons refuse in the most emphatic manner to give the slightest information.'

'It is almost self-evident, however, that had that particular organ not been removed the police would gladly have said so, if only to allay in some slight measure the panic which has again set in with painful intensity among the poor people in the crime-plagued district.'

'Sir Charles Warren arrived at Millers Court at a quarter to two o'clock on Friday afternoon (*incorrect* – my italics) and remained until the completion of the post mortem examination, which lasted two hours. The surgeon's report, in consequence, will be of an unusually exhaustive character.'

It should be noted here that, as far as can be ascertained, Sir Charles Warren resigned as Metropolitan police commissioner that very morning or the day before, and he never attended Millers Court, which was partially the reason for several hours' delay before Superintendent Arnold arrived and ordered the door to Kelly's room to be forced open. Also, much of the newspaper report is incorrect regarding the placing of flesh around the room and the removal of the victim's uterus; only the heart was missing.

The **East London Advertiser** of 17th November 1888 reports that 'the poor woman lay on her back on the bed, entirely naked. Her throat was cut from ear to ear, right down to the spinal column. The ears and nose had been cut clean off. The breasts had also been cleanly cut off and placed on a table which was by the side of the bed (*incorrect* – my italics).'

'The stomach and abdomen had been ripped open, while the face was slashed about, so that the features were beyond all recognition. The kidneys and heart had also been removed from the body, and placed on the table by the side of the breasts (*incorrect* – my italics). The liver had likewise been removed, and laid on the right thigh (*incorrect* – my italics). The lower portion of the body and the uterus had been cut out, and the thighs had been cut.'

'A more horrible or sickening sight could not be imagined. The clothes of the woman were lying by the side of the bed, as though they had been taken off and laid down in the ordinary manner. The bedclothes had been turned down, and this was probably done by the murderer after he had cut his victim's throat.' (*From the photographs it does appear that the bed clothes may have been rolled back, but as for clothes, it is not possible to say.*)

'There was no appearance of a struggle having taken place, and, although a careful search of the room was made, no knife or instrument of any kind was found. It was reported that Bloodhounds would be laid on to trace the murderer, but for some reason this project was not carried out, and, of course, after the streets became thronged with people, that would have had no practical result.'

These Bloodhounds were the earlier brainchild of Sir Charles Warren, who had borrowed two from a breeder and tested their tracking abilities in person – the dogs had been returned to their owner by the time of Kelly's murder, which was the second of two reasons for the delay breaking open the Millers Court door that day. One of the last acts from Sir Charles was the granting of a murder pardon – whereby the 'secretary of state would advise the granting of Her Majesty's pardon to any accomplice, not being the person who contrived or actually committed the murder (*of Mary Kelly* – my italics), who shall give such information and evidence as shall lead to the discovery and conviction of the person or persons who committed the murder.' Most ripperologists take this pardon document to be an admission of the final failure of the police to solve the ripper murders.

END OF VOL I

REFERENCES

[1] This is the only known photograph purporting to show Inspector Abberline; the only other thing to compare with is an artist sketch from the newspapers of the time, purporting to show the same man. There is some verisimilitude between them.

Abberline sketch

[2] Inquest report as reported in *The Times* newspaper 3rd September 1888.

[3] As reported in the *Times* 14th September 1888.

[4] Home Office file HO/144/220/A49301C f 8g

[5] Donald Rumbelow *The Complete Jack The Ripper* – he does not name the source but I would presume the memoirs of Major Henry Smith.

[6] Bob Hinton's research and also '*Uncle Jack*' (2005) by Tony Williams.

[7] A new study suggesting the ripper was Francis Spurzheim Craig, a 51-year-old reporter covering the murder inquests. Researcher Dr Wynne Weston-Davies claims Craig's intimate knowledge of how the police worked from covering the courts allowed him to get away with his crimes! (*Daily Express online* 4/8/2015)

INDEX

'Dear Boss', 93, 94, 95, 96, 119, 146
'From Hell', 95, 119
'Saucy Jacky's', 95, 119
29 Hanbury Street, 100
Albert Cadoche, 35, 106
Albert Collins, 39
Alexander Pedachenko, 144
Alfred Long, 51, 64, 66
Alice Mackenzie, 14
Amelia Palmer, 30, 31
Amelia Richardson, 27, 28, 32
Amos Simpson, 149, 150, 152
Annie Chapman, 6, 14, 23, 24, 26, 30, 31, 33, 34, 35, 36, 37, 100, 106, 108, 146, 153
Annie Phillips, 52, 62
Arthur Dutfield, 39
Bagster Phillips, 33, 34, 35, 43, 54, 62, 71, 76, 78
Baxter Hunt, 11, 51, 114
Berner Street, 4, 6, 14, 37, 39, 41, 42, 44, 45, 46, 47, 50, 93, 109, 110, 111, 112, 114, 147
billycock, 121, 126, 153
Bishopsgate police station, 50, 52, 53, 54
Brights Disease, 96
Britannia public house, 123
Brown's Stable Yard, 4, 14, 17, 18
Buck's Row, 14
Bucks Road, 97
Captain Young, 34
Caroline Maxwell, 76, 123, 125
Catherine Eddowes, 6, 9, 11, 12, 14, 44, 52, 53, 54, 61, 66
Catherine Lane, 42
Central News Agency, 91, 93, 94, 95, 146, 147
Charles Brittain, 21
Charles Cross, 14, 16, 22, 24, 25
Charles Pinhorn, 11
Charles Preston, 43
Chief Inspector West, 46
Church Passage, 48, 53, 54, 63
City of London police, 91, 96, 114, 115, 116, 117, 131
Cloak Lane police station, 112
Commercial Street Police Station, 106
Crossingham's lodging house, 100
Croydon Times, 79
Daniel Halse, 12, 50, 51, 65
Detective Constable Daniel Halse, 114
Donald McCormick, 144
Donald Neilson, 152

Donald Sutherland Swanson, 9
Donald Swanson, 8, 9
Dorset Street, 4, 7, 14, 30, 31, 52, 54, 67, 68, 72, 73, 74, 75, 76, 77
Dr Blackwell, 40, 42, 43, 46
Dr Brown, 11, 50, 51, 54, 59, 60, 61
Dr Llewellyn, 17, 18, 19, 20, 21, 23, 24, 97
Dr Saunders, 61
Dr Sequeira, 50, 54, 61
Dr Thomas Bond, 92, 120, 123
Dr. Brown, 94
Duke Street, 48, 50, 53, 57, 63
Durward Street, 97
Dutfield's Yard, 91, 109, 110, 111, 112
East London Advertiser, 80
Edmund John James Reid, 10
Edmund Reid, 10, 46, 47
Edward Badham, 33
Edward Johnston, 40, 46
Edward Marriott, 50
Edward McKenna, 34
Edward Spooner, 39, 42
Edward Walker, 19
Edward Watkins, 48, 57
Eliza Cooper, 34
Eliza Gold, 52, 54, 55
Elizabeth Fisher, 52
Elizabeth Long, 34, 106
Elizabeth Prater, 75, 76
Elizabeth Stride, 6, 14, 37, 38, 40, 41, 42, 43, 44, 45, 46, 47, 48, 66, 93, 95, 109, 111, 112, 131, 147
Elizabeth Tanner, 42
Ellen Holland, 19, 22, 23
Emily Birrell, 51
Emma Green, 17, 18, 21, 23
Emma Jones, 52
Emma Smith, 14, 35
Ernest Elliston, 10
Eva Harstein, 44
Fanny Mortimer, 45
Flower and Dean, 42, 52, 55, 56
Fountain Smith, 31
Frances Coles, 14
Frances Wright, 33
Francis Tumblety, 144
Frederick Blackwell, 42
Frederick Deeming, 141
Frederick George Abberline, 10
Frederick Gordon Brown, 50, 72

83

Frederick William Blackwell, 40
Frederick William Foster, 58
Frederick William Wilkinson, 56
George Bagster Phillips, 12, 30, 35, 40
George Chapman, 141
George Godley, 21
George Henry Hutt, 62
George Hutchinson, 121, 126, 148
George Hutt, 53
George James Morris, 50, 63
George Lusk, 66, 67, 95, 96, 118, 119
George Oldfield, 92
George Simmons, 53
George William Sequeira, 50
Gerard, 3, 90
Gilbert, 3, 90
Golden Lane, 44, 50, 51, 54
Goulston Street, 4, 6, 11, 12, 51, 54, 58, 61, 64, 65, 91, 112, 113, 114, 115, 116, 117, 118, 130, 131, 147
Grand and Batchelor, 109
Hanbury Street, 3, 4, 14, 16, 22, 24, 26, 27, 29, 32, 34, 35
Hansi Weissensteiner, 151
Harriet Hardiman, 27, 32
Harry Douglas, 44
Harry Harris, 53, 63
Harry Owen, 125
Harry the Hawker, 31
Henry John Holland, 29, 32
Henry Lamb, 39, 42
Henry Matthews, 9, 13
Henry Moore, 10, 35, 44
Henry Tomkins, 21
Herbert Stanley, 144
Herendeen, 3, 90
Hindley and Brady, 152
HO 144/221, 147
Inspector Abberline, 33, 45, 71, 72, 73, 77, 78, 82
Inspector Beck, 77
Inspector Chandler, 30, 32, 33, 100
Inspector Edward Collard, 50, 58
Inspector Helson, 23
Inspector Pinhorn, 46
Inspector Spratling, 97, 146
International Working Men's Educational Club, 109
Isaac Kozebrodsky, 39
Israel Lipski, 45
Israel Schwartz, 45, 110
J K Stephens, 143

James Brown, 46, 110, 111, 119, 125
James Byfield, 62
James George Byfield, 53
James Green, 29, 32
James Hatfield, 21, 24
James Kent, 29, 31, 32
James Maybrick, 142
James McWilliam, 51
James McWilliams, 11
James Monro, 8, 9
James Mumford, 21
Jari Louhelainen, 150
Jill the Ripper, 145
John Davis, 27, 28, 29, 31, 32, 100
John Evans, 31
John Humble, 92
John Kelly, 52, 55, 56
John McCarthy, 67, 71, 74
John Neil, 17, 19
John Pizer, 23, 31, 32, 100, 106
John Richardson, 28, 29, 32, 33, 35, 36, 100, 107
John Spratling, 18, 21
John Thain, 17, 18
John Thomas Stride, 40
John West, 10
Jonas Mizen, 16, 97
Joseph Barnett, 73, 74, 77, 120, 124, 125, 132
Joseph Chandler, 11, 29, 32
Joseph Drage, 43
Joseph Fleming, 124, 125
Joseph Henry Helson, 22
Joseph Lave, 41
Joseph Lawende, 53, 63
Joseph Levy, 53, 63
Karen Miller, 151
Kate Eddowes, 47, 52, 54
Kearley and Tongue, 48, 49, 50
Keylers, 75, 76
Kosminski, 139, 150, 151, 152
leather apron, 100, 106
Lee, 3, 90
Leman Street, 6, 31, 39, 43, 45, 51, 65, 86
Leon Goldstein, 45
Lewis Robinson, 62
Lizzie Albrook, 74, 120
Louis Diemschutz, 37, 42
Louis Robinson, 52
Louis Stanley, 41
M J Druitt, 139

84

Maguire, 3, 90
Major Henry Smith, 11, 82, 96, 112
Major Smith, 65
Mannis van Oven, 151
Maria Harvey, 74, 77, 120
Martha Tabram, 14, 24, 35
Mary Ann Cox, 75, 120, 137
Mary Ann Monk, 22
Mary Ann Nichols, 14, 19, 22, 24, 35
Mary Elizabeth Simonds, 33
Mary Jane Kelly, 14, 54, 67, 73
Mary Kelly, 6, 13, 67, 69, 71, 73, 74, 75, 76, 77, 78, 81, 92, 93, 114, 120, 121, 123, 124, 125, 130, 131, 132, 134, 137, 144, 148, 152, 153
Mary Malcolm, 42
Mary Monk, 19
Matthew Packer, 43, 44, 46, 109
Melville Leslie MacNaghten, 9, 14
MEPO 3, 146, 147, 148
Merritt, 3, 90
Michael Kidney, 40, 43, 109
Michael Ostrog, 139
Millers Court, 4, 14, 67, 68, 69, 71, 72, 73, 74, 75, 76, 78, 80
Miriam Angel, 45
Mitre Square, 4, 6, 11, 12, 14, 48, 49, 50, 51, 52, 53, 54, 57, 58, 59, 63, 64, 65, 80, 91, 96, 112, 114, 115, 116, 118, 147
Morris Eagle, 39, 41, 42
Moylan, 3, 90
Mr Brough, 129, 130
Mr Thompson, 27, 28, 32
Mr Walker, 27
Mr. Crawford, 56, 57, 64
Mr. McWilliams, 58
Mrs Copsey, 27
Mrs. Darrell, 35
Mrs. Mortimer, 45
Netley, 143
Otto Penzler, 152
Patrick Enright, 21
Patrick Mulshaw, 23, 25
Payne, 3, 90
PC Harvey, 54, 115
PC Holland, 50
PC Lamb, 42
PC Long, 114, 115, 117
PC Mizen, 17, 22
PC Pearce, 49
PC Thain, 18, 21, 24, 97

PC Watkins, 50, 53
Peter Sutcliffe, 89, 92, 152
Philip Kranz, 46
Philip Sugden, 91, 133, 134, 155
Polly Nichols, 97, 98, 99, 100, 146
Porter, 3, 90
Prince Albert Victor Christian Edward, 140
Professor Jeffreys, 151
Professor Walther Parson, 151
Recorder, 3, 90
Reno, 3, 90
Robert Donston Stephenson, 144
Robert Mann, 19, 21, 24
Robert Outram, 50
Robert Paul, 16, 22, 24
Roderick Macdonald, 13, 72, 73, 77
Royall, 3, 90
Russell Edwards', 148, 149
Samuel Frederick Langham, 54
Sarah Cox, 27
Sarah Harrison, 44
Sarah Lewis, 75, 76, 121, 123
Scotland Yard, 8, 9, 10, 13, 33, 44, 78
Sergeant Jones, 149
Sergeant Kerby, 17, 18, 20
Sergeant Thick, 32
Severin Antoniovich Klosowski, 141
Sidgwick & Jackson, 151
Simon Wood, 91, 132, 133, 134, 135, 136, 155
Sir Charles Warren, 3, 6, 8, 9, 12, 13, 44, 51, 71, 78, 80
Sir James Fraser, 11
Sir Robert Anderson, 8, 9, 92, 93, 129
Sir William Gull, 140, 142
Spitalfields, 5, 6, 26, 28, 30, 31, 32, 34, 35, 51, 54, 58, 62
St. James's Place, 48, 50
Stephen Adams, 152
Stephen White, 44
Steve Connor, 150
Sussex Regiment, 30, 34
Ted Stanley, 34, 106
Thomas Arnold, 10, 51, 71
Thomas Bond, 13, 72, 74
Thomas Bowyer, 67, 74
Thomas Conway, 52, 62
Thomas Coram, 43
Thomas Neill Cream, 140
Thomas Oppenshaw, 96
Thomas Richardson, 32
Thomas Stowell, 140

Thrawl Street, 97, 107, 111, 119, 121, 125
Timothy Donovan, 30, 31
Varnum, 3, 90
Wallace, 3, 90
Walter Beck, 11, 71
Walter Dew, 71
Walter Purkiss, 17, 20, 23
Walter Sickert, 143
Walter Simon Andrews, 10
Whitechapel, 1, 3, 5, 6, 9, 10, 12, 18, 19, 20, 22, 23, 24, 25, 30, 31, 33, 35, 43, 44, 50, 52, 56, 64, 66, 67, 75, 87

Whitechapel Vigilante Committee, 95
William Le Queux, 144
William Marshall, 46, 110
William Nichols, 19, 22
William Sedgwick Saunders, 54, 96
William Smith, 46
William Stevens, 34
William West, 41
Williams and Co, 50
Wynne Edwin Baxter, 12, 31
Yorkshire Ripper, 89, 92

Leman Street Police Station

Autumn 1888 – London's east end – Whitechapel – and a spate of ghastly murders go unsolved by police. The killings, by a person or person's unknown, give birth to the world's first serial killer – Jack the Ripper! In volume I the author goes through in detail the facts of each case, using photographs and street maps of the areas where they still exist today. In volume II the author explores the oddities about each case, and the thoughts of other ripperologists. In the end, however, you'll never find out just who Jack the Ripper was, nor will you ever know.

Stephen Bloom 2017

Ripperologist II

A new look at Whitechapel serial killer Jack the Ripper using modern day evidence, photographs and maps.

Stephen Bloom

CONTENTS

PREFACE	90
PHOTOGRAPHS OF THE PEOPLE INVOLVED	91
LIST OF ILLUSTRATIONS	92
7. PAPER AND INK	93
8. ABOUT POLLY NICHOLS	98
9. ABOUT ANNIE CHAPMAN	101
10. ABOUT ELIZABETH STRIDE	110
11. ABOUT CATHERINE EDDOWES	113
12. ABOUT MARY KELLY	121
13. NEMESIS OF FAILURE	128
14. DASTARDLY SUSPECTS	140
15. CONCLUSIONS	147
BIBLIOGRAPHY	155
REFERENCES	156
INDEX	157

PREFACE

No! We still don't know who Jack the Ripper was, although there are some pretty convincing theories out there. I think I first became interested in the case after watching that Barlow & Watts TV series on the case in 1973 (still available on YouTube). I remember riding my motorcycle up to London from my parent's house in West Sussex sometime in 1976/77 and using an old Polaroid camera to photograph the murder sites – the pictures I no longer have. A year later I joined the RAF and on my journey to my training base my car gave up near Wolverhampton and I abandoned it at a garage, along with many of my belongings that I could not carry – including my ripper notes and books. A few years later the police asked me to drop by to explain the books – it was then the height of the Yorkshire Ripper investigation: Peter Sutcliffe!

But I was too young when the first Yorkshire Ripper murders took place to be involved and the police discharged me with a smile; it was a pity they never returned to me the items taken from my broken down car by the garage attendants in Wolverhampton. Amongst them were my hand written notes from the Metropolitan police files that I had read at the public records office. So I have always held a deep interest in the original Jack the Ripper case; me, and dozens of other ripperologists and theorists. Anyone who is keen can become one. What you need to do though is something slightly different from everyone else, and hopefully I have done so with this book 'Ripperologist.' Okay, the photographs are few and far between and nobody has yet done a house clearance and come across a load of new pictures, diaries or police notes dated 1888. But modern technology, for example, enables us to accurately measure distances from one murder site to the next and calculate whether the murderer could have killed twice in one night in the time scale reported by police.

So 'Ripperologist' will examine closely the killings, the time sequencing as well as the men involved, both civilians, police and in the last instance, brief theories as to who may have been responsible for the murders and the failure to apprehend the person or persons guilty. Where possible, I have added maps of the various locations plus modern day aerial shots; also photographs or newspaper drawings where available of those who dealt with the crimes – for after all, it's nice to put a face to a name, isn't it?

Stephen Bloom, England 2017

PHOTOGRAPHS OF PEOPLE INVOLVED

All photos freely available on the world wide net, unless otherwise specified in the text.

LIST OF ILLUSTRATIONS

Facsimile of the 'Dear Boss' letter

The Central News Agency post card from Jack

The 'From Hell' letter

Polly Nichols grave marker

Unflattering impression showing facial bruising on Polly and body covered in sheet in coffin

Layout of no. 29

The passageway; rear yard door not quite visible right of stairs, door on right is entrance to the kitchen

The yard seen from houses; not from police files so likely computer enhanced

The rear yard shed; not from police files so likely computer enhanced

Another view of passage and steps; not from police files so likely computer enhanced

Close knit community – Nichols and Chapman lived just 270 yards apart

Berners Street (now Henriques Street) towards Commercial Road; Dutfield's Yard was near the second tree

108 – 119 Wentworth Buildings Goulston Street today and in Jack's time (below)

Note in police files from Sir Charles Warren

Purported photo of Sergeant James Byfield, City of London police, Bishopsgate, who was in charge when Eddowes was brought in for being drunk on the evening before she was murdered

Purported photo of PC George Hutt, who was jailer and looked after Eddowes until she was sober and released from Bishopsgate police station and met her death in Mitre Square

Map of the court and some of the occupants

Computer enhanced picture of Millers Court; note water pump on left and rag in broken lower window pane

Simon Wood's diagram

Philip Sugden's drawing

Feint chair outline above flesh on table

7. PAPER AND INK

You might remember the terrible Yorkshire Ripper killings of the 1970's/80's? Well, there was one man who decided, in his infinite wisdom, to send taunting letters and a tape recording to the police. His hoax may have cost several women their lives at the hands of the real ripper, because it was a further two years before Peter Sutcliffe was arrested. The police, led by George Oldfield, were led up the garden path and in the wrong direction, by hoaxer John Humble. Twenty-five years after this event, a tiny DNA match led Humble to eight years' imprisonment for perverting the course of justice. It was similar back in 1888, when Jack the Ripper terrorized the east end of London. Only, there was no DNA, no blood grouping, and no finger printing in those days. A few psychiatrists had started to develop offender profiling, but nobody was seriously asked by police to assist in the hunt.

Dr *Thomas Bond*   Sir *Robert Anderson*

Criminal profile

Dr Thomas Bond, who conducted the Mary Kelly post mortem, was the A Division police surgeon (Westminster), and an advocate of offender profiling. So much so that, on the 25th October, Sir Robert Anderson, head of C.I.D Scotland Yard, wrote him to examine material connected with the Jack the Ripper investigation. Anderson enclosed copies of evidence given at the inquests into the murders of Nichols, Chapman, Stride and Eddowes, and asked Bond to deliver his opinion. Bond's remarks showed a lot of coincidence between the murders and the *modus operandi* of the killer; something Anderson's detective department seemed unable to comprehend. Bond believed the five killings at that time (Mary Kelly had just been murdered and Bond conducted her post mortem), were all by the same hand – with all throats cut left to right (although it was not possible with Kelly to determine the initial cut, due to the savagery of the attack).

The women, Bond said, were all lying down and their throats were cut first. There was no indication of a struggle, so sudden had been the ripper's attack – in the case of Kelly, a bed sheet may have been used to smoother her face as the throat was cut, thus preventing the perpetrator from being covered with blood. The women were all attacked from their right side – except Kelly; because of the bed being in the way, she was likely attacked from the front or her left side. The murderer would not necessarily be covered in blood because of his position in relation to the victims, although his hands and arms could have blood about them.

The object of the attacks was mutilation, Bond surmised, except in the case of the Berner Street victim Elizabeth Stride – likely the attacker was disturbed by the arrival in the yard of the pony and cart. The killer did not possess any specific scientific or anatomical knowledge; nor that of a butcher or slaughterer. The murder weapon was a very sharp knife, six inches long, one-inch wide, with a pointed end. The killer must have been a man of great physical strength, great coolness and daring. There is no evidence of any accomplice. He must be a man subject to periodical attacks of homicidal and erotic mania. The character of the mutilations indicate that he may be in a condition sexually when murdering; that is, satyriasis.

It is possible that the homicidal impulse may have developed from a revengeful or brooding condition of the mind, or that religious mania may have been the original disease. The murderer, in external appearance, is quite likely to be a quiet, inoffensive looking man, probably middle aged and respectably dressed. He must be in the habit of wearing a cloak or overcoat. The killer would probably be solitary and eccentric; also, he is likely to be a man without regular occupation, but with some small income or pension. He is possibly living among respectable persons who have some knowledge of his character and who may have grounds for suspicion. Such persons would probably be unwilling to communicate their suspicions to the Police for fear of trouble or notoriety, whereas if there were a prospect of reward, it might overcome their scruples. Bond's response to Sir Robert Anderson was delivered on the 10th November, the day after Mary Kelly was murdered. There is no indication as to any response to the report from the head of the C.I.D, nor the detective department.

A few good letters

As the murders reached a peak, the police were receiving letters from the public at about 1000 a week! Most were filed away by police with comments scribbled across them such as 'ignore,' and 'the man must be a lunatic.' Some letters made suggestions as to who the murderer was, or where he might be found. Others included crude descriptions of how to capture the killer, or suggestions that policemen should dress as women and patrol the streets at night – clean shaven chins, of course! A careful checking of viable letters produces only three of any interest. The first is known as the 'Dear Boss' letter, sent to the City of London **Central News Agency** and received on the 27th September 1888. It reads as follows:

'Dear Boss,
I keep on hearing the police have caught me but they wont fix me just yet. I have laughed when they look so clever and talk about being on the right track. That joke about Leather Apron gave me real fits. I am down on whores and I shant quit ripping them till I do get buckled. Grand work the last job was. I gave the lady no time to squeal. How can they catch me now. I love my work and want to start again. You will soon hear of me with my funny little games. I saved some of the proper red stuff in a ginger beer bottle over the last job to write with but it went thick like glue and I cant use it. Red ink is fit enough I hope ha. ha. The next job I do I shall clip the ladys ears off and send to the police officers just for jolly wouldn't you. Keep this letter back till I do a bit more work, then give it out straight. My knife's so nice and sharp I want to get to work right away if I get a chance. Good Luck.
Yours truly
Jack the Ripper
Dont mind me giving the trade name
PS Wasnt good enough to post this before I got all the red ink off my hands curse it No luck yet. They say I'm a doctor now. ha ha'

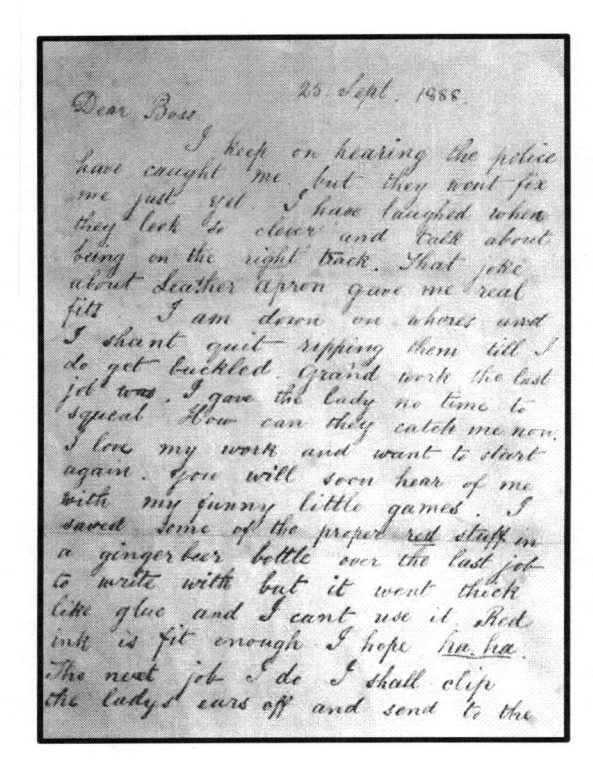

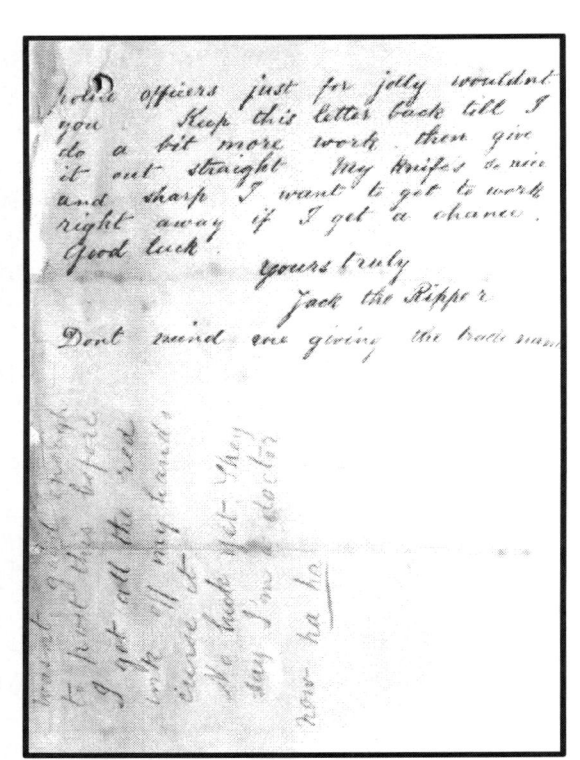

Facsimile of the 'Dear Boss' letter written in red ink (police files)

If this was from the real killer, there are some interesting points. Excusing his lack of grammar, punctuation and spelling, this was the first time the name 'Jack the Ripper' had been used – until then, he had been known simply as the Whitechapel murderer. Second, he says that his next victim will have her ears clipped off and sent to police. When the post mortem on Kate Eddowes was concluded, Dr. Brown noted that the 'lobe and auricle of the right ear was cut obliquely.'

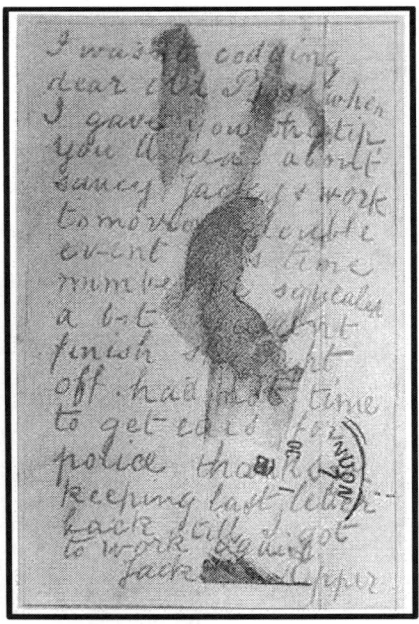

The Central News Agency post card from Jack (police files)

95

However, although cut, the ear was not sent to police. Perhaps Jack had no time to complete his mission before the distant plodding of an approaching copper interrupted his grisly work? Nevertheless, this is a possible ripper letter – there was time enough for a follow up letter, perhaps, apologising for the lack of ear in the post? Was there another letter posted to the CNA? On the 1st October, the day following the double murder, the **Central News Agency** in London received another note in the post, this time a post card, from Jack the Ripper. The hand writing is similar to that of the 'Dear Boss' letter, and it arrived the same day it was posted. It reads as follows:

'I was not codding (kidding?) *dear old Boss when I gave you the tip, you'll hear about Saucy Jacky's work tomorrow double event this time number one squealed a bit couldn't finish straight off. Had not got time to get ears off for police thanks for keeping last letter back till I got to work again.*
Jack the Ripper'

A double event is mentioned this time; likewise, 'Boss.' Number one victim (Elizabeth Stride), apparently squealed a bit, leaving no time to get ears off for police. However, the writer does not mention victim number two (Kate Eddowes), where an attempt was made to cut off her right ear. Is it possible that this card was written by someone with first-hand knowledge of the crime, such as a journalist or police officer? Most ripperologists believe the 'Dear Boss' letter and the 'Saucy Jacky's' post card to be written by one hand. But there seems to me to be one glaring error in the text. The use of the words 'Saucy Jacky's' rather than simply 'Saucy Jack's.' It is possible that the 'y' should really be a simple 's'? But it will prove difficult to judge whether it was a spelling mistake by the author – because the original card has gone missing from the file. Only a copy exists. The third and final letter worth looking at is the infamous 'From Hell' letter. It was enclosed inside a small box, addressed to George Lusk, who was the head of the **Whitechapel Vigilante Committee**. It arrived on the 16th October, and also inside the box was half a human kidney!

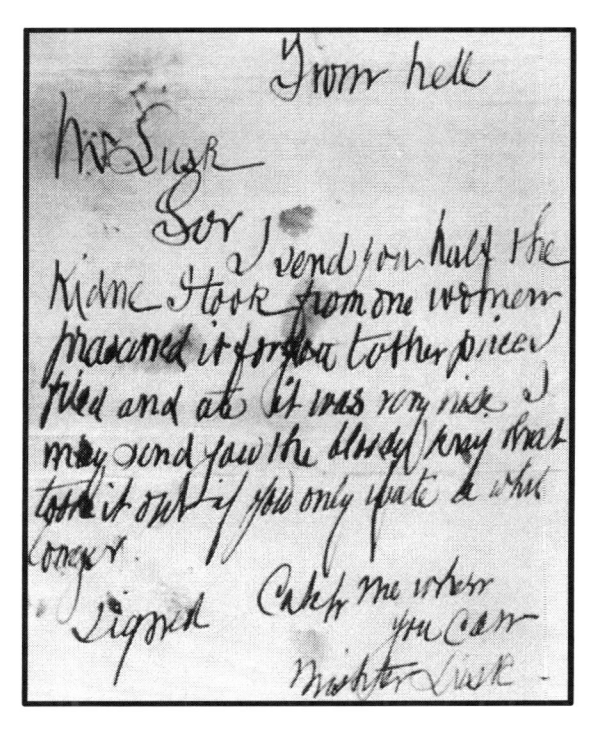

The 'From Hell' letter (police files)

It reads as follows:

'From hell
Mr Lusk,
Sor
I send you half the Kidne I took from one women prasarved it for you tother piece I fried and ate it was very nise. I may send you the bloody knif that took it out if you only wate a whil longer
signed
Catch me when you can Mishter Lusk'

This letter is littered with spelling mistakes – the main ones are the word 'Sor' instead of sir, 'Kidne' instead of kidney, 'Prasarved' instead of preserved, 'Nise' instead of nice, 'Wate' instead of wait, and 'Mishter' instead of mister. Also, it is not signed. The piece of kidney had been preserved in alcohol, and was that of a 45-year old female. It was examined by Dr Thomas Oppenshaw, who deduced that information.

Thomas Oppenshaw   George Lusk

Oppenshaw believed the kidney came from a woman who had a disease called Brights Disease, which is associated with heavy drinking. One of Kate Eddowes' kidneys had been taken by the murderer, and she was known as a heavy drinker. However, despite four doctors examining the body of Eddowes, nowhere in any evidence is there mention of her suffering Brights Disease. Most ripperologists believe this episode was a medical prank played by student doctors or the like, who had access to such gruesome body parts. Against this was Major Henry Smith, acting commissioner of the City of London police, who received the kidney (since it applied to his victim, Catherine Eddowes murdered in Mitre Square) and handed it to his police surgeon for analysis. Smith says, in his memoirs, that the human renal artery is 3" long – and that 2" had been left in Eddowes' corpse, with 1" still attached to the George Lusk kidney.

Dr William Sedgwick Saunders examined the contents of the stomach of Catherine Eddowes for poisons, but with negative results. He did not examine the Lusk kidney, but commented that there was no difference between the kidneys of men and women, nor for that matter most animals, too. It was to be assumed that, if the surviving kidney in Eddowes showed no sign of disease, then the other kidney would, in all likelihood, also be free of disease. We cannot confirm if what Major Smith says was the case regarding the renal artery. In all probability then, the George Lusk kidney was a hoax, as were most of the letters sent to the police. It did not help matters when the police released the 'Dear Boss' / 'Saucy Jacky' letter and post card to the press – all manner of crank would soon put pen to paper.

8. ABOUT POLLY NICHOLS' DEATH

The Whitechapel murders really began in earnest with the murder of 42-year old Polly Nichols in Bucks Road (now Durward Street). This took place right outside a house, where none of the occupants, although probably asleep or dozing at the time of the murder, heard a thing. The two men discovering the body thought the victim to be drunk; what they could not see was blood oozing from her neck wound. They both set off in search of a policeman, but also in the direction of their places of work. None thought to call for help in the Row. The beat bobby was actually coming up behind them, from the direction of Brady Street. It was further minutes before they came across the first police officer, who was Jonas Mizen. He set off immediately to Bucks Row – an approximate distance of 270 yards. When he arrived there, the beat officer (Neil) had already summoned help from PC Thain, who rushed off to summon medical assistance from Dr Llewellyn in Whitechapel Road; Mizen was sent for further assistance from Bethnal Green police station, which was nearly a mile away.

The doctor wanted to get back to his bed, for he pronounced life extinct and told the police to take the body to the Old Montague Street mortuary. Time of death: 3:30 a.m. During inventory of the dead woman's clothing, Inspector Spratling discovered further body mutilations, and ordered the doctor aroused from his slumbers once more. The victim was quickly identified and had been living at 18 Thrawl Street in a doss house. Polly was a family woman, although not living with her husband, like many of the victims. She had four children. According to police the victim's hat lay by her side when she was discovered; also there was very little blood on the cobblestones – no more than six inches' diameter; two wine glasses full or half a pint at most.

Speculation regarding this was that Polly had been murdered elsewhere and dumped where she was discovered – the blood had, in fact, been absorbed by her clothing. The post mortem revealed facial bruising – there was a bruise running along the lower part of the jaw on the right side of the face; that might have been caused by a blow from a fist or pressure from a thumb. There was a circular bruise on the left side of the face, which also might have been inflicted by the pressure of the fingers. Seemingly the murderer grabbed her face, from front or more likely rear, whilst cutting her throat. Prostitute sex in those days was nearly always conducted standing up, with the man face on or from behind. From that last position, it would be easy for the assailant to smother the face with a hand whilst welding the knife; thus keeping any blood lost on his body at a minimum. Alternatively, the victim may have laid down on her back.

Regarding the neck wound, on the left side of the neck, about 1" below the jaw, there was an incision 4" in length, and ran from a point immediately below the ear. On the same side, but an inch below and commencing about 1" in front of it, was a circular incision, which terminated at a point about 3" below the right jaw. That incision completely severed all the tissues down to the vertebrae. The large vessels of the neck on both sides were severed. The incision was about 8" in length. Jack, it seemed, required two attempts to cut the throat of his first victim. There were other, bodily wounds. Two or three inches from the left side was a wound running in a jagged manner. The wound was a very deep one and the tissues were cut through. There were several incisions running across the abdomen. There were also three or four similar cuts, running downwards, on the right side. Interestingly, no attempt was made at this early stage of his career for the killer to remove any body organs. The medical evidence suggested a four or five-minute time scale to complete these mutilations, but considering the number of cuts, I would think a much smaller time limit – perhaps just two minutes.

Polly Nichols grave marker (unknown)

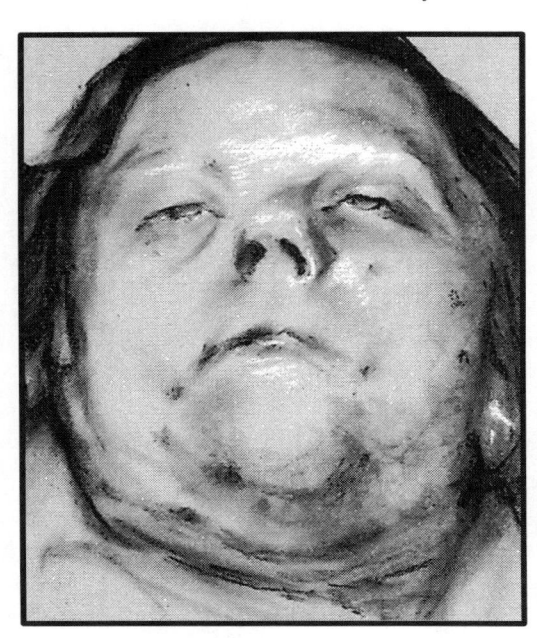

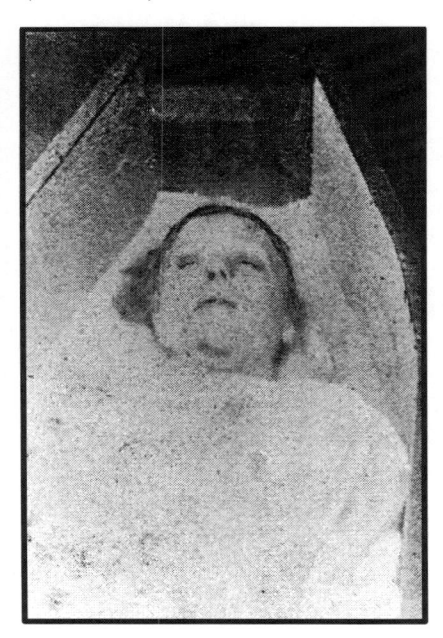

Unflattering impression (left) showing facial bruising on Polly and body covered in sheet in coffin (unknown and police files)

How was it done? The lack of blood to the chest area of the victim suggests she was actually lying down on her back at the time her throat was cut. The murderer squatted by her right side, slashing the throat from left to right – indicting a left handed killer. This method made sure any spurting blood went away from him. As for the body wounds, the medical evidence suggests cuts downwards and towards the knife welding maniac – or, a right handed killer! Either Jack was ambidextrous or more likely, changed position during his attack on Polly. Despite the attempt at disembowelment, nothing was taken from the body. The victim had a 'jolly new bonnet' about her, which was found next to her body. Some ripperologists suggest she had two hats, which was likely since women like Polly carried all their world goods about them. There was no evidence of sexual intercourse prior to death, and although Polly's movements were well documented up until when she began her death walk to Bucks Row, she was not seen with any suspicious men prior to death. Not so other victims of Jack the Ripper.

9. ABOUT ANNIE CHAPMANS' DEATH

There was not too much to conclude about the murder of Polly Nichols on 31st August 1888. A plain looking woman of forty-two, with front teeth missing and an old scar on her forehead, she drank a lot and on her final night on earth had drunk her doss house money several times over. This indicates she might well have been sexually active with several men that evening. With the remaining ripper victims, however, we will try and find any similar traits common to all victims, including wounds, possible suspects, and so on. Annie Chapman was victim number two of Jack the Ripper. She was found disemboweled in the rear yard of 29 Hanbury Street. What a risk her killer took in entering that yard with Annie, for there were at least seventeen people asleep in that house. There seems a lot of discrepancy as to the time this victim was killed – there was much movement within the house that night, beginning with a carman leaving early for work at 3:30.

The passageway to the rear yard was checked clear of persons when John Richardson called by at 4:45 to assist his mother's business. Richardson found one of his boots hurting, so says he opened the back door and sat on the top step to cut away an irritating bit of leather. Now bearing in mind the time of day, how is it possible that Richardson was able to see what he was doing, without additional light from a candle or gas lamp? Without additional light there was the danger of him cutting his fingers in the darkness. Since his report was not made to police until much later, I find it difficult to imagine that Richardson did as he said. John Davis was the man who discovered the body in the rear yard. It was six o'clock when he descended the stairs and headed for the back yard, noticing on his way that the front door had been left open. He then discovered Annie's body in the yard.

George Bagster Phillips, police surgeon, gave the time of death as 4:30 in the morning! This would mean the body was there when Richardson stood there to cut a piece of leather from his boot, although Richardson said he saw nothing – if it was so dark, how could he see to cut his leather boot? Close to Annie's feet had been laid a small piece of coarse muslin, a small toothed comb as worn in the hair, and a pocket comb in a paper case. Near where her head had been lay a small portion of an envelope containing two pills, which wasted a hell of a lot of police time. The type of pills was never explained, but were likely the 1888 equivalent of aspirin or similar. Inspector Chandler, at the scene, did not, according to his report, discover any rings or coins next to the victim, although it was possible she wore brass rings (because gold was so expensive) which had been wrenched off her fingers and taken away by the killer.

The victim lived at the Crossingham's lodging house at nearby 35 Dorset Street. This she had in common with Polly Nichols. She had been married with three children, and was fond of the old drink. However, she had not been well of late and visited a hospital for treatment for her ails. During a search of the rear yard, a leather apron was found next to the water tap – hence the connection with John Pizer, aka Leather Apron. He was released by police on the 11th, when no evidence was found against him. The apron belonged to John Richardson, he of the leather boot trimming fame who, when questioned that day by Inspector Chandler, did not even mention his boot incident! From the medical evidence, 'the uterus and its appendages, with the upper portion of the vagina and the posterior two-thirds of the bladder had been entirely removed.' One must deduce that 'removed' meant taken away by the murderer, as opposed to thrown about the ground. This was Jack's first successful attempt at disembowelment and taking away of body organs.

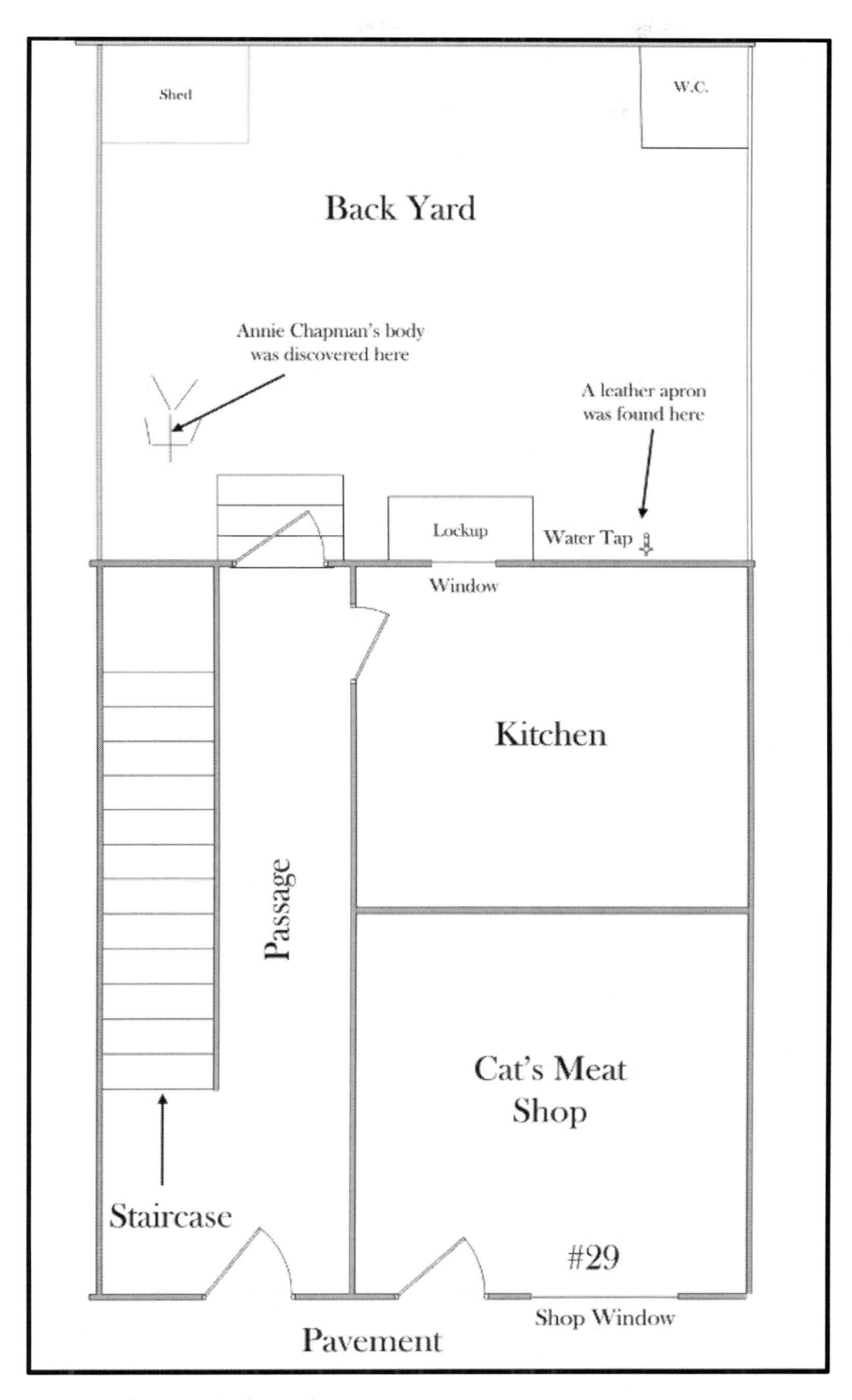

Layout of no. 29 (unknown)

The passageway, rear yard door not quite visible right of stairs, door on right is entrance to the kitchen (unknown)

The yard seen from houses behind; not from police files so likely computer enhanced (unknown).

The rear yard shed; not from police files so likely computer enhanced (unknown).

Another view of passage and steps, not from police files so likely computer enhanced (unknown).

The doctor suggested that the killer was a medical expert, or at least one who 'had such knowledge of anatomical or pathological examinations as to be enabled to secure the pelvic organs with one sweep of a knife.' It seems to me that Jack had a rough idea of where the body organs were located, similar in fact to that you and I might have from having studied biology at school. On 14th September, Ted Stanley, also known as 'the Pensioner,' called at Commercial Street Police Station. He had been mentioned at the inquest as a close friend of the dead woman, but up to this point the police had been unable to trace him. It was Ted with whom Annie had fisticuffs over, with another woman, regarding some soap.

Stanley gave a satisfactory account of his movements and said he had last seen Annie on the corner of Brushfield Street on 2nd September, at which time she was wearing two brass rings on one of her fingers. Since the police had not found them, we must assume that Jack had added them to his ghoulish trophy collection. Of the two murders so far, this one was a first for another reason; a witness had seen the victim with a man who may well have been her killer just before discovery of her body. This was Elizabeth Darrell, also referred to as Durrell or Elizabeth Long. She lived at 32 Church Street, but on the morning of 8th September, at 5:30, she was walking along Hanbury Street on the same side as no. 29 on her way to Spitalfields Market.

Close to the shutters of that house she saw a man and a woman talking. The man had his back towards Brick Lane and the woman was facing Mrs Darrell. She had seen the dead woman since and was sure that the woman she saw was the same person – Annie Chapman. As she passed, Mrs Darrell heard the man say 'will you?' and the woman replied 'Yes.' Although she never saw the man's face, Darrell was able to give a partial description. He was dark, wore a brown deerstalker hat and looked to be over forty. He had a shabby, genteel appearance, was a little taller than Annie and appeared to be a foreigner. Annie Chapman had been five feet tall, putting her companion at a short 5 feet 2". There is no facial description.

The second useful witness from the day of the killing was Albert Cadoche, who lived next door to the murder site at no. 27 Hanbury Street. On the morning that Annie's body was found, Albert got up at 5:15 and soon afterwards went out into his yard. The water closet was at the rear of most houses in the street, so it was natural to enter the yard first to use the toilet. As he returned to his house, Cadoche heard a voice say 'no' from behind the wooden fence dividing the two houses, although he was not absolutely certain it came from that yard. Three or four minutes later, he was again in his yard and heard a sound as if something was falling against the dividing fence. He did not attempt, however, to look over to see what was going on. Since he heard no further noises, he soon left his house to go to work.

This sound was likely Jack laying Annie Chapman on the ground and commencing his butchery. Cadoche passed Spitalfields Church at about 5:32, so the murder must have taken place a few minutes earlier, at about 5:25. The distance from no. 27 to the church is 200 yards. Mr Cadoche does not describe whether the voice he heard was male or female. Allowing for errors in the timings given, if these two new witnesses were telling the truth then this information pins down the time of the attack on Annie Chapman to between 5:25 and 5:30 in the morning. This time frame, if correct, was contrary to the estimation of Dr Bagster Phillips by one whole hour!

According to the coroner, the killer seized Annie by the chin, pressing her throat and thus preventing the slightest cry – partial strangulation; he produced insensibility and suffocation. Regarding Annie's clothes not being torn during the attack, the pocket of her underskirt had been cut open at the front and side. No doubt the killer took the contents thereof and laid them on the ground, or kept them as souvenirs. There are only three suspects as a result of police inquiries: John Pizer (leather apron – eliminated), the man seen with Annie by the witness Mrs Darrell (not enough descriptive information), and one other – John Richardson, he of the boot mending who didn't see a body in the yard but had a knife on him, and did not disclose all this to the police when first questioned.

Detectives did hold views that Richardson was a prime suspect, although his clothes were examined and he had alibis for his whereabouts. There was no evidence that he was involved in anyway. Because the police simply accepted the time of death given by Dr Phillips, they ignored and eliminated the statements given by Darrell and Cadosch. The most likely reason for the doctor's inaccuracy was the chilly September morning, and the vast blood loss the victim suffered.

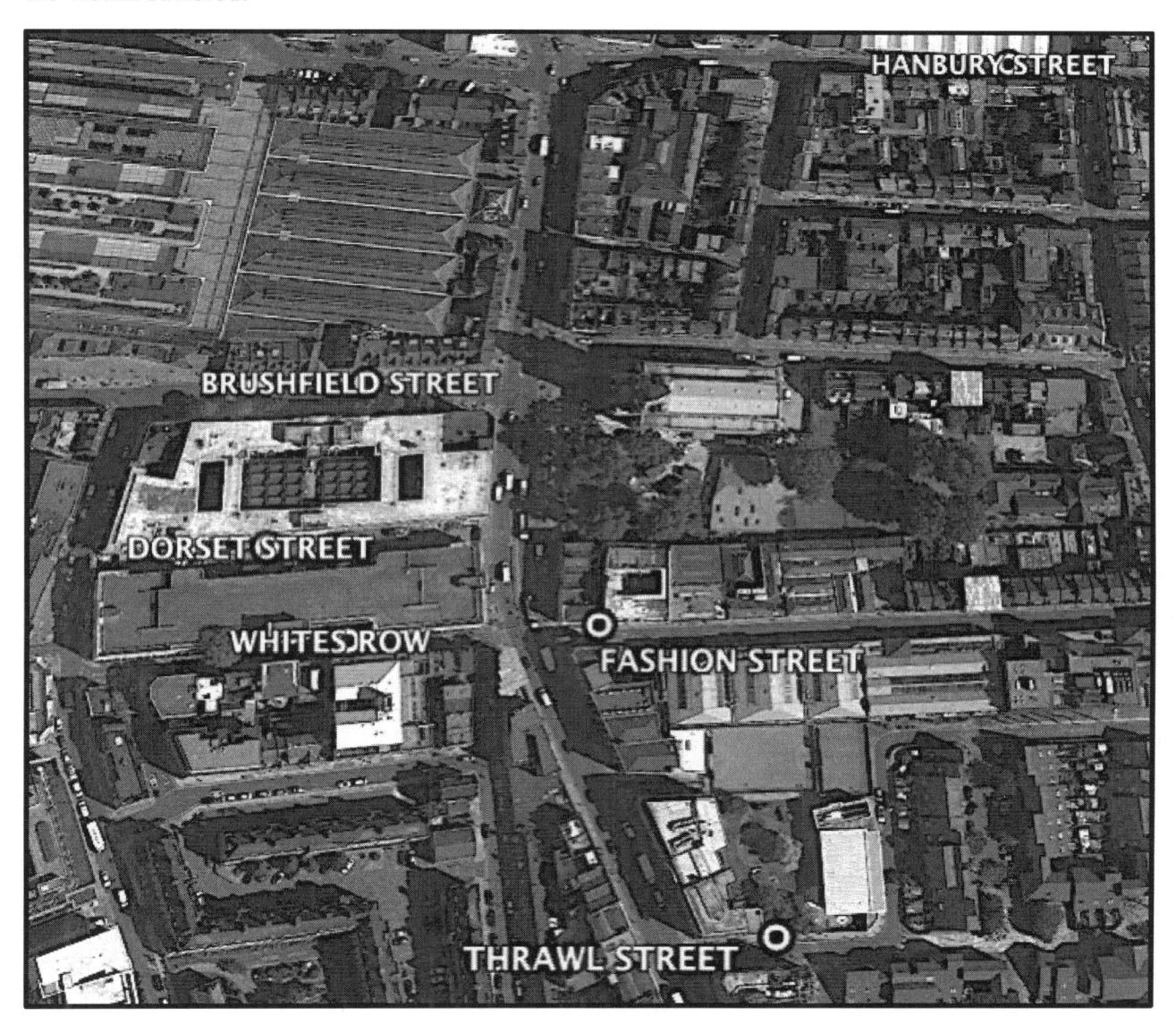

Close knit community – Nichols and Chapman lived just 270 yards apart

Comparison between Nichols/Chapman

This would be a good time to see if there are any similarities between the first two ripper murders. There isn't much information to play with. **Ages**: Nichols 42 – Chapman 47. **Occupations**: prostitutes. **Housing**: Nichols 18 Thrawl Street – Chapman 35 Dorset Street. **Injuries**: Nichols throat cut with two cuts, jagged cut to belly but no disembowelment, no body parts missing. Her hat was left on ground by killer – Chapman throat cut once but very deep, almost beheading. Body disembowelled. Body parts taken away by killer, including two brass rings wrenched from finger. **Witnesses**: Nichols – up to two hours before death was documented. No suspects seen with her after that time. Chapman – up to three hours before death was documented. One suspect was seen with her – described as dark, wore a brown deerstalker hat and looked to be over forty with a shabby genteel appearance, a little taller than Annie and appeared to be foreign. Just one curious last question I must ask regarding Annie Chapman's murder. How did the killer see what he was doing in the dark? If Cadosch was correct, he heard sounds but saw no indication of a light beyond the fence. How did Jack operate in pitch darkness?

10. ABOUT ELIZABETH STRIDES' DEATH

Elizabeth Stride is not always counted as a genuine ripper killer by some ripperologists; others do count her, but do so as an 'interrupted' killing which drove the murderer into a rage to the City of London, where he came across the unfortunate Catherine Eddowes. Jack had originally struck twice in eight days, but now there was a large gap of twenty-two days before he surfaced again. This was in the early hours of Sunday 30th September. The Met police always considered Stride's murder as a ripper killing, and as such sent their top men to Berner Street to investigate; the Leman Street police HQ was only 600 yards or so away. It had been a breezy and drizzly night when Louis Diemschutz turned his pony and cart into the gates of the International Working Men's Educational Club in Berner Street – there was a space between the open gates and the yard at the sides and back of the club of about twenty-yards in complete darkness. It was about one a.m. when Diemschutz's pony shied to the left in this dark space. Had anybody been hiding next to the gates, Diemschutz would not have seen them; nor did he see the body lying on the ground next to the club wall. This was, of course, Elizabeth Stride.

At first members of the club thought she was drunk, and moved the body a little; reports suggest both her hands were tucked beneath her body. On closer inspection they saw that she was murdered, with a cut throat and blood on her right hand; the left hand gripped a bag of cachous sweets, some of which had spilt on the cobbles. Her checked silk scarf around her neck had the bow turned around to the left and pulled very tight. The line of the cut to the throat followed closely the line of the scarf. There was just one wound, and no attempt at disembowelment. Two doctors attended Stride at Berner Street: Dr Blackwell, who gave his estimate to the time of death as 12:46 to 12:56, and Dr Bagster Phillips, the police surgeon who arrived half an hour after Blackwell, who gave an estimate to the time of death as 12:44 to 12:54. Two minutes' difference may not seem a lot in the scheme of things, until various witnesses were interviewed later by police.

Bagster Phillips examined the hands and clothing for blood of everyone in Dutfield's Yard; later, the residents of the cottages facing the club had to endure a police search of their homes. This was concluded at about five o'clock in the morning, when news had already circulated of a second body found in the City of London. Stride was forty-five years old, 5'2" tall with two front teeth missing, and separated from her husband, who had since died. She then lived with another man, Michael Kidney, like other victims of Jack. Divorce in those days was rare for the poor. The couple resided at a common lodging house at 32 Flower and Dean Street. There was much talk about Stride having consumed grapes prior to death, or held a grape stalk in her hand.

This came about because of greengrocer Matthew Packer of 44 Berner Street; he who told police he had closed his shop at 12:30 that night and had seen nothing and knew nothing about any murder until the next day. Three other people at no. 44 also heard and saw nothing. Yet Matthew Packer, however, changed his story, after two private detectives named Grand and Batchelor of the Whitechapel Vigilance Committee, spoke to him. Packer now suddenly swore that at 11:45 in the evening of 29th September he had sold half a pound of black grapes to a man and a woman who were standing outside his shop. He was not, however, considered trustworthy enough to be called to Stride's inquest, for he was changing his story to fit the circumstances as they unfolded in the newspapers.

Packer gave a description of the grape buyer: middle-aged (but then he qualified the estimate later to age twenty-five to thirty), about 5'7" tall, stout, squarely built and wearing a 'wide-awake' hat and dark clothing. Packer's big mistakes, however, showed him to be a liar was when he got the colour of the flower pinned to Stride's jacket wrong, saying it was white when in fact it was red – also, he gave no description of the woman who was with the grape buyer, which might or might not have been Stride. Israel Schwartz of 22 Ellen Street made a statement to police as early as 30th September indicating that he might have seen the murderer attack Stride and that the killer might have had an accomplice; Schwartz was never called as a witness. Schwartz's police statement said he turned into Berner Street from Commercial Road at 12:45 in the morning of 30th September. As he drew closer to the entrance to Dutfield's Yard he saw a man stop and speak to a woman who was standing in the gateway.

Berner Street (now Henriques Street) towards Commercial Road; Dutfield's Yard was near the second tree (courtesy Google earth).

Schwartz could not hear what was said but the man tried to pull the woman out into the street, turned her around and threw her down to the pavement. If this was Jack, why would he pull the woman into the street, rather than into the darkness of Dutfield Yard? Also, why do this when people like Schwartz were still about? No wonder the police were not really interested in this story. One man who was called to the coroner's inquiry was William Marshall of 64 Berner Street, and he too had viewed the body in the mortuary. He was sure it was a woman he had seen at 11:45 in the evening of 29th September. He had gone to his front door at 11:30 and noticed a man and a woman on the pavement between his house and the club but on the other side of the road. The couple were kissing and he heard the man say 'you would say anything but your prayers.' After that, the couple walked up the street towards Dutfield's Yard. Marshall described the man as middle aged, about 5'6" tall, rather stout and looking like a clerk. He wore a small black coat, dark trousers and a round cap with a small peak.

Another witness was James Brown of 35 Fairclough Street. At 12:45 in the morning he left home to go to a chandler's shop for his supper. The shop was at the corner of Berner Street and Fairclough Street, and as he was crossing the road he saw a man and a woman standing together by the wall at the school opposite Dutfield's Yard. Brown was sure that the woman was Elizabeth Stride. He heard her say to the man 'no, not tonight, some other night.' The man was described as stout and about 5'7" tall, wearing a long coat. Police Constable William Smith was the Berner Street beat officer. On his 12:30 visit to the street, Smith had seen a man and a woman standing across from Dutfield's Yard. The woman had a flower on her jacket, which indicated that she was Elizabeth Stride. The man held a newspaper parcel in his hand about eighteen inches long and six or eight inches broad. He was 5'7" tall and wore a hard felt deerstalker hat and dark clothes; he was about twenty-eight years old and had no whiskers.

There are several eye witness reports here, describing Stride standing with a man. We can check details now against those of Nichols and Chapman: **Ages**: Nichols 42 – Chapman 47 – Stride 45. **Occupations**: All prostitutes. **Housing**: Nichols 18 Thrawl Street – Chapman 35 Dorset Street – Stride 32 Flower and Dean Street. (Within about 200 yards of each other.) **Injuries**: Nichols throat cut with two cuts, jagged cut to belly but no disembowelment, no body parts missing. Her hat was left on ground by killer – Chapman throat cut once but very deep, almost beheading. Body disembowelled. Body parts taken away by killer, including two brass rings wrenched from finger – Stride throat cut once, neck scarf pulled very tight, blood on right hand, hat near head, packet of cachous held in left hand. **Witnesses**: **Nichols** – up to two hours before death was documented. No suspects seen with her. **Chapman** – up to three hours before death was documented. One suspect was seen with her – described as dark, wore a brown deerstalker hat and looked to be over forty with a shabby genteel appearance, a little taller than Annie and appeared to be foreign. **Stride** – documented until about seven p.m. on evening before her death, after which whereabouts unknown. There were three main descriptions by witnesses who thought they saw Stride with a man just prior to her murder.

From William Marshal: middle aged, about 5'6" tall, rather stout and looking like a clerk. He wore a small black coat, dark trousers and a round cap with a small peak. From James Brown: stout and about 5'7" tall, wearing a long coat. From PC William Smith: the man held a newspaper parcel in his hand. He was 5'7" tall and wore a hard felt deerstalker hat and dark clothes; he was about twenty-eight years old and had no whiskers. Police Constable William Smith was probably the only person to see Stride with her killer, recognizing her by the red flower pinned to her jacket. However, this was likely not Jack the Ripper, but a copycat murderer who was, like Jack, never caught by police.

11. ABOUT CATHERINE EDDOWES' DEATH

Elizabeth Stride was counted by police as the ripper's third victim since he first struck on 31st August 1888. Many ripperologists place Stride as an opportune or copycat killing, and the true third victim of Jack the ripper was Kate (or Catherine) Eddowes, on the same night that Stride was killed. The Eddowes murder was discovered only three-quarters of an hour after Stride was found in Dutfield's Yard. Was there time then for Jack, if he had killed Stride (but failed to disembowel her), to seek out a new victim in the City of London, and disembowel her instead? The distance is about two-thirds of a mile from Berner Street to Mitre Square. It would take a brisk twenty or twenty-five-minute walk to reach the city. Jack was now on very dangerous ground, for, like the Met, city police adopted a rigid series of beats for their patrolling police officers. On top of it, the head of the force, acting commissioner Major Henry Smith, had detectives in plain clothes out in the streets at night.

'I put nearly a third of the force into plain clothes, with instructions to do everything which, under ordinary circumstances, a constable should not do,' Sir Henry wrote in his memoirs in later years (*From Constable to Commissioner – 1910*). 'It was subversive of discipline; but I had them well supervised by senior officers. The weather was lovely, and I have little doubt they thoroughly enjoyed themselves, sitting on door-steps, smoking their pipes, hanging about public-houses, and gossiping with all and sundry.' Sir Henry spent an uncomfortable night at Cloak Lane police station when the alert was sounded. A few minutes later, Sir Henry, a large superintendent and three detectives hanging on the back took a hansom cab ride to Mitre Square. The murderer had taken tremendous risks in selecting Mitre Square – the approaches to Mitre Square are covered by three passages, by Mitre Street, Duke Street Passage, and St. James's Place Passage. In the south-western corner, to which there is no approach other than Mitre Street, lay the body of a woman.

'I was convinced then,' Sir Henry wrote, 'and am convinced now, that had my orders been carried out in the spirit – they may have been to the letter – the reign of terror would have ceased that night. The orders were to account for every man and woman seen together. It may be that the man and woman, having made an appointment, went separately and met in the square.' Today, Mitre Square still exists, along with the spot where Eddowes died, but the old Kearley and Tongue warehouses have gone; and so has St James's Place and possibly the Duke Street Passage (building works continues there at the moment). According to Sir Henry Smith: 'By this time a stretcher had arrived, and when we got the body to the mortuary, the first discovery we made was that about one-half of the apron was missing. It had been severed by a clean cut.'

This was Eddowes' infamous apron cut, discovered later in Goulston Street. Sir Henry continued: 'My men, thoroughly awake at last, were scouring the whole neighbourhood, and one of them, Halse by name, who had been with us in Mitre Square, thinking he had a better chance down Whitechapel way, ran at his best pace in that direction.' Goulston Street, Whitechapel, is a broad thoroughfare running parallel with the Commercial Road, just one-third of a mile from the Square. It still exists today, although the dwelling where the apron and graffiti was found have been converted into shops; the white lintels are still there, however. These buildings were model workmen's dwellings, erected by Peabody. Just inside the entrance to 108 – 119, was discovered the bloody apron segment belonging to Kate Eddowes, and the graffiti on the wall.

108 – 119 Wentworth Buildings Goulston Street today and in Jack's time (below) (unknown).

What occurred next only adds to the air of mystery about Jack. Detective Constable Daniel Halse, City of London police, went searching for Eddowes' murderer from Mitre Square. He made his way to Goulston Street but saw nothing, despite it being but half an hour or so after the event. According to Sir Henry Smith's memoirs: 'He (*Halse* – my italics)) saw a light, and, halting, found a constable of the Metropolitan force looking at the missing piece of apron. It was folded up, and immediately above, on the wall, written in chalk, were the words, 'The Jews (*sic*) are the men that won't be blamed for nothing.' It was thus proved beyond doubt that the murderer, on that evening at any rate, made, in the first instance, for Whitechapel.'

Sir Henry here spells the word 'Jews' wrong; all other witnesses to the event suggest it was spelt 'Juwes.' Detective Halse must have gone from one end of the street towards Dorset Street, which stood near the end of Goulston Street, before turning back and seeing the torch light of the Met police officer, Alfred Long, outside 108 – 119 Wentworth Buildings. The constable would not have known the significance of the bloody apron he had just found discarded there, since he did not know of the city murder. It is also quite likely that Long may not have been aware of Stride's murder at Berner Street, too. Halse acquainted Long of the killing in the city. He would not have known, however, that part of the dead woman's apron had been cut off and taken away by the killer. What caught their attention next was the chalk writing on the wall just inside the doorway to the flats. As more police arrived at the scene, PC Long carried the bloody apron piece to Commercial Street police station.

Daniel Halse sent a fellow detective, Baxter Hunt, to inform their inspector (McWilliam) at Mitre Square of the finds – the inspector told them the writing should be photographed, and that the two detectives should search the buildings, which they did. As usual, they found nothing. At last, a serious clue had been found, and a police photographer was called. But according to Sir Henry Smith, 'Sir Charles Warren was instantly apprised of this discovery, and, coming down himself, ordered the words to be wiped out, alleging as his reason for so doing that he feared a rising against the Jews. This was, I thought, a fatal mistake, as Superintendent McWilliam (*sic*) plainly told Sir Charles when he called about seven o'clock, accompanied by Superintendent Arnold. It is just possible the words, if photographed, might have afforded an important clue.'

Some detectives present suggested that the writing be simply covered up until a photograph could be taken at first light; other suggestions included erasing just the word 'Juwes.' But the senor Met police there would not have it – despite the fact that the writing was placed in such a position that it could not be seen by the general public, who were just getting up to go about their daily routines. Despite Daniel Halse's protestations, the writing was erased, some same by Sir Charles himself, at about 5:30 that morning. According to Sir Henry, 'The assassin had evidently wiped his hands with the piece of apron. In Dorset Street, with extraordinary audacity, he washed them at a sink up a close, not more than six yards from the street. I arrived there in time to see the bloodstained water.' Mary Kelly, the ripper's final victim, also lived in Dorset Street.

Meanwhile, that important piece of apron was handed over to Dr Brown, the city police surgeon, who took it to the Golden Lane mortuary to compare it with the clothing of the dead woman. The match was exact, even down to a seam that corresponded in both pieces. Without blood grouping, finger prints and DNA, the police were severely hindered in their search for Jack. However, don't let some modern ripperologists fool you into believing that Eddowes' apron still exists today, and that DNA can be extracted from it! (More later.) Back to Sir Henry. 'At the exit leading direct to Goulston Street, opposite the corner where the murder was committed, there was a club, the members of which were nearly all foreigners. One, a sort of hybrid German, was leaving the club – he was unable to fix the hour-when he noticed a man and woman standing close together. The woman had her hand resting on the man's chest. It was bright moonlight, almost as light as day, and he saw them distinctly. This was, without doubt, the murderer and his victim.'

A description was given as follows: 'young, about the middle height, with a small fair moustache, dressed in something like navy serge, and with a deerstalker's cap – that is, a cap with a peak both fore and aft.' This German witness also said he had only a short glimpse of the man. If this was Eddowes, it could not have been the night of her murder but some earlier time. The reason? As Sir Henry commented, 'it was bright moonlight, almost as light as day, and he saw them distinctly.' However, we know that it was breezy and drizzly on the night Stride and Eddowes died, and so hardly likely to be bright moonlight, almost as light as day – clouds must have covered London in the small hours. Do not forget that Sir Henry Smith, acting commissioner of the City of London police, put pen to paper *twenty-two* years after the murders!

There were others who thought they saw Eddowes with her killer: Joseph Lawende, Joseph Levy and Harry Harris. They had frequented the small hours of the 30th September at the Imperial Club, 16-17 Duke's Street (renamed Duke's Place in 1939). They waited for a rain shower to pass before leaving. Two of the men could not give any description of a man and a woman seen together at the corner of Church Passage. Lawende, however, did take a look at them, and noticed that the woman, who had her back to him, was wearing a black jacket and bonnet and was quite small. She was resting one hand on the man's chest and their conversation was hushed. Her companion was facing Lawende so his description was detailed. He was about thirty years old, 5'7" or 5'8" tall and of medium build, with a fair complexion and moustache. He wore a pepper-and-salt loose jacket, a grey cloth cap with a peak and a reddish neckerchief tied in a knot. Lawende thought he looked like a sailor.

Lawende had not seen the woman's face clearly, however, but was later shown Eddowes's clothing and believed them to be the same. If true, then we know that Eddowes was alive with a man at the top of Church Passage at 1:35 that morning, twenty-five minutes after she first arrived near Mitre Square and just nine minutes before her body was found by PC Watkins. The other witness that night was PC Harvey, who reckoned he walked down Church Passage at 1:41 or 1:42 and looked into the square, seeing nothing. Harvey's timings are approximate, as most timings are. He most likely guessed the time, and looked into Mitre Square when he was passing the post office clock, which was then reading about 1:28 or 1:29.

If Harvey's timing was accurate, then when he looked into Mitre Square, Eddowes's body must surely have been lying in that darkened far corner, straight in front of the officer? Jack might have still been there, panting from his exertions and hiding in the shadows, perhaps behind those gates in ripper corner? Alternatively, Eddowes' body was already lying in the dark and her killer had made good his escape. PC Harvey simply did not notice them in the dark, or more likely cut out that part of his beat covering Church Passage. The distance from the square to Goulston Street and the Wentworth Buildings was about 550 yards; Jack could not have gone there immediately because of the time line and discovery of Eddowes' cut apron – that, or both PC Long (who found the apron) and Detective Daniel Halse (who saw Long find it, along with the writing on the wall), had their timings wrong. The times are between 2:20 that morning, when Alfred Long inspected Wentworth Buildings but saw nothing, and 2:55, when he found the bloody apron. Whereabouts was Jack, having killed Eddowes, until he dropped the apron in the Goulston Street buildings sometime after 2:20 that morning?

What was the apron used for? Many ripperologists believe Jack wiped his hands, and probably his knife upon it. His hands must have been in a terrible state, covered in wet blood and smelly faecal matter. But would Jack be wiping his hands and knife all the way from Mitre Square to Goulston Street, a particularly noticeable and dangerous thing to do? The distance between Mitre Square and the Goulston Street buildings is about 550 yards, or a third of a mile. No, the killer could only have used the apron cut from Eddowes' body to carry the bodily organs obtained – her uterus and kidney. Was the writing on the wall a genuine ripper artefact? Many ripperologists believe such graffiti would not be on the wall for very long, especially in a Jewish quarter of Spitalfields, and would be erased quickly. This is likely true; however, the writing was there at 2:55 a.m. and the police believed it to be a message from the person who also dropped Eddowes' bloodstained apron at the entrance to the stairs. Sir Charles Warren certainly thought it important enough to have the writing erased before a photograph could be made at first light. So confident was he that, at about seven o'clock that morning, both he and Superintendent Arnold arrived at City of London police HQ to tell the acting head of the city force, Sir Henry Smith, what they had done and why.

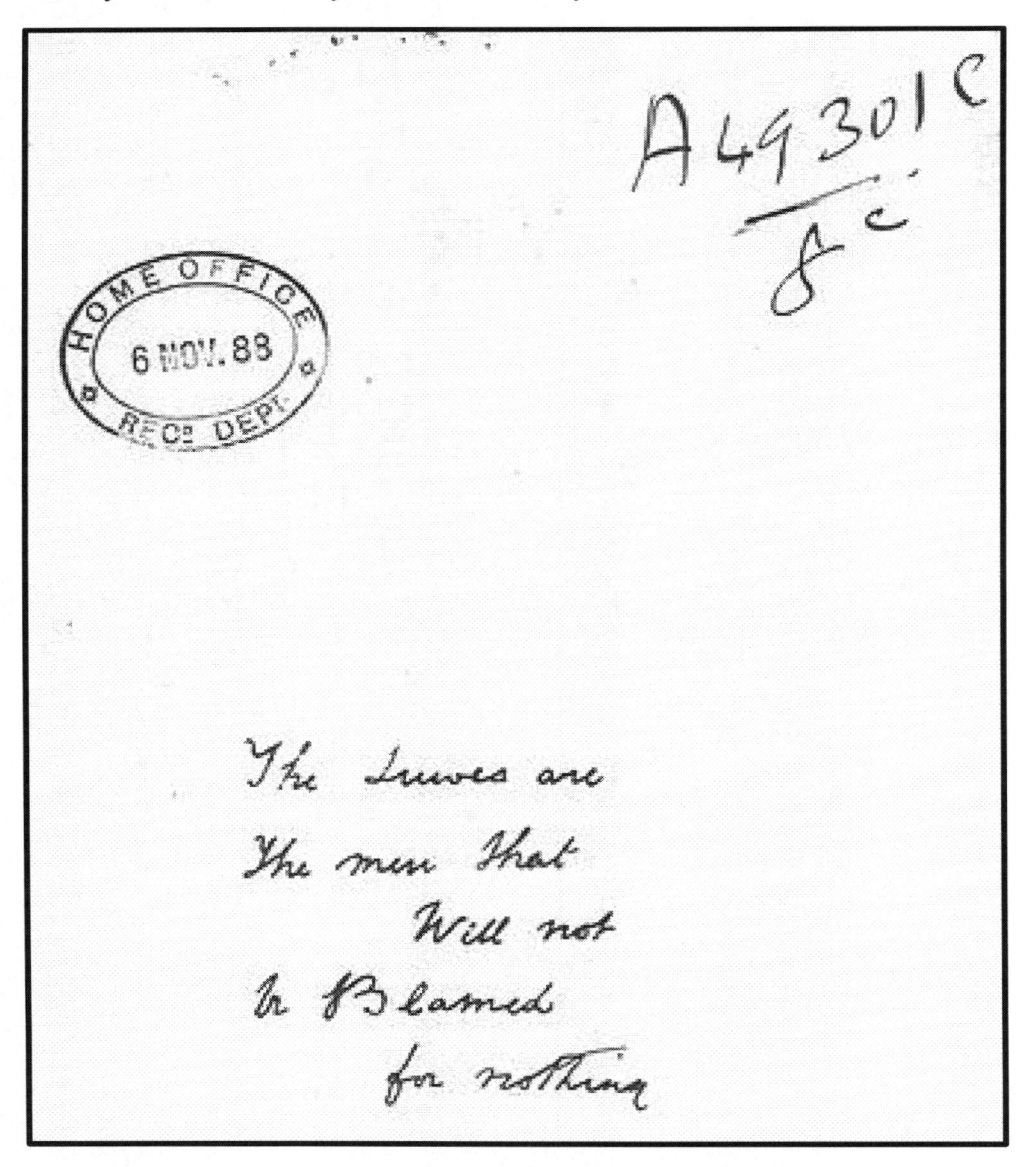

Note in police files from Sir Charles Warren (police files)

Everyone from the city police force thought it a bad error on behalf of Sir Charles, who was of the opinion that rioting against Jews may have followed had the general public seen the writing. As it was there was no rioting. In a confidential memorandum to Henry Mathews, Home Secretary, from Sir Charles Warren, we find specific mention of the location of the writing on the wall: 'Subject: 'The writing on the wall.' I accordingly went down to Goulston Street at once before going to the scene of the murder; it was just getting light, the public would be in the streets in a few minutes, in a neighbourhood very much crowded on Sunday mornings by Jewish vendors and Christian purchasers from all parts of London. There were several police around the spot when I arrived, both Metropolitan and City. The writing was on the jamb of the open archway or doorway, visible to anybody in the street and could not be covered up without danger of the covering being torn off at once.'

The words, once copied down by several police officers, were erased, and here further problems arose at the inquest as to what was written down. The spelling of the word 'Jews' has been open to question, and even at the inquest there were four different recorded versions of it. As mentioned, the actual wording was disputed, Detective Daniel Halse recorded it as 'The Jews are not the men that will be blamed for nothing.' PC Alfred Long's version was 'The Jews (Juews) are the men that will not be blamed for nothing.' There were other versions but these two are the ones mentioned during the inquest. PC Long said, 'I copied the words from the wall into my report – I could not say whether they were recently written – I wrote down into my book and the Inspector noticed that Jews was spelt Juews, there was a difference between the spelling.'

Purported photo of Sergeant James Byfield, City of London police, Bishopsgate, who was in charge when Eddowes was brought in for being drunk on the evening before she was murdered (unknown).

Purported photo of PC George Hutt, who was jailer and looked after Eddowes until she was sober and released from Bishopsgate police station to meet her death in Mitre Square (unknown).

Daniel Halse said he noted it down before it was erased, but here we also have Alfred Long stating not only that he recorded it before it was erased from the wall, but it was witnessed by his inspector. The inspector read his notes and apparently compared what was recorded with what was on the wall. Whose version do we feel was likely to be the more accurate? Detective Halse said: 'There were three lines of writing in a good schoolboy's round hand. The size of the capital letters would be about 3/4 of an inch, and the other letters were in proportion.' Halse also reported that 'when Detective Hunt returned, inquiry was made at every door of every tenement of the model dwelling-house, but we gained no tidings of anyone who was likely to have been the murderer.' The city police made a search of the buildings in Goulston Street, but the Met, in whose patch the buildings stood, did not. This was mentioned by the city solicitor (Mr Crawford) during the Eddowes inquest. 'As to the premises being searched, I have in court members of the City police who did make a diligent search in every part of the tenements, the moment the matter came to their knowledge.'

Because of Dr Brown's remarks at the inquest regarding Eddowes' remaining kidney (right kidney was pale, bloodless, with slight congestion of the base of the pyramids), the piece of kidney sent to George Lusk (purporting to have come from Eddowes) could not belong to her – that piece had, according to experts who examined it, Bright's disease, which would also be present in *both* kidneys in life. Eddowes' remaining kidney did not have that disease, as Dr Brown testified. We can only conclude that the kidney sent to George Lusk of the Whitechapel Vigilance committee was a hoax, and with it one of the letters sent to police. The 'From Hell' letter accompanying the Bright's Disease kidney piece is also a hoax, and can be eliminated. That leaves only two likely letters from the murderer – the 'Dear Boss' letter and the 'Saucy Jacky's' post card, both of which are of similar handwriting style; one predicts a killing and the other describes after the event. Neither of these, nor the writing on the wall, led police to the killer.

Ages: Nichols 42 – Chapman 47 – Stride 45 – Eddowes 46 **Occupations**: All prostitutes. **Housing**: Nichols 18 Thrawl Street – Chapman 35 Dorset Street – Stride 32 Flower and Dean Street – Eddowes 55 Flower and Dean Street. **Injuries**: Nichols throat cut with two cuts, jagged cut to belly but no disembowelment, no body parts missing. Her hat was left on ground by killer – Chapman throat cut once but very deep, almost beheading; neckscarf tied around throat. Body disembowelled. Body parts taken away by killer, including two brass rings wrenched from finger and her uterus – Stride throat cut once, neckscarf pulled very tight, blood on right hand, hat near head, packet of cachous held in left hand – Eddowes severely disfigured, disembowelled, nose and one ear lobe cut off, body parts taken by killer included uterus and left kidney. **Witnesses**: **Nichols** – up to two hours before death was documented. No suspects seen with her. **Chapman** – up to three hours before death was documented. One suspect was seen with her – described as dark, wore a brown deerstalker hat and looked to be over forty with a shabby genteel appearance, a little taller than Annie and appeared to be foreign. **Stride** – documented until about 7 p.m. on evening before her death, after which whereabouts unknown. There were three main descriptions by witnesses who thought they saw Stride with a man just prior to her murder.

From William Marshal: middle aged, about 5'6" tall, rather stout and looking like a clerk. He wore a small black coat, dark trousers and a round cap with a small peak. From James Brown: stout and about 5'7" tall, wearing a long coat. From PC William Smith: the man held a newspaper parcel in his hand. He was 5'7" tall and wore a hard felt deerstalker hat and dark clothes; he was about twenty-eight years old and had no whiskers. William Smith was probably the only person to see Stride with her killer, recognizing her by the red flower pinned to her jacket. However, this was likely not Jack the Ripper, but a copycat murderer who was, like Jack, never caught by police. **Eddowes** – only one reliable witness here: Joseph Lawende, who describes a man as about thirty years old, 5'7" or 5'8" tall and of medium build, with a fair complexion and moustache. He wore a pepper-and-salt loose jacket, a grey cloth cap with a peak and a reddish neckerchief tied in a knot. Lawende thought he looked like a sailor.

12. ABOUT MARY KELLY'S DEATH

So to the final killing, the climax to Jack's murderous career and the end of the ripper killings. The murder of Mary Jane Kelly was not greatly documented, due to Coroner Macdonald's inexplicable decision to cut short her inquest. The medical evidence was suppressed, although, thanks to Dr Thomas Bond's recently discovered autopsy report, we are able to read one doctor's view of the injuries sustained by the unfortunate victim.

Sketch of John McCarthy   *Sketch of Joseph Barnett*

Mary Kelly remains an enigma. Far younger and more attractive than the other dead women, she is described as stout, or heavy boned, with fair or auburn hair. Like the others, she drank a lot and was a prostitute, but with one difference – she rented a room at McCarthy's rents in Millers Court, rather than live in a lodging house. She had a steady man friend – Joseph Barnett, but had fallen recently out with him and he had moved out of Millers Court. This was probably because she was in arrears with her rent and McCarthy may have insisted she share her room with another money making prostitute – Maria Harvey.

Harvey spent only two nights with Mary Kelly, plus the evening of the day before Kelly was murdered. She left behind a pile of clothing, which was discovered the next day burnt in Kelly's fireplace. Detective Inspector Abberline said the ashes in the fire grate consisted of remnants of clothing, a portion of a brim of a hat and a skirt. 'It appeared as if a large quantity of women's clothing had been burnt.' There are some interesting sightings of Mary on her last day alive. We have documentary evidence that Kelly saw her estranged friend Joseph Barnett in the evening of the 8th November. He said he last saw her at 8 p.m. When he first arrived at Room 13, Mary had a friend present with her – Lizzie Albrook. Also, there was the source of poor Barnett's problems, Maria Harvey plus clothes bundle.

Barnett said he arrived at the room at 7:30 or 7:45 in the evening; Harvey said it was 6:55 that night. Either way, since neither had a chain watch and relied upon local church bells to give them the time, Maria Harvey left right away when Barnett arrived. The next sighting of Kelly was by Mary Ann Cox, the widow who lived at 5 Millers Court and had known Kelly about nine months. Cox was returning to her room to warm herself at about 11:45. As she turned into Dorset Street she saw Mary Kelly walking in front of her in the company of a man. By the time Cox reached the archway to Millers Court, Mary and her male friend were just going into Room 13. Mary Cox got a good look at the man, whom she describes as about thirty-six years old and 5'5" tall.

He was stout with a fresh complexion but had blotches on his face. He had a thick, carroty moustache and was dressed in rather shabby dark clothes, with a dark overcoat and a black billycock hat. He carried a quart can of beer and Cox later heard Mary Kelly singing inside her room. Cox went out again at about midnight and when she returned for the last time at three o'clock, there was no light from the windows of Room.13 and all was quiet. Sarah Lewis from Great Pearl Street had argued with her husband and walked out of their house. She decided she would stay with friends at 2 Millers Court. It was 2:30 when she passed Christ Church and was soon in Dorset Street. Here she saw a man standing by a lodging house that was directly opposite Millers Court; she described him as not tall but stout, and stated he was wearing a black wide-awake hat.

As she looked at him, another young man with a woman passed along the street. The man near the lodging house appeared to be looking up Millers Court, as if waiting for someone to come out. The couple were likely Mary Kelly with a man, and the other person standing by the lodging house was probably George Hutchinson, who came forward after the inquest had concluded. Star witness for the prosecution, had the police arrested Jack! An unemployed laborer and former groom of military appearance, George Hutchinson lived at the Victoria Working Men's Home, Commercial Street. At six p.m. on 12th November 1888, George went into the Commercial Street police station and gave a statement to Sergeant Edward Badham. He said this: 'About two a.m. 9th I was coming by Thrawl Street, Commercial Street, and saw just before I got to Flower and Dean Street the murdered woman Kelly. And she said to me Hutchinson, will you lend me sixpence. I said I can't, I have spent all my money going down to Romford. She said good morning, I must go and find some money. She went away toward Thrawl Street. A man coming in the opposite direction to Kelly tapped her on the shoulder and said something to her. They both burst out laughing. I heard her say alright to him. And the man said you will be alright for what I have told you. He then placed his right hand around her shoulders. He also had a kind of a small parcel in his left hand with a kind of strap around it. I stood against the lamp of the Queen's Head Public House and watched him.

They both then came past me and the man hid down his head with his hat over his eyes. I stooped down and looked him in the face. He looked at me stern. They both went into Dorset Street I followed them. They both stood at the corner of the court for about three minutes. He said something to her. She said alright my dear come along you will be comfortable. He then placed his arm on her shoulder and gave her a kiss. She said she had lost her handkerchief; he then pulled his handkerchief, a red one, out and gave it to her. They both then went up the court together. I then went to the court to see if I could see them, but could not. I stood there for about three-quarters of an hour to see if they came out. They did not so I went away. Description: age about 34 or 35. height 5'6" complexion pale, dark eyes and eye lashes, slight moustache, curled up each end, and hair dark, very surly looking, dress long dark coat, collar and cuffs trimmed astrakhan. And a dark jacket under. Light waistcoat, dark trousers, dark felt hat turned down in the middle. Button boots and gaiters with white buttons. Wore a very thick gold chain, white linen collar. Black tie with horse shoe pin. Respectable appearance, walked very sharp. Jewish appearance. Can be identified.' (*I must ask how Hutchinson knew this man had dark hair when he wore a felt hat which he pulled down over his eyes, plus it was dark – my italics.*)

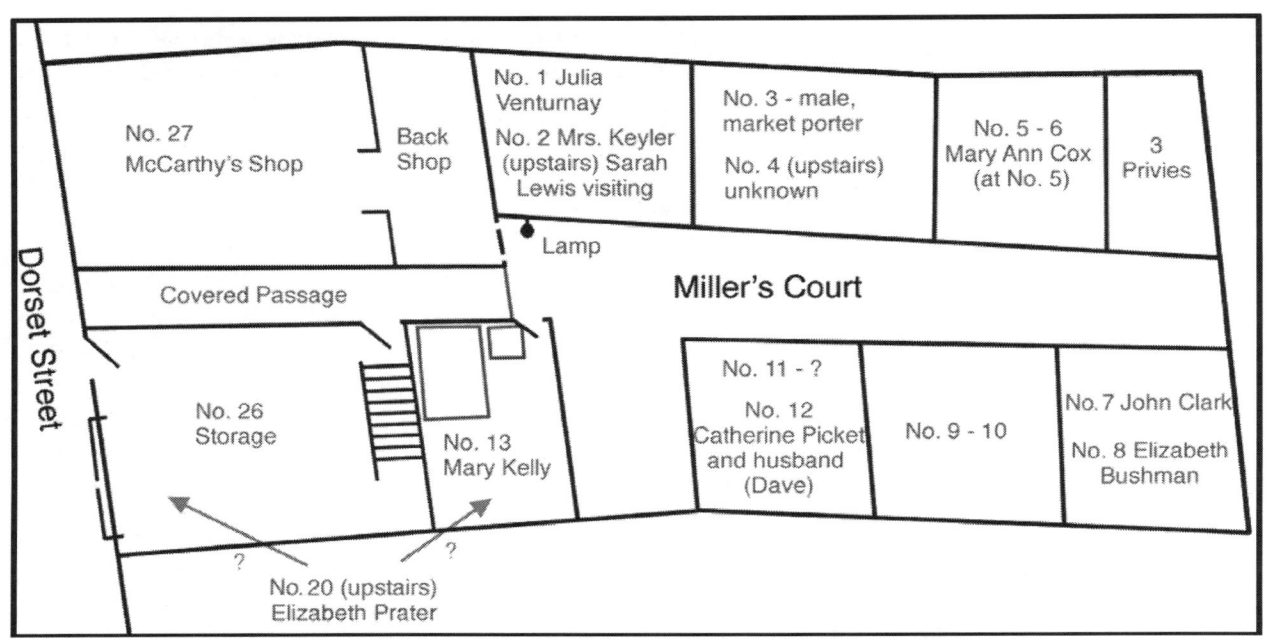

Another map of the court and some of the occupants (unknown).

Computer enhanced picture of Millers Court; note water pump on left and rag in broken lower window pane (unknown).

No wonder with such a description that the statement went straight to Detective Inspector Abberline, who commented: 'I have interrogated him this evening and I am of opinion his statement is true. He informed me that he had occasionally given the deceased a few shillings, and that he had known her about three years. Also, that he was surprised to see a man so well dressed in her company, which caused him to watch them.' Hutchinson was the man Sarah Lewis saw standing outside the lodging house opposite Millers Court between two and three a.m. on the morning of the murder. Can we believe Hutchinson's statement? There are a number of inconsistencies. Firstly, why did George take so long to inform the police? It was three days after Kelly was killed, apparently, that he went to Commercial Street police station. That was the 12th November; the Kelly inquest concluded on the 11th. Secondly, why did he spend so long loitering outside the Dorset Street lodging house, attracting attention and suspicion from the likes of Sarah Lewis? Where were the police that night? And lastly, and perhaps most important, how in the dark night conditions, was he able to give such a detailed description of the man accompanying Mary Kelly up Millers Court?

My opinion is that, if Hutchinson did see anyone walking with Mary Kelly (with whom he was acquainted enough to lend money), his description of the man seen was exaggerated considerably. Some ripperologists have suggested that Hutchinson may have been the killer, but there is nothing to connect him to any of the previous victims. Contentious to many was the testimony of Caroline Maxwell, who also lived in Dorset Street. The consensus was that Mary Kelly had been killed sometime in the early hours of the 9th November; however, Mrs Maxwell claims to have seen Mary Kelly after this time. She had known Mary Kelly for only four months and had spoken to her only twice, but Maxwell stated that between eight and 8:30 on the morning of the 9th she saw Kelly standing on the corner of Millers Court.

The two women, as we know, spoke and Kelly admitted that she was feeling the worse for drink; she pointed out some vomit in the gutter that she said was hers. One hour after this, at about 9:30, Maxwell saw Kelly again, talking to a stout man wearing dark clothes outside the Britannia public house. Many ripperologists seized upon this as being some sort of Masonic conspiracy and that someone other than Mary Kelly had died in 13 Millers Court. If so, surely Kelly would want her room back once the police had finished? The only likely explanation was that Maxwell was mistaken about the date. Some ripperologists have even suggested that this vomiting episode was an indication that Mary Kelly was pregnant. This theory can be put to rest when we check Dr Thomas Bond's autopsy report:

'The viscera were found in various parts (*places*): the uterus and kidneys with one breast under the head, the other breast by the right foot, the liver between the feet, the intestines by the right side and the spleen by the left side of the body. The flaps removed from the abdomen and thighs were on a table.' The uterus, kidneys with one breast were found under the head. This is the moment when Dr Bond would have noticed if the uterus was in a pregnant state – he does not mention it. Kelly was not pregnant when she died; this places several other theories as to who killed her and why out of the window, as we shall see later.

Dr Bagster Phillips gave very limited testimony about the murder of Mary Kelly. He described her room as 'it had two windows in the court. Two panes in the lesser window were broken, and as the door was locked I looked through the lower of the broken panes and satisfied myself that the mutilated corpse lying on the bed was not in need of any immediate attention from me, and I also came to the conclusion that there was nobody else upon the bed, or within view, to whom I could render any professional assistance.' The police surgeon had spoken to the coroner before the inquest began, and illegally suggested suppressing the medical evidence by giving just the immediate cause of Kelly's death – this being the severance of the right carotid artery. All other injuries were done after death. But in the previous paragraph above, Dr Phillips says 'as the door was locked I looked through the lower of the broken panes and satisfied myself that the mutilated corpse lying on the bed was not in need of any immediate attention from me.'

The door was mysteriously locked. Joseph Barnett reported to police that the key had been lost some weeks before. Normal entry into the room was as follows: remove rag from broken window pane, draw back curtain, reach in and operate the latch. And yet, somebody must have had a key, which explains why police had to order McCarthy to break open the door. Unless Kelly had found the key, or another had been made, then in all likelihood it was the murderer who let himself out of the property and locked it, taking the key with him. An alternative would be to exit the room via one of the windows – which was likely to make a bit of noise late at night. But since the door to room 13 was locked, Jack must have had it about his person. Another ripper mystery unsolved. Was it possible that, when the key was lost, Jack had acquired it then? Did he have a plan to murder Mary Kelly all along?

Joseph Barnett was praised by the coroner for the way he gave his evidence at the inquest. Here are some further pieces of his testimony that shed a little light on his relationship with Mary Kelly. He had lived with the deceased one year and eight months. Her name, he said, was Marie Jeanette Kelly, with the French spelling. Kelly was her maiden name. Barnett had seen the body in the mortuary, and identified it by the ear and eyes, which were all that he could recognize. He was positive it was the same woman he knew. He had lived with her in room 13 Millers Court, for eight months. He had separated from her on 30th October. The coroner asked why did he leave her. Barnett replied because she had a woman of bad character there, whom she took in out of compassion, but he objected to it. That was the only reason they separated. He left her on the Tuesday between five and six p.m. He last saw her alive between 7:30 and 7:45 on Thursday night, when he called upon her. He stayed there for fifteen minutes.

Were you on good terms, the coroner asked? Yes, Barnett replied, on friendly terms. He had no work at that time, and so nothing to give her, for which he was sorry. Did they drink together, Macdonald asked? No, she was quite sober that evening. Was she, generally speaking, of sober habits? When she was with Barnett, he found her of sober habits, but she had been drunk several times in his presence. Was there anyone else there on the Thursday evening, the coroner asked? Yes, replied Barnett, a woman who lived in the court. She left first, and he followed shortly afterwards. The coroner asked if Barnett had any conversation with Kelly about her parents? Yes, he replied, frequently. She said she was born in Limerick, and went when young to Wales. She did not say how long she lived there, but that she came to London about four years ago. Her father's name was John Kelly, a foreman in an iron works in Carnarvonshire, or Carmarthen. Mary said she had one sister, who was respectable, who travelled from market place to market place.

This sister was very fond of Mary. There were also six brothers living in London, and one was in the army. One of them was named Henry. Barnett never met the brothers. Mary said she was married when very young, in Wales, to a collier, by the name of Davis or Davies. She said she had lived with him until he was killed in a mining explosion. Her age was sixteen when she married him. About a year later Mary Kelly was in a gay house in the west-end of London, but in what part she did not say. A gentleman came there to her and asked her if she would like to go to France. She did not remain long with this man in France, perhaps two weeks. She returned to England, and went to the Ratcliffe Highway. Mary lived with a man opposite the Commercial Gas Works, Stepney, named Morganstone. Mary had told Barnett of another man named Joseph Fleming, who came to Pennington Street, London, a bad house where she stayed. She was very fond of him, apparently. He was a mason's plasterer and lodged in Bethnal Green Road. After Fleming, she teamed up with Barnett. After this testimony, the coroner had turned to the jury and said:

'The doctor has sent a note asking whether we shall want his attendance here today. I take it that it would be convenient that he should tell us roughly what the cause of death was, so as to enable the body to be buried. It will not be necessary to go into the details of the doctor's evidence; but he suggested that he might come to state roughly the cause of death.' The jury acquiesced in the proposed course, hence cutting short the medical testimony. Throughout the remainder of this short inquest, various tiny snippets of information give us a clearer picture of Mary Kelly. From John McCarthy, Kelly was described 'when sober she was an exceptionally quiet woman, but when in drink she had more to say. She was able to walk about, and was not helpless.'

From Mary Cox 'I have often seen the woman the worse for drink.' From Caroline Maxwell to the coroner 'I have seen her in drink, but she was not a notorious character.' From Julia Vanturney of 1 Millers Court, a charwoman living with a man named Harry Owen, 'I knew the deceased for some time as Kelly, and I knew Joe Barnett, who lived with her. He would not allow her to go on the streets. Deceased often got drunk. She said she was fond of another man, also named Joe. I never saw this man (*this was Joseph Fleming, who visited Mary at the 'bad' house, obviously a brothel – my italics*).' Mary was not as bad as often made out then; drinking yes, and picking up casual clients for sex when money circumstances required it – this must have been more frequent, since she was 29s in arrears with her rent. It could have been a reason for separating from Joseph Barnett. Her broken window pane may well have come about as a result of an argument between the two of them.

Ages: Nichols 42 – Chapman 47 – Stride 45 – Eddowes 46 – Kelly 25 **Occupations**: All prostitutes. **Housing**: Nichols 18 Thrawl Street – Chapman 35 Dorset Street – Stride 32 Flower and Dean Street – Eddowes 55 Flower and Dean Street – Kelly Room 13 Millers Court, 26 Dorset Street. **Injuries**: Nichols throat cut with two cuts, jagged cut to belly but no disembowelment, no body parts missing. Her hat was left on ground by killer – Chapman throat cut once but very deep, almost beheading; neckscarf tied around throat. Body disembowelled. Body parts taken away by killer, including two brass rings wrenched from finger and her uterus – Stride throat cut once, neckscarf pulled very tight, blood on right hand, hat near head, packet of cachous held in left hand – Eddowes severely disfigured, disembowelled, nose and one ear lobe cut off, body parts taken by killer included uterus and left kidney – Kelly severely disfigured, disembowelled, and body parts placed around bed and bedside table, only the heart was missing.

Witnesses: **Nichols** – up to two hours before death was documented. No suspects seen with her. **Chapman** – up to three hours before death was documented. One suspect was seen with her – described as dark, wore a brown deerstalker hat and looked to be over forty with a shabby genteel appearance, a little taller than Annie and appeared to be foreign. **Stride** – documented until about seven p.m. on evening before her death, after which whereabouts unknown. There were three main descriptions by witnesses who thought they saw Stride with a man just prior to her murder: From William Marshal: middle aged, about 5'6" tall, rather stout and looking like a clerk. He wore a small black coat, dark trousers and a round cap with a small peak. From James Brown: stout and about 5'7" tall, wearing a long coat. From PC William Smith: the man held a newspaper parcel in his hand. He was 5'7" tall and wore a hard felt deerstalker hat and dark clothes; he was about twenty-eight years old and had no whiskers. William Smith was probably the only person to see Stride with her killer, recognizing her by the red flower pinned to her jacket. However, this was likely not Jack the Ripper, but a copycat murderer who was, like Jack, never caught by police.

Eddowes – only one reliable witness: Joseph Lawende, who describes a man as: about thirty years old, 5'7" or 5'8" tall and of medium build, with a fair complexion and moustache. He wore a pepper-and-salt loose jacket, a grey cloth cap with a peak and a reddish neckerchief tied in a knot. Lawende thought he looked like a sailor. **Kelly** – several witnesses: Mary Cox, who saw Kelly with a man at about 11:45 p.m. with the man described as short, stout, shabbily dressed wearing a longish coat, very shabby, and carrying a pot of ale in his hand. He wore a round, hard billycock hat and had a blotchy face and full carroty moustache. George Hutchinson, he who reported late to the police of seeing Kelly with a man at about two a.m. and described him as: age 34 or 35, height 5'6" complexion pale, dark eyes and eye lashes, slight moustache, curled up each end, and hair dark, very surly looking, dress long dark coat, collar and cuffs trimmed astrakhan, dark jacket under, light waistcoat, dark trousers, dark felt hat turned down in middle, button boots and gaiters with white buttons, wearing a very thick gold chain, white linen collar, black tie with horse shoe pin, of respectable appearance, walked very sharp, Jewish appearance.

13. NEMESIS OF FAILURE

The murderous campaign that began on 31st August 1888 and ended on 9th November 1888 after just seventy days can only be described as a nemesis of failure. Yes, the fledgling police force of fifty-nine years and its more junior detective department of about ten years had never dealt with this sort of crime before. Jack was unheard of in his time. The satirical magazine Punch called it the 'nemesis of neglect' – the way the poor were being treated in the east end of London.

There floats a phantom on the slum's foul air,
Shaping, to eyes which have the gift of seeing,
Into the Spectre of that loathly lair.
Face it – for vain is fleeing!
Red-handed, ruthless, furtive, unerect,
'Tis murderous Crime – the Nemesis of Neglect!

So, we know now of the crimes, we've seen the murder photos, we've read about the inquests and met the people involved. Today, more than 129 years after events, we still don't know who murdered those women, and we are still no closer to finding out. Some ripperologists claim to know who the killer was, and some make very good cases for their man – but most can be shown to be wanting. I don't pretend to be one of those ripperologists – I don't know who the killer was and I don't accept some of the theories as to who the killer was; frankly, I'm not bothered. I'm just happy for Jack to remain a mystery, wearing a black top hat, shrouded in the fog of time. We will look at a few of the other ripperologists ideas just as to who Jack might have been later – bear in mind, there must be dozens of books out there by keen ripperologists which, if you read them, would totally confuse you. So for now, this chapter is about the nemesis of failure, and who was responsible for the failure to apprehend the killer. We must start at the very top, of course, excluding the politicians who allowed neglect of the poor to breed the types of women that would roam the alley-ways of Whitechapel at night, with a killer on the loose, to earn a few pennies for a bed, food or drink.

Sir Charles Warren

Sir Charles Warren

The senior Met police officer of the events. Forty-eight years old at the time of Jack's reign, he was formally a soldier and so a perfect candidate for Met Commissioner. He was commissioned in 1857 as a lieutenant in the Royal Engineers, so was quite intelligent. He was a keen archaeologist and worked for the army in Palestine and Syria from 1867 before returning home due to poor health. He next was sent to survey Africa and experienced his first battle in the Transkei War (1877–78), where he was badly wounded at Perie Bush. For this, he was mentioned in dispatches and promoted lieutenant colonel. He was then appointed special commissioner to investigate native questions in Bechuanaland (British crown colony in South Africa), and commanded the Northern Border Expedition troops by quelling rebellion. By 1879, he was administrator for Griqualand West (central South Africa).

By 1880, Sir Charles was back home as chief instructor of surveying at the School of Military Engineering, interrupted in 1882 when he was sent to Sinai to discover what had happened to Professor Edward Palmer's archaeological expedition. He discovered that they had been robbed and murdered, found their remains and brought their killers to justice. For this, he was created a Knight Commander of the Order of St Michael and St George (KCMG). In 1884 Lieutenant-Colonel Warren was sent as special commissioner to command a military expedition to Bechuanaland to assert British sovereignty in the face of encroachments from Germany and the Transvaal, who were stealing land and cattle from the local Tswana tribes. Known as the Warren Expedition, a force of 4,000 British and local troops headed from Cape Town, accompanied by the first three observation balloons ever used by the British Army.

The expedition achieved its aims without bloodshed and Warren was recalled in September 1885 and appointed a Knight Grand Cross of the Order of St Michael and St George (GCMG). In 1885 Sir Charles stood for parliament, but lost. The following year, prior to resuming his military duties in Sudan, he became Metropolitan Police commissioner. The reasons why he was selected are unknown, but it was likely a case of jobs for the boys. All previous commissioners were selected from the ranks of the military, and Sir Charles was no exception. The Met Police was in a bad state when Warren took over, due to the previous incumbent's inactivity over the past years. Economic conditions in London were bad, leading to demonstrations. Warren appears genuinely concerned for his men's welfare, but much of this went unheeded by his superiors. Sir Charles was described as rather aloof, although he had good relations with his senior police officers.

To make things worse, Sir Charles, a Liberal, did not get along with Conservative Home Secretary, Henry Matthews. Matthews appeared to support the desire of Assistant Commissioner (Crime), James Monro, to remain independent of the Met police commissioner, and also supported the Official Receiver, the force's chief financial officer, who continually clashed with Warren. Home Office Permanent Secretary, Godfrey Lushington, did not get on with Warren either. Warren was criticized in the press for his extravagant dress uniform, his concern for the quality of his men's boots and his reintroduction of drill. The press completely turned against him after Bloody Sunday on 13th November 1887, when a demonstration in Trafalgar Square was broken up by 4,000 police on foot, 300 infantrymen and 600 mounted police and the Life Guards!

Now to 1888, when Sir Charles introduced five chief constables, ranking between superintendent and assistant commissioner. James Monro insisted that the chief constable of the Criminal Investigation Department (CID), who was his deputy, should be a friend of his, Melville Macnaghten, but Sir Charles opposed this on the grounds that, during a riot in Bengal, Macnaghten had been 'beaten by Hindoos', as he put it. This grew into a major row between Warren and Monro, with both men offering their resignation to Home Secretary Matthews, who accepted Monro's resignation. Instead, Monro was moved to the Home Office, allowing him to keep command of the Special Branch. Sir Robert Anderson was appointed Assistant Commissioner (Crime) and Superintendent Adolphus Williamson appointed Chief Constable (CID). Both men, of course, were encouraged to liaise with Monro behind Warren's back.

This then, is a brief snap shot on the life of Sir Charles Warren, until he took over the Met police. As commissioner, he got rid of James Monro, but instead found Monro heading the Special Branch and Robert Anderson the C.I.D, all answerable direct to Home Secretary Matthews behind Warren's back. Until Jack arrived in August 1888, Sir Charles to his name had used brute force against a demonstration in London, and got rid of Monro. Now came Jack. Sir Charles was criticized frequently for never offering a financial reward for information leading to the arrest of the murderer – in fact, he was in favour of such a move but apparently it was blocked by the Home Office! No surprise there, then? Sir Charles was also accused of not putting enough police officers on the ground; in fact, Whitechapel was swamped with them, both uniformed and plain clothed!

Warren was accused of being more interested in uniformed policing than detective work, which was probably true, but this failed to take into account the fact that he allowed his more experienced detectives to conduct their own affairs without interference. Detective work, of course, was not really his domain – it was that of Sir Robert Anderson and the C.I.D. He was accused of not using Bloodhounds,' which had been tested by Sir Charles in person. He had sought the assistance of a bloodhound breeder, Edwin Brough, of Scarborough. Mr Brough was asked to bring a couple of trained Bloodhounds to London for the purpose of testing their capabilities in following the scent of a man. These hounds were named Barnaby and Burgho.

Edwin Brough

They were tried in Regent's Park on the morning of Monday 8th October. The ground was frosty, but *The Times* reported that they did their work well, successfully tracking a man who had been given a fifteen-minute head start, for nearly a mile. Further trials took place on the evening of the same day in Hyde Park. It was dark and this time the Bloodhounds were hunted on the leash, as would be the case if they were employed in Whitechapel. They were successful in performing this task, and so on the following morning, Tuesday 9th October, another trial took place, this time before Sir Charles Warren himself. That morning trial was reported to be a much better one for scenting purposes than had been the Monday trials. In the end, half a dozen runs were made, with Sir Charles Warren himself twice acting as the bait. In every instance, the dogs hunted persons who were complete strangers to them. So, *The Times* for 10th October reported that Warren expressed satisfaction at the result of these trials.

Negotiations for the purchase of two hounds began, but Sir Charles Warren could not give any definite assurance about purchase; he said that he required more trials to be carried out before making a final decision. Critics were now mocking him over the bloodhound trials once reports appeared in the press, and so Mr Brough insisted that the hounds be returned to him. According to experts, the use of Bloodhounds in the Whitechapel area was feasible, providing that the body was found when the streets were not crowded. That would hardly be the case unless the next victim was found in the middle of the night. In this, Sir Charles Warren was a maverick, for it was not until the 1930's before the official police dog arrived! However, he could not decide whether to use them, and by the time Mary Kelly was killed the dogs had been sent home.

Another serious error by Sir Charles was his decision to erase the Goulston Street writing on the wall, as we have already seen. He now began to publicly complain about his lack of control of the C.I.D, which brought an official Home Office reprimand for discussing his office publicly without their permission. He finally resigned the day before the murder of Mary Kelly, on 9th November 1888. Every superintendent on the force visited him at home to express their regret, apparently. His resignation hindered the investigation for half a day. He had given an order that if another murder occurred, nobody was to enter the scene – an odd thing to say since the previous victims had all been found in open streets – until he arrived to personally direct the investigation. As a result, when the murder of Kelly was discovered, the police did not enter the room for three hours because, unaware of his resignation, they were waiting for Warren to arrive in person, perhaps with his Bloodhounds.

Barnaby and Burgho (unknown).

Sir Charles, as we have seen, was a very good archaeologist, surveyor and military engineer – but was he a good policeman? He certainly put extra police and plain clothed detectives on the streets of Whitechapel – if you go through the police and Home Office files you will see numerous receipts for the costs of employing the extra men. He was seriously hampered by Matthews, the Home Secretary, who was his direct boss – such that no reward was offered for the capture of the killer. Perhaps his experience with the London riots in 1886, when he was criticized for being heavy-handed with demonstrators, made him more cautious about such an event reoccurring again, when he made the decision to erase the infamous writing on the wall in Goulston Street? His last duty before resigning as head of the Met was to issue a free pardon for anyone giving information leading to the arrest of the actual murderer. Needless to say, nobody came forward.

The photographs

Much has been written about the scant number of photographs in the police and Home Office files – the lack of them, considering photography had been in existence since about the late 1830's. The first three victims (including Elizabeth Stride) each have only one mortuary photograph. Kate Eddowes, investigated by the City of London police, had a few more mortuary pictures – four at least, including full body shots after post mortem. Mary Kelly, the final victim, until the late 1980's had only one photograph, plus one other, the only known picture of Millers Court itself. Then in the 1980's, another photo was sent to police from an unknown source, and this picture was of Kelly taken from the 'opposite' side of the bed. Somebody had taken photos from the files and had returned one. Perhaps there might be others, in due course?

The Kelly photos are worth examining further, since all the others are mortuary photos. Kelly has no known mortuary photos. Yet Detective Constable Walter Dew, who looked through the Millers Court window, claimed that several photographs were taken that gloomy day, including close-ups of Kelly's eyes! There was a misinformed theory in Victorian times that by photographing a murder victim's eyes close-up, the image of the last thing seen in life – presumably the murderer, would still be on the eye lens! Kelly's eyes were apparently photographed, with negative results. More on her eyes shortly. Perhaps more interesting are the two pictures of Mary Kelly *in situ* taken by a police photographer – probably a City of London photographer, according to various ripperologists including Donald Rumbelow. Remember the police were pacing around at Millers Court that morning waiting for Sir Charles Warren and his Bloodhounds to turn up. According to Rumbelow in his revised book *The Complete Jack the Ripper*, a window at Millers Court was removed before the door was axed by John McCarthy. From there, a photograph could have been taken, obviously the full side on view of Kelly on her bed. We can call that picture MK1 and the second photo taken from the other side of the bed MK2. The outdoor photo of Millers Court we will call MK3.

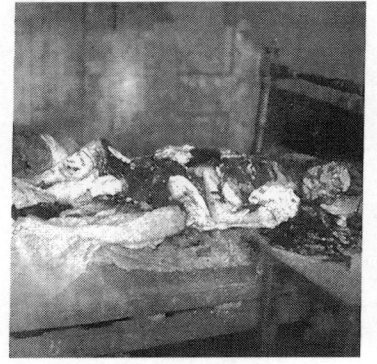

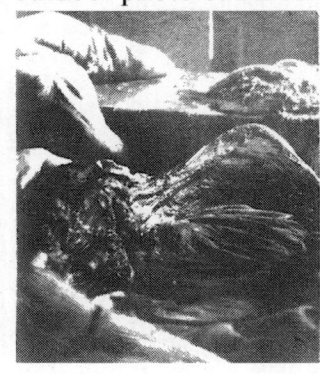

MK1 *MK2* *MK3*

MK1 must have been taken either through a window, or inside once the door had been broken open. We don't know which for definite, but if a window had to be removed, as Donald Rumbelow suggests, would it not likely be the smaller of the two windows in MK3, since the lower glass pane was broken? If the picture had been taken from the larger left hand window, then the angle would be such that much less of Kelly's bedside table would be in view. As it is, only a part of the front leading edge and about fourteen inches of the side edge of the table are visible. I think, as do others, that the bigger, left hand window was from where photo MK1 was taken, otherwise the whole of that small bedside table would be in view, side on.

Simon Wood, in his theory of 2005, shows various angles from which the photos could have been taken from. MK2 would have been taken after the bed had been pulled away from the wall for the purpose of placing a camera tripod there by police. We'll look at MK2 in just a moment, but for now let's look at just room 13 first. For this, we have Simon's scale drawing of the room; ignore the camera and camera angles in this first picture for now, but consider the small size of Kelly's room: 12' by 10'. For the door (top right of the drawing) to open in normal circumstances, the head of Kelly's bed and table must be placed up in the top left corner of the room, against that partitioned wall, otherwise the entrance door would forever be banging against that small table. No witnesses (such as Joseph Barnett) suggest at any time that the door was ever a problem, other than having to reach through a small broken window to use the latch.

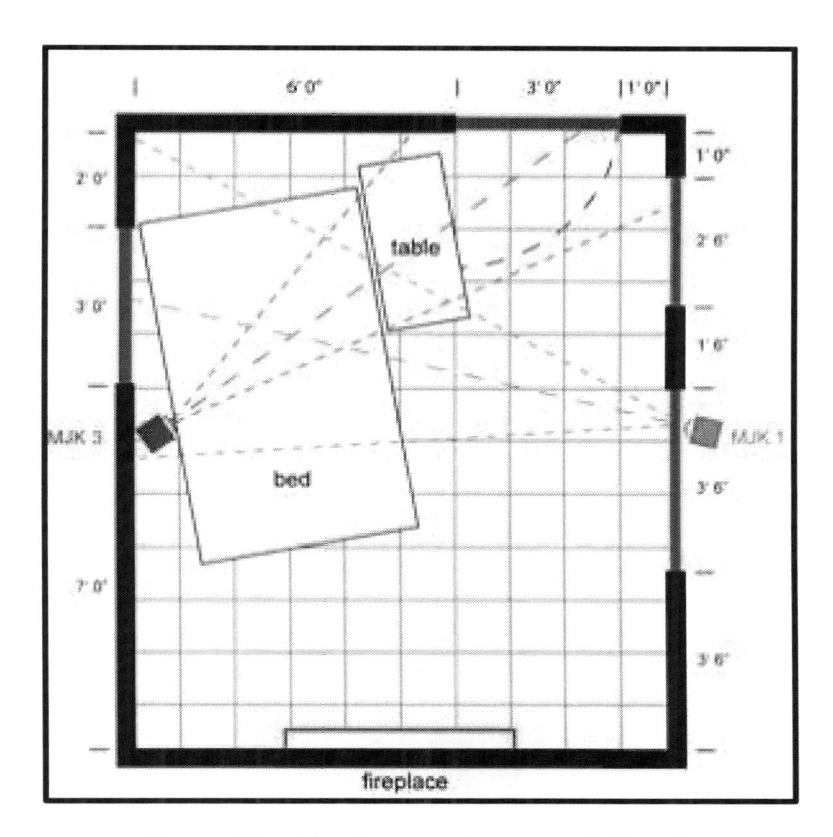

Simon Wood's diagram (courtesy S Wood).

Of course, the small table may have been moved from elsewhere inside the room, but being so small a room, and with a bigger table also towards the fireplace (see below), there isn't much room to place that small table other than beside the bed. Note also the location of the fireplace and another door (presumably locked) in the partition wall in Simon's diagram, coming from number 26 next door.

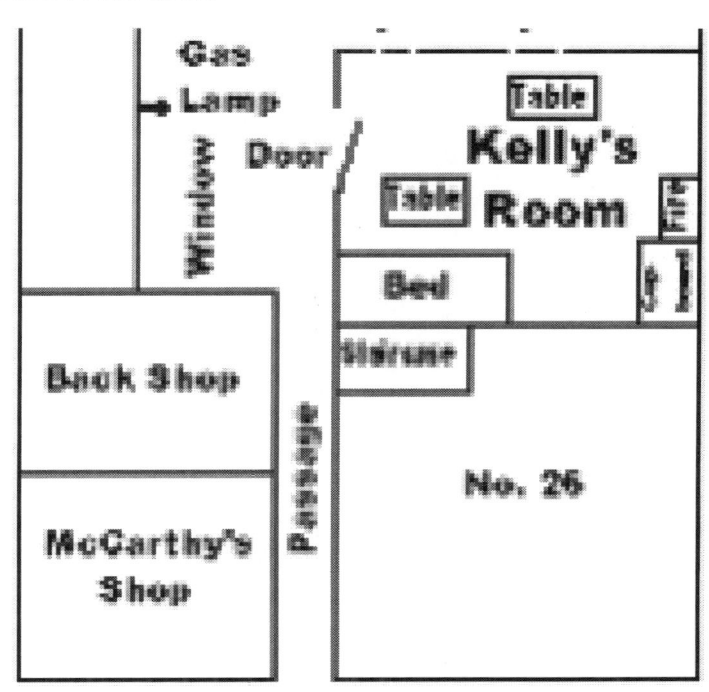

Philip Sugden's drawing (courtesy P Sugden).

Philip Sugden, in his book *the complete history of Jack the Ripper*, provides this drawing above, probably taken from various newspaper sketches of the time, and showing the lay out of room 13 at Millers Court. It does not show a door into room 13 from number 26, and does provides a staircase going up from number 26 right next to Kelly's bed. It also shows two tables and probably a cupboard. If MK1 was taken from the bigger window, as suggested by Simon Wood, then, in all probability the second table would have been in view, plus the whole bed and more of the bedside table. Why would the police remove a perfectly good window, when a broken window was available and nearer to the body? I understand Simon's camera angles, but then those angles assume Kelly's bed had already been pulled away from the partition wall when MK1 was taken, probably by the killer so he could get on the far side to mutilate further. A close study of MK1 seems to show the bed up against the partition wall. However, quite rightly there is a definite angle to the bed, judging by the headboard.

MK1

The bed base (above), built of wood, is fairly low to the ground compared to the top of the bedside table, which towers probably eight inches higher than the mattress. Above the dark headboard you can see paneling marks; the whole place was in need of redecoration! The staining above the right knee of the victim is probably age damage to the photograph. There looks like a circular bowl, perhaps a bed pan, beneath the bed. The mattress, to me, appears to be a single or very small double bed. There is one vertical line, commencing just below the knee junction and rising up, which *might* be the hinged edge of the dividing door from number 26. Around Kelly's right ankle is a pile of bed clothes, it seems, rolled back. Simon Wood suggests this was wedged down the side of the mattress, making a gap at the bottom of the bed of about eleven inches from the partition wall. Just enough space, perhaps, for the killer to operate?

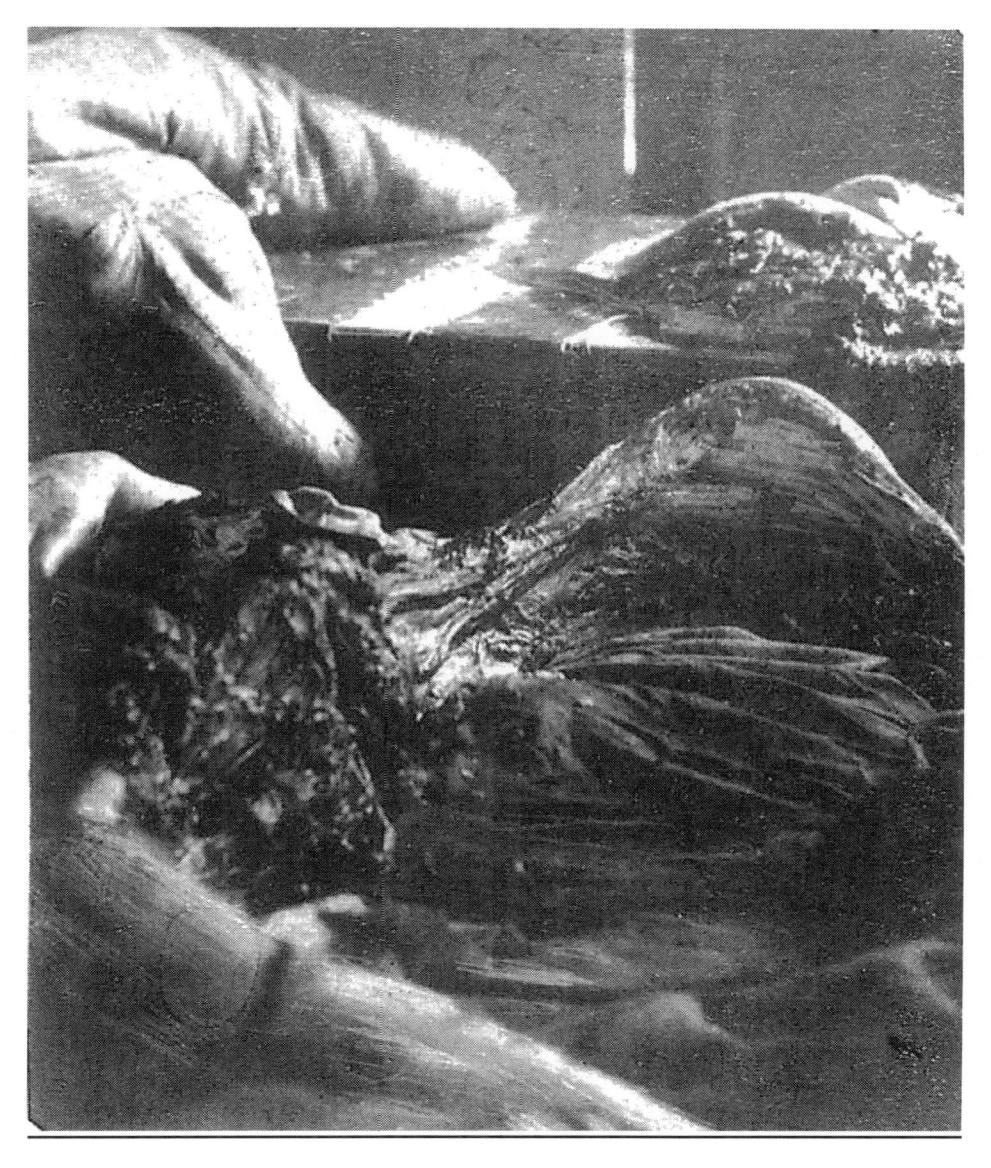

MK2

Now to that second photograph, MK2. Taken inside the room, the camera must have been up against the partition wall and the bed pulled out at an angle to enable it to be taken, or the dividing internal door from number 26 was opened and the picture taken from the doorway (I should expect more light if the dividing internal door was opened). That door between number 26 and room 13 must be in a slightly wrong location in Simon Wood's scale drawings. Picture MK2 warrants further close examination.

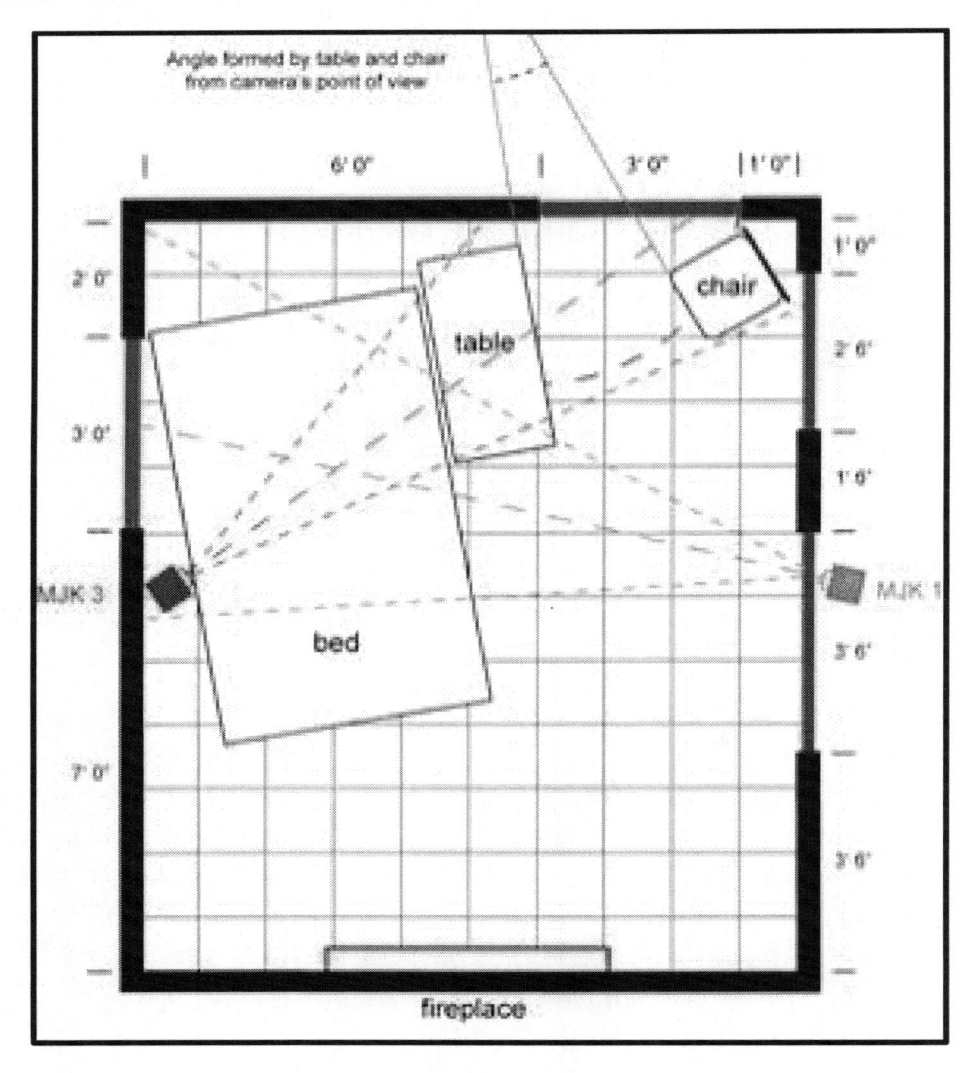

Simon Wood's diagram (courtesy S Wood).

The diagram above suggests both the front door and a chair are in view in MK2. To gain entry, McCarthy had to axe the door open, during which it banged against the bedside table. To keep the door shut so that MK2 could be taken, the police must have wedged a chair, the only one in the room, against it. This, it is suggested, is just visible in the photograph. I have enhanced the picture below as best as I can and the nearest outline of a chair I can see is just above the flesh on the table. Ignore the white triangle top right and vertical white line centre right of photo.

Now to the mystery of the white vertical line centre right of the MK2 photograph, mentioned above. A shaft of door light, perhaps? Nope! Several newspapers reported that the murderer had draped entrails around the room. Simon Wood says 'it's not a strip of light. Tweaking revealed it to be in a different plane to the door (nearer the camera), and I believe it to be something dangling from the ceiling that has been caught in the bright light source (just visible) coming from the right of the photo. (*This is likely light from the window* – my italics.) I have no knowledge of the working parts of the human body, but would suggest that it is something internal. Notice how it is slightly bulbous at its base and appears stretched in places as though sagging on its own weight.'

Feint chair outline above flesh on table (police photo).

I agree that it is probably something dangling from on high, and likely intestinal. At the very bottom front left of photograph MK2 is Kelly's lower right thigh; it is suggested that this was painted in afterwards, because the camera was just too close to focus, and I agree with that assumption. Either way, it does not distract from the horror captured of the moment. The rest of MK2 shows the inside of her left thigh, at the knee, stripped of flesh, and her left hand partially stuffed into her open stomach. On the bedside table is a sort of pillow, plus what looks like flesh from Kelly's thighs and skin flaps. What we can deduce, especially from MK1, is that the corpse on the bed does not appear to be very stout, as Mary Kelly has been often described.

Entry and Exit

Just how did Jack get in and out of room 13? It doesn't take much imagination to work things out. He was either picked up by Mary Kelly and brought home, or he came to the room and either she let him in, or he let himself in, using the lost key. It is interesting that, in such a thin walled tenement as Millers Court, nobody heard Jack arrive. Mary Ann Cox returned for the last time to Millers Court at about three a.m. and reported that there was no light from the windows of room 13, and all was quiet. Cox slept fitfully after this; she heard several men entering and leaving the court and finally heard someone leave at about 5:45 in the morning, although she could not say from which room. Kelly was found dead on her bed wearing some kind of night dress, undergarment or chemise, contrary to many press reports that she was naked. In MK1 you can quite clearly see the puffy sleeve at her left shoulder. The rest of her clothes, including a velvet bodice she had been seen wearing earlier that night, were arranged by the fireplace. What does this suggest? I believe she (and probably her killer) striped down to their undergarments, Victorian modesty being what it was in those days.

From his point of view, Jack could say he was paying for Mary's services if somebody called at the room – in all likelihood, he would not get blood on his main escape garments at the same time. So, how did he escape once the deed was done? Perhaps through the windows? Well, most windows in that Victorian period were sash windows, which would certainly make a noise when opened upwards. The other tenants were likely to remember if a window had been forced opened in that cold November night. Nobody reported a sound, other than the feint cry of 'murder' at around four o'clock that morning. In all probability, Jack had the key to Mary's room, and used it on exit, locking the door when he left, which was why it had to be axed open by McCarthy.

14. DASTARDLY SUSPECTS

Most books about Jack's murderous campaign report who their authors believe to be likely suspects to be Jack the Ripper. Some are pretty convincing, until you begin to realize that there really isn't much evidence presented by the ripperologists. I present to you no suspect suggestions of my own, because I am currently of the belief that Jack will never be disclosed; it doesn't mean to say I can't bring a few suspects to your attention. We should begin with Sir Melville MacNaghten's memorandum of 1894 (written six years after events and not made public until 1959), which gives us the names of three police suspects. Sir Melville says 'no one ever saw the Whitechapel murderer; many homicidal maniacs were suspected, but no shadow of proof could be thrown on any one. I may mention the cases of three men, any one of whom (*sic*) may have committed this series of murders:

(1)　**M J Druitt**, said to be a doctor and of good family – who disappeared at the time of the Millers Court murder, and whose body (which was said to have been upwards of a month in the water) was found in the Thames on 31ˢᵗ December, or about seven weeks after that murder. He was sexually insane and from private information I have little doubt but that his own family believed him to have been the murderer.

Druitt

(2)　**Kosminski** – a Polish Jew and resident of Whitechapel. This man became insane owing to many years' indulgence in solitary vices. He had a great hatred of women, specially of the prostitute class, and had strong homicidal tendencies: he was removed to a lunatic asylum about March 1889. There were some circumstances connected with this man which made him a strong suspect.

Kosminski

(3)　**Michael Ostrog**, a Russian doctor, and a convict, who was subsequently detained in a lunatic asylum as a homicidal maniac. This man's antecedents were of the worst possible type, and his whereabouts at the time of the murders could never be ascertained.

Ostrog

There is little evidence that any of these men were operating in Whitechapel in 1888.

Prince Albert Victor Christian Edward (known as Eddy)

Duke of Clarence

Dr Thomas Stowell in 1970, an early ripperologist, published an article in *The Criminologist* called 'A Solution' suggesting Prince Eddy could be the ripper on account of his insanity due to syphilis. The royal family were aware of his activities, along with the royal doctor, Sir William Gull. Eddy was the son of the future King Edward VII, and grandson of Queen Victoria. However, we can discount Eddy straight away, when you consider the royal archives giving Eddy's whereabouts during the murders: 29th August – 7th September: Prince was staying with Viscount Downe at Danby Lodge, Grosmont, Yorkshire (Nichols murdered 31st August). 7th – 10th September: Prince was at the Cavalry Barracks in York (Chapman murdered 8th September). 27th – 30th September: Prince was at Abergeldie, Scotland, where Queen Victoria recorded in her journal that he lunched with her on 30th September (Stride and Eddowes both murdered between 1.00 and 2.00 A.M., 30th September.) 1st November: arrived London from York. 2nd – 12th November: Prince was at Sandringham (Kelly murdered 9th November).

Dr Thomas Neill Cream

Thomas Cream

A poisoner as opposed to a ripper, Cream was serving a prison sentence from 1881 to 1891 in Joliet, Illinois, and therefore could not possibly have been in London in 1888. He had bragged about the Whitechapel murders, however, hence his inclusion by many ripperologists as a possible suspect. He was hung in 1892 and as the trap opened, was heard by witnesses to say 'I am Jack...'

Frederick Deeming

Deeming

In 1888, Deeming, a sailor, moved his family to Capetown, South Africa, quickly earning the reputation of a cheat. He then moved to Johannesburg, where his moral behavior apparently grew no better. Deciding it best for his family to move to England, he sent them to live in Merseyside. Deeming himself soon followed. They lived what seemed to be a relatively normal existence until it soon became apparent to neighbors that his family had 'disappeared'. Deeming contended that his wife and children had simply gone away. Returning to Australia, Deeming remarried but after a while, left the house, saying his wife had gone away. Attempting to re-let the property, a smell was noticed in the dining room. Police were called to lift the floor boards, and there lay the new Mrs Deeming, in an advanced stage of decomposition and with her throat cut. Police in England went to Deeming's former home and lifted the floor boards there, sadly to find the remains of the first Mrs Deeming and their four children, all with their throats cut. Deeming was tried in Australia in 1892 and hung. For ripperologists, the only connection to Jack was that Deeming was in Liverpool sometime in 1888 and murdered by throat cutting. There was nothing connecting him with London.

George Chapman

Chapman

Also known as Severin Antoniovich Klosowski, he arrived from his native Poland in England in 1887 or 1888. He was seen running a barber shop on his own at 126 Cable Street, St. George's-in-the-East, this being about a third of a mile south of Berners Street (Stride). Chapman married, but he also had a legal wife in Poland, who promptly found out about his new marriage and came to England. Chapman and illegal wife went to America briefly, but soon returned in about 1892, settling in Whitechapel and then, as a separated couple due to his violent behavior, in Tottenham for him. Chapman's story was really a case of having several wives and girlfriends, who were beaten regularly and three of whom died. Arsenic was his pleasure, but after just 11 minutes' deliberation in 1903, Chapman was found guilty and hung. Is there really any connection here with Jack the Ripper, other than a man with a violent temper who used a sharp knife as part of his trade? Detective Inspector Abberline said to Chapman's arresting officer, 'you've got Jack the Ripper at last!' Why would Abberline say this? Only because Chapman arrived in England in 1887 or 1888, and settled in Cable Street. He had sharp knives, being a barber. He was, as discovered later, a poisoner, not a ripper. He was also twenty-three years of age, far younger than any witness who saw a victim with a suspect – the youngest guess was about twenty-eight years of age. It wasn't until 1890 that Chapman was known to live and work in Whitechapel Road. I cannot personally see why Chapman, a poisoner, could be seriously considered a true ripper suspect.

James Maybrick

Maybrick

Discard him right away, since all evidence against him is based upon a diary which appeared in 1990. Michael Barrett, who originally discovered Maybrick's diary, has confessed on numerous occasions that he forged the document. These confessions have been retracted and restated many times in the years. This is a case of finding Jack the Ripper's diary – forged, of course.

Sir William Gull

William Gull

Controversial Ripper theories was made by Stephen Knight in his 1978 book, *Jack the Ripper: The final solution*. The portly doctor was attending the royal family and Queen Victoria. The book is a good read actually, but flawed. Read it and find out for yourself, but to cut a long book short, I'll summarize briefly. This book does revolve around the royals, masons, gay men (illegal in those days) and a place of scandal: Cleveland Street in London. Sadly, these houses of ill repute had been pulled down at the time events unfolded, apparently! A young male royal, probably Eddy Duke of Clarence, picks up a venereal disease or makes a woman pregnant and marries her in secret. Naturally, this needs to be covered up, so Sir William Gull, royal surgeon, rides around the east-end of London in a conveyance driven by a man called Netley, searching out the wedding witnesses and murdering them. Improbable, with, according to Knight, a child of this illegal wedlock being whisked away but surviving. Believe me, it has been about twenty-five years since I read Knights book, and if I were to fully explore every suspect here in detail this book would be three times longer. Still, a carriage would make it easier to not be seen, and even murder women inside it. No witnesses ever describe hearing a pony and carriage during the nights of any of the murders.

Walter Sickert

Walter Sickert

The iconic British painter appears in Stephen Knight's book and also in a book by Patricia Cornwell called *Portrait of a Killer: Jack the Ripper - Case Closed.* This is about DNA from Sickert being found on some of the Jack the Ripper correspondence. Patricia Cornwell apparently had a forensics team, who performed DNA testing on the backs of envelopes and stamps from Jack's correspondence, as well as from some of Sickert's correspondence. DNA testing of material over a century old has never before been done, plus I would have to question where was permission sought to do this? Nuclear DNA testing is the usual form of testing, and this came back negative. End of theory, surely? The forensics team then attempted mitochondrial DNA (mtDNA) testing, which apparently provided some results. Sequences of mtDNA were found in both the Ripper correspondence and Sickert's correspondence. Of course, this correspondence, being handled as it must have been for more than a century, may well have picked up another person's DNA. Likewise, did Sickert lick his own stamps, or did he have one of those damp sponge things to do it with? Inconclusive, I'm afraid. There remains no concrete evidence that connects Sickert with any ripper letters. Further, it is believed Sickert was away in France during the nights of the first four murders (including Stride.)

J K Stephens

J K Stephens

What the deuce! Old Etonian, attended Cambridge University where he read history with Prince Edward of Wales, he was a Poet, he was called to the bar as trainee barrister, newspaper editor – sent to Wales by his father, who appointed him Clerk of Assize for the South Wales Circuit in 1888. He received a head injury in 1886 or 1887. Ripperologist Michael Harrison suggested Stephens was the ripper in his biography of Prince Albert Victor, *Clarence*. But on what grounds? Stephens was a known misogynist (having a hatred or dislike of women) and a lunatic, apparently, perhaps due to his earlier head injury. However, he was not known to have been a violent man, and had no connections with the East End of London!

Other ripper suspects

Dr Herbert Stanley

Rule him out immediately! Stanley was the fictitious name given to Jack by Leonard Matters in his 1929 book *The Mystery Of Jack The Ripper*. It is said Stanley took revenge on a prostitute, who on boat race night 1886, gave his son Herbert, a particularly virulent form of syphilis that killed him within two years. The prostitutes name was Mary Kelly! However, no records exist in any London hospital of a Dr Stanley, nor of his residence in Portman Square. Syphilis takes far longer to kill than the two years it took to kill Stanley's son; there is no evidence to substantiate the claim that Mary Kelly had syphilis, nor why Stanley should kill the other Whitechapel victims.

Dr Alexander Pedachenko

Pedachenko was first named as Jack by William Le Queux in 1923 in his memoirs, then later by ripperologist Donald McCormick, in *Identity of Jack the Ripper*. Typically, he was a mad Russian doctor, supposedly sent by the Russian Secret Police to discredit Scotland Yard by murdering a bunch of women. There is no evidence that Pedachenko even existed, and he is thought to have been made up by a man who was known for inventing sensational stories. I can only conclude that Alexander Pedachenko was not Jack the Ripper.

Robert Donston Stephenson

Robert Stephenson (also known as Roslyn D'Onston) was a journalist and writer interested in the occult and black magic. He admitted himself as a patient at the London Hospital in Whitechapel shortly before the murders started, and left shortly after they ceased. He authored a newspaper article claiming that black magic was the motive for the killings and alleged that the Ripper was a Frenchman. Stephenson's strange interest in the crimes resulted in an amateur detective reporting him to Scotland Yard on Christmas Eve, 1888. Two days later, Stephenson reported his own suspect, a Dr Morgan Davies of the London Hospital. Subsequently, he fell under the suspicion of newspaper editor William Thomas Stead. In his books on the case, author and historian Melvin Harris argues that Stephenson was a leading suspect, but the police do not appear to have treated either him or Morgan Davies as serious suspects. The London Hospital night-shift rosters indicate that Stephenson was not able to leave on the nights of the ripper murders and hence could not be Jack the Ripper.

Francis Tumblety

He earned a fortune posing as an Indian Herb doctor throughout the United States and Canada, and was commonly perceived as a misogynist and a quack. He was connected to the death of one of his patients but escaped prosecution. In 1865 he was arrested for alleged complicity in the assassination of Abraham Lincoln, but no connection was found and he was released without charge. Tumblety was in England in 1888 and was arrested on 7th November, apparently for engaging in homosexuality, which was illegal then. It was reported by his friends that he showed off a collection of 'wombs' from every class of woman. Awaiting trial, he fled to France and then to the United States. Already notorious in the States for his previous criminal charges, his arrest was reported as connected to the ripper murders. American reports that Scotland Yard tried to extradite him were not confirmed in the British press or by the London police. New York City Police said that there was no proof of his complicity in the Whitechapel murders, and the crime for which he was under bond in London was not extraditable. Tumblety was only mentioned as a ripper suspect by Chief Inspector Littlechild in a letter to journalist and author George Sims. Other than Littlechild's letter, there is no evidence pointing to him being Jack.

Jill the Ripper

The obvious one. A lady, perhaps an abortionist, would find it easy to be on the scene of a murder with good excuse and alibi. Would Jill, however, have the nerve to commit such atrocious mutilations on a fellow woman? I doubt it, but I suppose it is remotely possible.

Making your mind up

At the end of this volume is a short bibliography of books related to Jack. There you will find the ripperologists, the authors, the book titles and also the name of the suspect some authors put forward. My advice is that, if you're interested in a particular suspect, look them up if you are able too. Personally, I don't believe any of these suspects could be Jack. The mystery of the murders will endure for all time, as it should be.

15. CONCLUSIONS

And so to the end. We do not know who Jack the Ripper was, nor are we any closer to knowing or ever know. All we have are clues and writers putting pen to paper with their best guestimates. All are wrong, but try nevertheless to push their theories forward. Some just cannot accept that their ideas are simply flawed. Some theories are beyond belief. None of them give the true identity of Jack the Ripper; how can we ever know, when he (or she) was never caught?

Police reports

Have you ever seen the police files? They are there at the public records office if you go down there. Most are full of either public letters to the police, or money requests from the police for extra men, overtime payments, and so on. There are two main files, as you probably already know, because I have been harping on about them. These are the Metropolitan Police files and the Home Office files – the latter closed for about 100 years, although with written consent (such as I received in 1976) you could view them – permission is probably not required today since it has been 129 years.

Documents at the National Archives

The ripper documents that are available are held at The National Archives. The hard facts available to ripperologists are few; the evidence lost is considerable. All of the City of London Police files were destroyed in the Blitz during World War II. What remains of the Metropolitan Police files are available to the public but the files are sparse, with most remaining material now saved on microfilm. The files include the following:

MEPO 3/140: a report by Inspector Spratling on the murder of Mary Ann Nichols (31st August 1888). It fell to Inspector John Spratling of J Division (Bethnal Green) to make the initial police report on the first generally recognized ripper murder; that of Polly Nichols. In a three-page, hand-written report, Spratling details the finding of the body by the beat officer, PC97 Neil. A description is given of the initial police activity and the injuries and appearance of the deceased.

Also in **MEPO 3/140**: A report by Inspector Abberline of Scotland Yard on the Nichols and Chapman murders (8th September 1888). Inspector Frederick George Abberline was the Scotland Yard detective assigned to lead the on-the-ground investigation into the ripper murders. He has enjoyed the highest profile of all the officers involved in the investigation. His report describes the police investigation into the murders of Polly Nichols and Annie Chapman. Inspector Abberline details the identification of the victims and the questioning of witnesses, and reveals the early police suspect, Joseph (Jacob) Isenschmid (*later found insane and incarcerated during the nights of the final murders, so not a true suspect*).

MEPO 3/3153: The 'Dear Boss' letter (25th September 1888). This is a colour copy of the important two-page letter purporting to come from the murderer and signed 'Jack the Ripper', the first known use of this name. It was received at the Central News Agency on 27th September 1888 and forwarded to the police two days later. It is by no means certain that the letter was actually written by the killer. Sent three days before the 'double murders' of 30th September (Stride and Eddowes), the letter includes threats to commit more murders and 'to clip the lady's ears off.' In view of these subsequent murders, and the fact that part of Eddowes' right ear was cut off, some believed it genuine.

MEPO 3/3156: Modern copy of an original mortuary photograph of Elizabeth Stride taken after the discovery of her body in Berner Street, Whitechapel, on 30th Sept 1888. Treated as third canonical victim of 'Jack the Ripper.'

HO 144/221/A49301C: Overall summary of the murder of Elizabeth Stride by Chief Inspector Swanson (19th October 1888). Swanson was the Scotland Yard chief assigned to overall supervision of police enquiries into the Whitechapel murders. He collated the all reports, statements, and correspondence. The handwritten report summarizes the events surrounding the murder of Elizabeth Stride and the resulting extensive police enquiries carried out. It gives an excellent insight into police procedures and thinking at that time, and lists the complicated sequence of events on the night of the Stride murder, as recounted by the many witnesses.

HO 144/221/A49301C: Report by Inspector McWilliam, City of London Police, into the murder of Catherine Eddowes. James McWilliam was head of the detective department of the City of London Police. This report by McWilliam is of special significance, as the City Police records have not survived. It is an eight-page handwritten report and provides a rare insight into the Mitre Square murder, and the City Police investigation. The possible sighting of the killer with the victim at the entrance to Church Passage is described, and details of the receipt of the 'Lusk letter and kidney' are given. The liaison between the City and Metropolitan police forces in the ongoing investigation is also described.

MEPO 3/142: Letters from individuals signed 'Jack the Ripper'. Includes 'Saucy Jacky' postcard (1st October 1888). This was the second communication received by the Central News Agency just after the double murder, and again purporting to come from Jack the Ripper. This postcard includes the use of the name saucy Jacky and speaks of the double event. The original postcard is now missing from Scotland Yard. All there is are the colour facsimiles held at the National Archives.

HO 144/221/A49301C: Report by Sir Charles Warren regarding his actions on the morning of the Stride and Eddowes murders. This handwritten report from Sir Charles, chief commissioner of the Metropolitan Police, to the Home Office, pays special regard to his erasure of the chalk written message on the wall in Goulston Street. A controversial figure, Warren resigned in November 1888 at the height of the murders, after ongoing disputes with the Home Office. Greatly criticized over the failure to capture the murderer, Warren was often required to justify his actions.

Also in **HO 144/221/A49301C**: Report by Chief Inspector Swanson regarding Metropolitan Police knowledge of the Mitre Square murder. This handwritten report by Swanson relates the facts known to the Metropolitan Police surrounding the murder in Mitre Square, which fell under the jurisdiction of the City Police. Importantly, it includes a variant of the message on the wall, and gives the witness Lawende's description of the suspect seen with a woman identified as Catherine Eddowes. Also, details of the 'Lusk letter and kidney' incident are given.

MEPO 3/142A: A Jack the Ripper letter (8th October 1888). The initial Jack the Ripper correspondence sent to the Central News Agency resulted in a flood of similar correspondence, much of it colourful and imaginative, such as this example sent to Scotland Yard from, of all places, Birmingham.

MEPO 3/142: A letter from Philadelphia, USA, signed Jack the Ripper (October 1888). This letter was sent from America and, purporting to come from the killer, threatens more murders. It is a good example of the international notoriety attained by the name Jack the Ripper and the Whitechapel murders, demonstrating that the press coverage in the USA was extensive and affected the American public.

MEPO 3/140: Statement of George Hutchinson regarding a last sighting of Mary Jane Kelly (written on 12th November 1888). A rare survival is this original witness statement of George Hutchinson, which gives Hutchinson's important account of his sighting of Mary Kelly on the morning of her murder, together with his very detailed description of the suspect he saw with her.

Also in **MEPO 3/140**: Report by Inspector Abberline on the Kelly murder and inquest, and the witness Hutchinson (12th November 1888). This important report, written in Abberline's own hand, gives details of the Kelly murder inquiry and inquest, and comments on the important witness George Hutchinson.

MEPO 3/141: Macnaghten report, identifying three police suspects (23rd February 1894). Although not contemporary with the murders, this handwritten report by Sir Melville Macnaghten, chief constable, is rightly held as a very important document by many students of the ripper crimes, and has greatly influenced Ripper studies. Macnaghten was second-in-command (to Robert Anderson) in the CID at Scotland Yard, and held a great interest in the case throughout his career. The report defines the popularly accepted five victims, and names three persons regarded by the police as suspects.

So, these are some of the files included in the national archives. The important thing to note is this – the daily or weekly written reports by the detectives investigating the murder cases, are, in the main, not there. That is a big shame. We know of some suspects the police believed responsible, but there are, no doubt, many others who we don't know of. No thanks to WWII and the bombing of London. Occasionally, a new theory comes to light, but is quickly knocked down as false or impossible. I offer no theories here of my own in these volumes; as far as I am concerned, Jack was never caught and therefore he is still just a phantom, disappearing into the fog of Whitechapel. Perhaps that is the way it should always be?

A new theory I just cannot accept – The Eddowes shawl

That's Russell Edwards' 2014 book *Naming Jack the Ripper*. In this, he will have us believe he bought at auction a shawl belonging to Kate Eddowes! The shawl was in two sections; the biggest part 73.5" in length and 25.5" wide, whilst the smaller piece 24" by 19". The colour was dark brown, with golden brown on the reverse. At both ends of them were blue sections two feet long, patterned with Michaelmas daisies and golden lilies in red, ochre and gold. Pieces had been cut from it at some time. There was a small fringe of tassels at both ends of both section. There were a number of dark stains on the shawl, possibly blood. Before we proceed further in a police like manner, we should list all the clothing and belongings found on Eddowes' body at the mortuary:

A black straw bonnet trimmed in green and black velvet with black beads, black strings worn tied to the head; black cloth jacket trimmed around collar and cuffs with imitation fur and around the pockets in black silk braid and fur; large metal buttons; dark green chintz skirt, three flounces, brown button on waistband; **skirt patterned with Michaelmas daisies and golden lilies**; *man's white vest, matching buttons down front; brown linsey bodice, black velvet* *collar with brown buttons down front; grey petticoat with white waistband; very old green alpaca skirt worn as an undergarment; very old ragged blue skirt with red flounces, light twill lining also worn as undergarment; a white calico chemise; no drawers or stays; a pair of men's lace up boots, mohair laces, right boot repaired with red thread; 1 piece of red gauze silk worn as a neckerchief; 1 large white pocket handkerchief; 1 large white cotton handkerchief with red and white bird's eye border; 2 unbleached calico pockets with tape strings; 1 blue stripe bed ticking pocket;* **1 piece of old white apron,** *and brown ribbed knee stockings, darned at the feet with white cotton.* These were her clothes.

Her possessions consisted of the following: *2 small blue bags made of bed ticking; 2 short black clay pipes; 1 tin box containing tea; 1 tin box containing sugar; 1 tin matchbox, empty; 12 pieces of white rag, some slightly bloodstained; 1 piece coarse linen, white; 1 piece of blue and white shirting, 3 cornered; 1 piece red flannel with pins and needles; 6 pieces soap; 1 small tooth comb; 1 white handle table knife; 1 metal teaspoon; 1 red leather cigarette case with white metal fittings; 1 ball hemp; 1 piece of old white apron with repair; Several buttons and a thimble; 1 mustard tin containing two pawn tickets, one in the name of Emily Birrell, 52 White's Row, dated August 31st, 9d for a man's flannel shirt. The other is in the name of Jane Kelly of 6 Dorset Street and dated September 28th, 2s for a pair of men's boots. Both addresses are false; Printed handbill and a printed card for Frank Carter, 305 Bethnal Green Road; Portion of a pair of spectacles and 1 red mitten.* These were her possessions.

Like most of the poor people in London, Eddowes carried all her worldly goods about her person. During the inquest, Inspector Edward Collard was about to list the clothing found upon the victim at the City mortuary, but was stopped by the Coroner asking questions of a different kind regarding money. 'It (*Eddowes' body* – my italics) was then taken to the mortuary and stripped by Mr Davis, the mortuary keeper, in the presence of the two doctors and myself. I have a list of articles of clothing more or less stained with blood and cut.' The list was not read because the Coroner asked 'was there any money about her?'

An official listing of Eddowes' clothing was as follows: black jacket with imitation fur collar; three large metal buttons; brown bodice; **dark green chintz (with Michaelmas daisy and Gordon lily pattern) skirt (three flounces)**; (*a flounce: a strip of material gathered or pleated and attached at one edge, with the other edge left loose or hanging* – my italics), thin white vest; light drab linsey underskirt; dark green alpaca petticoat; white chemise; brown ribbed stockings mended at feet with piece of white stocking; black straw bonnet trimmed with black beads and green and black velvet; large white handkerchief round neck; a pair of men's old laced boots and a **piece of coarse white apron.**

At the murder scene, Sergeant Jones picked up from the foot way by the left side of the deceased, three small black buttons, such as are generally used for boots; a small metal button; a common metal thimble and a small penny mustard tin containing two pawn-tickets. They were handed to his inspector, Edward Collard. Back to Russell Edwards' theory of the Eddowes shawl, and who the murderer might have been; there appears to be no shawl listed amongst Eddowes' belongings. There is an apron, made of course white material, and several neckerchiefs. **The only item with Michaelmas Daisies on it is a dark green chintz skirt, not a shawl**. How was this so called shawl obtained, if it existed at all and nobody, policeman, doctor or pressman, felt fit to mention it? The theory is this. Acting Police Sergeant Amos Simpson, being on special duties and of the Metropolitan police, accompanied the body of Eddowes to the City mortuary in Golden Lane. He asked a senior officer if he could take it, since his wife might find the material useful for sewing!

I ask you this; a murder victim's shawl, probably covered in blood from her throat wound? An outrageous suggestion. Further, why was Amos Simpson working within the City police boundary, if he was on duty at all that breezy and damp night? Would not the item be washed by the excited wife, until she knew to whom it had belonged? Either way, it was rejected by Mrs Amos Simpson and stored away. The author of *Naming Jack the Ripper* does not mention, that I can see, the cost he paid at auction for this shawl. I hope it wasn't too much, for it did not take long for the scientific community to point out obvious errors in the DNA analysis conducted upon it. 'Error of nomenclature' undermines the case against Polish immigrant barber (Aaron Kosminski) accused of carrying out the atrocities in 1888 (*Independent*, Saturday 18th October 2014 by Steve Connor).

I'm no scientist either, so I can only try and translate in layman's terms. However, briefly, the scientist who carried out the DNA analysis had apparently made a fundamental error that fatally undermines his (Russell Edwards, the author) case against Kosminski – and once again throws open the debate over who the identity of the ripper was. This scientist, Jari Louhelainen, commissioned by Edwards to examine the shawl, is said to have made an 'error of nomenclature' when using a DNA database to calculate the chances of a genetic match. If true, it means his calculations were wrong, and that virtually anyone could have left the DNA that he insisted came from the ripper's victim.

This apparent error, first noticed by crime enthusiasts in Australia, has been highlighted by four experts with intimate knowledge of DNA analysis, including Professor Alec Jeffreys, inventor of genetic fingerprinting, who found that Dr Louhelainen made a basic mistake in analyzing the DNA extracted from a shawl supposedly found near the badly disfigured body of ripper victim Catherine Eddowes. The error means that no DNA connection can be made between Aaron Kosminski and Catherine Eddowes. Any suggestion therefore that the ripper and Kosminski are the same person appears to be based on conjecture and supposition – as it has been, ever since the police first identified Kosminski as a possible suspect more than a century ago.

The flurry of interest in Kosminski, who died in a lunatic asylum aged fifty-three, stems from that book, *Naming Jack the Ripper*, published by Russell Edwards, the businessman who bought the shawl in 2007 on the understanding that it was the same piece of cloth allegedly found next to Eddowes. 'I've got the only piece of forensic evidence in the whole history of the case. I've spent fourteen years working, and we have finally solved the mystery of who Jack the Ripper was. Only non-believers that want to perpetuate the myth will doubt. This is it now – we have unmasked him,' Edwards told *The Mail on Sunday* which serialized his book. I hope the paper did not pay him too much to serialize the book.

At the time, possessions and clothing were returned to the next of kin, like today, or buried with them. The only person who could have given acting Police Sergeant Amos Simpson any of Eddowes' clothing was John Kelly. But that did not happen, since Simpson was a Met officer and might not have been on duty 30th September 1888 – if Amos existed at all! Checking of records throws up this gem; Amos Simpson joined the Metropolitan Police in 1868 and he retired after serving his full term of twenty-five years in 1893. He was awarded a slightly inflated pension for a constable, no doubt because he was an acting sergeant for so long. In Hertfordshire, the town of Cheshunt was covered by the Metropolitan Police until the year 2000. Amos Simpson was living in Cheshunt in 1888, and he was based at Cheshunt Police Station. It has been checked. The distance from the town to Whitechapel is approximately thirteen miles, as the crow flies.

Back to Russell Edwards. He commissioned Doctor Louhelainen, a molecular biologist at Liverpool John Moores University, to carry out forensic analysis of the shawl, including extraction of any DNA that may be present within the cloth, which had been supposedly stored 'unwashed' all this time by the family of the London policeman (Simpson) who acquired the artefact. Louhelainen declined to answer any questions, but managed to extract seven incomplete fragments of mitochondrial DNA (mtDNA), and tried to match their sequences with mtDNA from a living descendant of Eddowes called Karen Miller. The work has not been published in a peer-reviewed journal (which is highly irregular), and the only detailed description by Louhelainen comes from Edwards' book.

'One of these amplified mtDNA segments had a sequence variation which gave a match between one of the shawl samples and Karen Miller's DNA only; in other words, the DNA sequence retrieved from the shawl did not match with control reference sequences,' Louhelainen wrote. 'This DNA alteration is known as *global private mutation* (314.1C) and it is not very common in worldwide populations, as it has frequency estimate of 0.000003506, or about 1: 290,000. This figure has been calculated using the database at Institute of Legal Medicine, GMI, based on the latest available information. Thus, this result indicates the shawl contains human DNA, identical to Karen Miller's for this mitochondrial DNA segment.'

But experts with detailed knowledge of the GMI's mtDNA database claim that Louhelainen made an 'error of nomenclature' because the mutation in question should be written as '315.1C' and not '314.1C'. Had Louhelainen done this, and followed standard forensic practice, he would have discovered the mutation was not rare at all, but shared by more than 99% of people of European descent! End of theory, to be honest. So to end this all: 'If the match frequency really is 90% plus, and not 1: 290,000, then obviously there is no significance whatsoever in the match between the shawl and Eddowes' descendant, and the same match would have been seen with almost anyone who had handled the shawl over the years,' Professor Jeffreys said.

'Dr Louhelainen appears to have made a basic error in calculating the frequency estimate. There are currently about 34,617 entries in the GMI database, and the figure would have been nearer to 29,000 when Dr Louhelainen carried out his research some time ago. So, failing to find a match for a non-existent mutation should have given a frequency of about 1: 29,000 – an error suggesting that he had placed a decimal point in the wrong place.'

'The random match probability of a sequence only seen once as claimed for the shawl, is therefore roughly 1: 34,617. With a database of this size, it is impossible to arrive at an estimate as low as 1: 290,000,' Professor Jeffreys said. Other scientists echoed Jeffreys' concerns, including Mannis van Oven, professor of forensic molecular biology at Rotterdam's Erasmus University; Professor Walther Parson of the Institute of Legal Medicine in Innsbruck, and Hansi Weissensteiner, also at Innsbruck and one of the scientists behind the computer algorithm used by Louhelainen to search the mtDNA database. A spokesperson for publishers Sidgwick & Jackson said 'the author stands by his conclusions. We are investigating the reported error in scientific nomenclature. However, this does not change the DNA profiling match and the probability of the match calculated from the rest of the haplotype data. The conclusion reached in the book, that Aaron Kosminski was Jack the Ripper, relies on much more than this one figure.'

Now if you understand any of this, well done. From my perspective, it means that the Eddowes descendent is not a descendent of Eddowes, or the blood on the shawl is not from

Eddowes. Either way, what seals it for me is that there **was** *no shawl listed in Eddowes' belongings,* and there is no proof that Amos Simpson was working in Whitechapel that night, nor that anyone else can confirm that a shawl was asked for by an acting sergeant from the Met, working within the City police boundaries.

The end

So, there you have my two volumes about Jack; volume I describes the killings and volume II adds a bit more detail, suspects and so on. Inevitably, there has to be a lot of information already published, due to the scant information still available after 129 years. Perhaps the latest theory is that of Russell Edwards, with Catherine Eddowes' shawl and Aaron Kosminski named as Jack. A refusal to publish the work (*scientifically*), and allow third-party investigation as is normal for all scientific research, is another dubious question mark against those who carried out the work. Another 2016 book is Bruce Robinson's *They All Love Jack: Busting the Ripper.* Here we have a cover up of Freemasonry, with a new suspect, Michael Maybrick, apparently a famous songwriter. Working under the name Stephen Adams, he released fifty songs in the 1880's; the author also suggests eight ripper victims, too.

Robinson's ingenious Ripper theory strains the limits of credibility, describing in forensic detail a cover-up of breathtaking audacity and a criminal conspiracy to conceal one of the worst crimes this country has ever seen – 'because the British state was rotten to the core, Bro Jack got away with it. Nothing could be allowed to threaten masonry, because the whole venal dinosaur of the Victorian ruling elite couldn't function without it.'

Still, at over 860 pages in length, it would have been better to save the rain forests. There are worse still; the 2016 book *Jack the Ripper* by Otto Penzler, a collection of essays from various people totaling over 920 pages! Back to the end again. Nobody saw or knew who Jack was, and no end of theories and names are going to change that. Why was he never caught? He probably would have been, had he continued his murderous spree, but he stopped. Most serial killers go on killing until captured – look at Hindley and Brady, Peter Sutcliffe or Donald Neilson. So, why did Jack stop? There are a few reasons: he died, or was committed to a mental asylum, or perhaps he had found the victim he really sought all along – Mary Kelly, in this case. Some suggest his brain gave way after his glut in Millers Court – quite probable.

Whatever his reasons for putting away in a drawer his knife, the police, fledglings as they were at the time, were in the main incompetent. From the very top, with Sir Charles Warren and his hare-brained scheme to use Bloodhounds in a dense city environment, down to the lowliest plod officer on his fixed patrol beat, who saw and heard nothing and carried an old fashioned rattle instead of a police whistle with which to summon help. The Whitechapel and Spitalfields area comprised the greater part of London's east-end. There were about 100,000 very poor people crowded here, including 1200 prostitutes of the lowest class, compared to the higher class of the west-end.

Jack had a field day, amongst the dimly lit alley's and over-crowded houses. He must have had good strength and nerve, as well as pleasantness of face to attract women and good word of mouth for his chat up lines. Perhaps he offered money? He knew the east-end well, being sure of his escape routes should anyone disturb him at his work, and was probably athletically fast and able to fight should it come to it. Since nobody really saw Jack, we don't know what clothes he wore, or where he hid his ripping knife. A long coat or cloak would cover any bloodstains, and provide a pocket for a knife or any trophies taken. Were any of the men seen by witnesses likely to be Jack? If we look at Annie **Chapman**, one witness describes a man as being: dark, wearing a brown deerstalker hat and looking to be over forty, with a shabby genteel appearance, a little taller than Annie and appearing to be foreign.

For Liz **Stride,** three people saw her with a man described as: middle aged, about 5'6" tall, rather stout and looking like a clerk, wearing a small black coat, dark trousers and a round cap with a small peak; also, stout and about 5'7" tall, wearing a long coat, and lastly, the man held a *newspaper parcel* in his hand about eighteen inches long and six or eight inches broad. He was 5'7" tall and wore a hard felt deerstalker hat and dark clothes; he was about twenty-eight years old and had no whiskers.

For Catherine **Eddowes**: thirty years old, 5'7" or 5'8" tall and of medium build, with a fair complexion and moustache. He wore a pepper-and-salt loose jacket, a grey cloth cap with a peak and a reddish neckerchief tied in a knot; looked like a sailor.

And lastly, Mary **Kelly**, two men: one short, stout, shabbily dressed wearing a longish coat, very shabby, and carrying a pot of ale, wearing a round, hard billycock hat with a blotchy face and full carroty moustache, and the later suspect aged thirty-four or thirty-five, height 5'6" complexion pale, dark eyes and eye lashes, slight moustache, curled up each end, and hair dark, very surly looking, dress long dark coat, collar and cuffs trimmed astrakhan, dark jacket under, light waistcoat, dark trousers, dark felt hat turned down in middle, button boots and gaiters with white buttons, wearing a very thick gold chain, white linen collar, black tie with horse shoe pin, of respectable appearance, walked very sharp, Jewish appearance.

If any of these men were Jack the Ripper, then we can profile him as being, by the law of averages, 5'6" to 5'8" tall (so of average height), aged 28 to 40 years of age, wearing a hat of some sort (deerstalker is mentioned several times, along with a cap twice and a specific hat description, a billycock); two wore whiskers and one didn't – the other witnesses failed to mention them. Stout was mentioned twice. One man was well dressed and the others of average clothing – one wears a jacket, two wear coats, one long and one short. Two or three men carried parcels with them. This is why nobody really saw Jack. Such a mixture of descriptions cannot belong to just one man; more likely, they just were clients of the victims who were prepared to pay for sex. It was unlikely that Jack was old, or very young, short or particularly tall. He might have been a bit on the chubby side. He may have worn a deerstalker cap and dark clothing, probably a coat of some kind, too.

What does seem probable is that Jack was unlikely to wear a black top hat and cape – running with a top hat will likely cause the hat to fly off the head, and I should know; I used to be in the police many moons ago, and when it came to running to an incident, we always took our helmets off and carried them, rather than try to run just using the chin strap! I should take most of the information you've read as gospel, since they come from old newspaper reports of the day and reports from the public inquests. Where other ripperologists have contributed, I mention them in the text and recommend their works.

End

BIBLIOGRAPHY

Donald Rumbelow – *the complete Jack the Ripper*

Simon Wood – *theory 2005*

Philip Sugden – *the complete history of Jack the Ripper*

Melville MacNaghten – *memorandum of 1894*

Thomas Stowell – *the criminologist – A solution*

Michael Barrett – *Maybrick's Diary*

Stephen Knight – *Jack the Ripper: The final solution*

Patricia Cornwell – *Portrait of a killer: Jack the Ripper – case closed*

Michael Harrison – *Clarence*

Leonard Matters – *The mystery of Jack the Ripper*

Donald McCormick – *identity of Jack the Ripper*

Melvin Harris – *Jack the Ripper: the bloody truth; the Ripper file (1989); the true face of Jack the Ripper (1994)*

Russell Edwards – *Naming Jack the Ripper*

Bruce Robinson – *They all love Jack: Busting the Ripper*

Otto Penzler – *Jack the Ripper* (2016)

REFERENCES

Any references are from old newspaper reports of the day, and published reports from the public inquests. Where other ripperologists have contributed, I mention them in the text and recommend their works. Special thanks to Simon Wood and Philip Sugden for their sketches.

INDEX

'Dear Boss', 6, 7, 8, 9, 32, 59
'From Hell', 8, 32
'Saucy Jacky's', 8, 32
29 Hanbury Street, 13
Albert Cadoche, 19
Alexander Pedachenko, 57
Amos Simpson, 62, 63, 65
Annie Chapman, 13, 19, 21, 59, 66
Baxter Hunt, 27
Berner Street, 6, 22, 23, 24, 25, 27, 60
billycock, 34, 39, 66
Brights Disease, 9
Britannia public house, 36
Bucks Road, 10
Caroline Maxwell, 36, 38
Central News Agency, 4, 6, 7, 8, 59, 60
City of London police, 4, 9, 27, 28, 29, 30, 44
Cloak Lane police station, 25
Commercial Street Police Station, 19
Crossingham's lodging house, 13
Detective Constable Daniel Halse, 27
Donald McCormick, 57
Donald Neilson, 65
Dr Llewellyn, 10
Dr Thomas Bond, 5, 33, 36
Dr. Brown, 7
Durward Street, 10
Dutfield's Yard, 4, 22, 23, 24, 25
Elizabeth Long, 19
Elizabeth Stride, 6, 8, 22, 24, 25, 44, 60
Francis Tumblety, 57
Frederick Deeming, 54
George Chapman, 54
George Hutchinson, 34, 39, 61
George Lusk, 8, 9, 31, 32
George Oldfield, 5
Gerard, 3
Gilbert, 3
Goulston Street, 4, 25, 26, 27, 28, 29, 30, 31, 43, 44, 60
Grand and Batchelor, 22
Hansi Weissensteiner, 64
Harry Owen, 38
Herbert Stanley, 57
Herendeen, 3
Hindley and Brady, 65
HO 144/221, 60
Inspector Chandler, 13
Inspector Spratling, 10, 59

International Working Men's Educational Club, 22
Israel Schwartz, 23
J K Stephens, 56
James Brown, 23, 24, 32, 38
James Maybrick, 55
Jari Louhelainen, 63
Jill the Ripper, 58
John Davis, 13
John Humble, 5
John Pizer, 13, 19
John Richardson, 13, 20
Jonas Mizen, 10
Joseph Barnett, 33, 37, 38, 45
Joseph Fleming, 37, 38
Karen Miller, 64
Kosminski, 52, 63, 64, 65
leather apron, 13, 19
Lee, 3
Lizzie Albrook, 33
M J Druitt, 52
Maguire, 3
Major Henry Smith, 9, 25
Mannis van Oven, 64
Maria Harvey, 33
Mary Ann Cox, 33, 50
Mary Kelly, 5, 6, 27, 33, 34, 36, 37, 38, 43, 44, 45, 47, 50, 57, 61, 65, 66
Matthew Packer, 22
MEPO 3, 59, 60, 61
Merritt, 3
Michael Kidney, 22
Michael Ostrog, 52
Mitre Square, 4, 9, 25, 27, 28, 29, 31, 60
Moylan, 3
Mr Brough, 42, 43
Netley, 56
Otto Penzler, 65
Payne, 3
PC Harvey, 28
PC Long, 27, 28, 30
PC Thain, 10
Peter Sutcliffe, 2, 5, 65
Philip Sugden, 4, 46, 47, 68
Polly Nichols, 10, 11, 12, 13, 59
Porter, 3
Prince Albert Victor Christian Edward, 53
Professor Jeffreys, 64
Professor Walther Parson, 64
Recorder, 3

Reno, 3
Robert Donston Stephenson, 57
Royall, 3
Russell Edwards', 61, 62
Sarah Lewis, 34, 36
Sergeant Jones, 62
Severin Antoniovich Klosowski, 54
Sidgwick & Jackson, 64
Simon Wood, 4, 45, 46, 47, 48, 49, 68
Sir Robert Anderson, 5, 6, 42
Sir William Gull, 53, 55
Stephen Adams, 65
Steve Connor, 63

Ted Stanley, 19
Thomas Neill Cream, 53
Thomas Oppenshaw, 9
Thomas Stowell, 53
Thrawl Street, 10, 20, 24, 32, 34, 38
Varnum, 3
Wallace, 3
Walter Sickert, 56
Whitechapel Vigilante Committee, 8
William Le Queux, 57
William Marshall, 23
William Sedgwick Saunders, 9
Yorkshire Ripper, 2, 5

Printed in Great Britain
by Amazon